LOST CITIES

An eminent British archaeologist and scholar here relates the fantastic discoveries of cities and whole civilizations that have been lost to white men for centuries, or survived as tiny settlements atop a buried ruin of incomparable splendor. From fragmentary remains, this skilled archaeologist rebuilds a fabulous city, repeoples its streets with the men and women who l...d there, and shares with the reader the fascination of rediscovering the past.

Under Leonard Cottrell's magic pen, the stone-lined chambers of Ashurbanipal's palaces in the Assyrian cities of Nimrud and Nineveh emerge after a darkness of nearly three thousand years. "The City of the Winged Bulls" appears frescoed with scenes of battle, conquest and violence. The Biblical Hittite civilization is found again in the truly buried cities of the wild Anatolian plateau of Central Turkey. The mud walls of Ur, Babylon and Nippur, on the even more ancient plain of Sumeria, reappear through reconstruction made possible by excavation.

The lesser-known civilizations of South and Central America, India and Ceylon are also brought to light. Mr. Cottrell tells the almost incredible story of the discovery of Macchu Picchu — the last magnificent capital of the Inca Empire — whose stone walls remained hidden in the Andes for nearly four centuries after the first Europeans arrived in Peru, and of the massive buildings of Chichen-Itza. He discusses the prehistoric civilization in the Indus Valley and the architectural achievements of the Singalese kings who were the contemporaries of the Roman emperors.

The stories of these lost cities and of many others are filled with the wonder and excitement that have made Leonard Cottrell's books so justly popular.

LOST CITIES

By LEONARD COTTRELL

UNIVERSAL LIBRARY • GROSSET & DUNLAP

NEW YORK

To

JOYCE *and* GORDON

CONTENTS

LOST CITIES

LOST CITIES

Introduction

My previous books on archæological subjects have had a more or less successfully concealed didactic purpose. The entertainment which some readers were kind enough to tell me they received from such books as *The Bull of Minos* and *The Mountains of Pharaoh* was really quite incidental to their main purpose, which was to inform. There is no such purpose in this book. It contains no chronicles or "King-lists", no detailed examinations of religious practices or political movements. It is a relaxed book, written for amusement, and though it does contain a lot of miscellaneous information—little of it new—its function is simply to entertain.

To most of us, if we are honest with ourselves, the words "Lost City" have a considerable nostalgic appeal. Rider Haggard realized this long ago when he wrote *She,* a Victorian best-seller which had all the ingredients of some modern "comic-strip" stories, including a "White Queen" ruling over a mysterious Lost City in the African jungle. More recently, James Hilton's mythical city "Shangri-la" has passed into our language as a symbol of romantic escapism. This present book is also frankly "escapist", except that all the cities it describes actually existed, and most can still be seen.

Some of these cities—such as those in the jungles of Peru and Yucatan—were physically "lost", at least to white men, for centuries. Others, like Hattusas, the capital of the Hittites in Asia Minor, survived as small settlements, their former greatness forgotten, until archæologists excavated and reidentified them. Some ancient cities were never lost in the physical sense, since their sites were always known; but these, plundered and then neglected for thousands of years, became mere heaps of rubbish. Yet, within the last hundred years archæologists, digging deep into those mounds of crumbled brick, have brought to light treasures of architecture and sculpture, domestic objects, and tomb-furniture which, with deciphered inscriptions, enable us to reconstruct these cities in our imaginations. To this class belong Nineveh and Babylon in Mesopotamia.

In many cases the adventures of the men who discovered or excavated these lost cities are as fascinating as the places themselves. Hiram Bingham's journey into Peru to find a lost city of the Incas, never seen by a white man (even by the Spanish Conquistadores), is a saga in itself. On another continent, the Mesopotamian explorations of such pioneers as Claudius Rich and Sir Henry Layard abound in personal adventures, hardships and dangers which rarely befall the modern archæologist. These adventures have been given liberal space in my book, even when they refer only indirectly to the lost cities which the explorers went to find.

Sometimes the fascination of a story lies not in the physical excitement of exploration, nor in the beauty and splendour brought to light by excavation; but in watching the patient skill with which a scientific archæologist rebuilds a lost city from the most fragmentary remains, and re-peoples its streets with the men and women who lived in it. Such a city was Tell-el-Amarna in Egypt.

This book does not aim to be comprehensive, and some well-known Lost Cities, such as Thebes, Palmyra, Mycenæ and Knossos have been deliberately omitted because they have been described in my earlier books. The only criterion I have used in selecting the examples is that of wonder, within the dictionary definition of that overworked word; "something that arrests the attention or strikes the mind by its novelty, grandeur or inexplicableness . . . something unusual, strange, great, extraordinary or not well understood". Though perhaps a better definition of my aim is contained in those well-known words of Sir Philip Sidney:

> *". . . with a tale forsooth he cometh unto you; with a tale which holdeth children from play, and old men from the chimney corner. . . ."*

LEONARD COTTRELL

Hampstead, London.
October, 1956.

CHAPTER ONE

City of the Winged Bulls

"Before I had reached my thirteenth year, I had read all the novels of Walter Scott then published. But the work in which I took the most delight was the *Arabian Nights*. I was accustomed to spend hours stretched upon the floor, under the greatest gilded Florentine table, poring over this enchanting volume. . . . My admiration for the *Arabian Nights* has never left me. I can read them even now with almost as much delight as I read them when a boy. They have had no little influence upon my life and career; for to them I attribute that love of travel and adventure which took me to the East, and led me to the discovery of the ruins of Nineveh. . . ."

Thus wrote Sir A. Henry Layard, G.C.B., D.C.L., recalling an episode in 1833, many years before those respectable initials were added to his name; a time when, as a rebellious schoolboy, unconventionally and haphazardly educated in Italy, France and England, he could have no idea that he was destined for adventures and achievements not incomparable with these in the book he loved so much. At the time he wrote those words he was Her Majesty's Ambassador at Madrid, an unlikely culmination of a career which included such episodes as the following:

"I was . . . accused" (at his English school) "of preaching sedition and revolution, and of attempting to corrupt my schoolfellows, and to incite them to rebellion. By way of chastising me for insubordination [my master] would make me stand with my jacket turned inside out on a stool, whilst the boys were at meals and give cheers for 'Hunt and Cobbett'—the two demagogues of the day whom he held most in aversion. I was not ashamed at my punishment; but was rather confirmed in my revolutionary principles, as I was very indignant at what I considered an undue and tyrannical interference with my political opinions."

Under the influence of the *Arabian Nights* he "thought and dreamt of little else but 'jins' and 'ghouls' and fairies and lovely princesses, until I believed in their existence and even fell in love with a real living damsel. I was deeply smitten with the pretty sister of one of my schoolfellows. I fancied I had a rival in an English boy of my own age. We quarrelled in consequence, and as we were both taking fencing-lessons we determined to settle our differences with foils without the buttons. How we were prevented carrying out our bloody intentions I now forget."

He was always a lad of spirit. When his parents moved to France and Henry was sent to a *lycée,* he explained to his schoolfellows that

"in English schools, boys were in the habit of resisting . . . ill-usage by rebelling against the author of it, and pelting him with books or any other missiles that might be at hand. I suggested the same mode of punishing our tyrant." (i.e. a sadistic master who "held our fingers in an iron grasp and then rapped the ends of them with an heavy ruler".)

"My suggestion was highly approved, and it was agreed unanimously that it should be carried out. It was arranged that at our evening class, at a given signal, the *professeur* was to be assailed by a shower of books and other objects. When the moment arrived for action, I seized one of the small leaden inkstands . . . and hurled it at the head of the obnoxious master, fortunately, however, missing it. There was dead silence. I looked around, and saw my co-conspirators to all appearances engaged intently in their studies, not one of them taking his eyes off his book, as if perfectly innocent and unconscious of the whole business."

This treachery on the part of the French boys naturally led to further violence. After the master had soundly whipped the *cochon d'Anglais* the *cochon* flew at his betrayers, and in the ensuing struggle "one of the boys cut my face open with the stiff leather rim of his *casquette.*"

Henry's father removed him from the school.

The more one reads of Henry Layard the more one likes him. He belongs to that class of young, nineteenth-century adventurers of whom Claudius Rich and James Silk Buckingham were other examples; men to whom the familiar command "Go West, young man" was reversed. They wanted to go East, because in their day the East was as little known as the Far West, and just as exciting.

These men were impelled to the East "by its quality of romance and mystery—a mystery, be it said, which has to-day been so largely dissipated by increased accessibility as to need emphasizing. Six centuries had passed since the end of the Last Crusade severed the connection between Europe and the Arab Empire. After the final fall of Acre, in Gibbon's words 'a profound and melancholy silence prevailed along the coast which had so long resounded to the World's Debate'. For the Westerner, Arabian Asia had been shrouded ever since in this silence, and remained so until rediscovered as a subject for 'debate' by the world of the nineteenth century." [1]

Born in 1817 of parents descended from Huguenot stock, Henry Layard's boyhood was divided between England, France, Italy and Switzerland; his father's health required constant changes of climate. His unconventional education gave him a background which was probably superior to that of most young men of his class, and one which suited him, for he had the eye of an artist, and, in his own words, he "acquired a taste for the fine arts, and as much knowledge of them as a child could obtain who was constantly in the society of artists and connoisseurs." He also developed a longing for travel, but this was at first frustrated when his parents sent him back to London at the age of sixteen to study

[1] Lloyd, Seton. *Foundations in the Dust.* Pelican Books.

law. He spent six years in a solicitor's office, and hated every one of them. At twenty-two, again in his own words, he "determined for various reasons to leave England and seek a career elsewhere." And as Mr. Seton Lloyd says in his delightful book *Foundations in the Dust,* "A glance at the coloured engravings of a young man in Bakhtiyari costume which forms the frontispiece to the *Early Adventures* is alone sufficient to suggest that the 'various reasons' were adequate ones".

He had read Rich's memoirs on Babylon. He had also been stirred by the stories then current of mysterious rock-cut inscriptions in the mountains of Persia; inscriptions in the wedge-shaped cuneiform writing which was just beginning to be deciphered. The East became an obsession with him, and when, in 1839, a relative offered to find him a post in Ceylon, he leaped at the chance. But the method by which he proposed to get there astounded his friends, who naturally supposed he would make the usual leisurely journey by sea. But this was too slow and boring for Henry, who was determined to take the overland route. This, of course, was before the days of railways. With a young and equally adventurous friend, named Mitford, Layard planned to travel via Central Europe to Dalmatia, Montenegro, Albania and Bulgaria to Constantinople. That would be the first stage. Then they would cross Asia Minor and Syria, Palestine and the Mesopotamian Desert to Baghdad.

"From Baghdad," he wrote, "we believed that we should be able to reach India through Persia and Afghanistan and so ultimately to Colombo."

Obviously Henry was determined that, before he finally ended as a tea-planter in Ceylon, he would have his fill of the countries which had taken such a hold on his youthful imagination. Or perhaps he had privately made up his mind that he would never go to Ceylon, but would find a more interesting and unconventional occupation somewhere en route. Anyway, that was what happened.

Lack of space forbids a full description of this crazy journey, which readers will find in Layard's own fascinating book, *Nineveh and its Remains,* published in 1849.[2] At Plovdiv, in Bulgaria, Layard developed gastritis, and was bled by a local physician, who drew a circle on his belly and filled the circle with leeches. He lost so much blood as a result that he was delayed for several weeks, and did not catch up with Mitford until he reached Asia Minor. There was more trouble in Jerusalem when Henry decided to go to Petra, passing through bandit-infested country and plagued by Bedouin. On his way to Aleppo, where he had agreed to rejoin the long-suffering Mitford, he visited Kerak, Jerash, and Amman, and was robbed twice, once near Kerak and again near Damascus. When, in pouring rain, he turned up at the home of the British Consul at Damascus, he was penniless, half-naked, and on foot. But he had seen what he wanted to see.[3]

Mitford, fuming in Aleppo, was eventually greeted after long delay by an excited Layard, who told him that he had also managed to see Beyrout and Baalbeck on the way. After a few days "to give my mare and myself a rest", the two resumed their journey, travelling southward through Urfah and Nisibis, and arrived on May 2nd at Mosul.

From the beginning Henry Layard loved Iraq, a country which has little physical appeal for most visitors, for there, as he writes:

> ". . . desolation meets desolation; a feeling of awe succeeds to wonder; for there is nothing to relieve the mind, to lead to hope or to tell what has gone by. . . . These huge mounds of Assyria made a deeper impression on me, gave rise to more serious thoughts and earnest reflection, than the temples of Baalbec, and the theatres of Ionia."

It must be realized that at this time Assyria was little more than a name mentioned in the Bible and by a few ancient authors. During the two or three centuries preceding Layard's visit, a hand-

---

[2] "Popular archæology" is nothing new. Layard's book, and those of Rich, Rawlinson and others, enjoyed a tremendous vogue a century ago.

[3] Nearly forty years later Layard returned to Damascus as the Queen's Ambassador.

ful of European travellers had passed that way. There was a certain John Eldred, who had travelled to Baghdad in the reign of Queen Elizabeth. There was a German physician, Rauwolff, who had travelled in Mesopotamia at about the same time; and there was the Abbé de Beauchamp, who in 1780 had been the Pope's Vicar-General in Babylonia. Gibbon had written about Babylon and Nineveh, but most of his knowledge was drawn either from the Bible or from classical authors like Herodotus. But the traditional sites of both Babylon and Nineveh were known, and visitors were sometimes taken to see the huge mounds of earth and crumbled brick which were apparently all that survived of these once-great cities.

However, before Layard's arrival there had been a slight stirring of interest in these ancient remains. The region formed part of the Ottoman Empire, with which the British Government had recently established regular diplomatic relations. Consular Agents were appointed at Baghdad and Mosul, and as these were often young men with a taste for adventure, and with time on their hands, they became interested in the antiquities of the area and even attempted a little amateur digging. A further stimulus came from attempts to decipher the wedge-shaped writing ("cuneiform") which could be seen in huge rock-cut inscriptions, and also on dried-mud bricks which were often dug out of the mounds and carried home by travellers as curiosities. Lord Byron has a satirical couplet about these in his *Don Juan*—referring to Claudius Rich, who had been Resident of the East India Company at Baghdad.

"Though Claudius Rich, Esquire, some bricks has got,
And written lately two memoirs upon't."

Rich, who died three years after Layard was born, had examined and sketched the ruins of Babylon (which is on the Lower Euphrates, south of Baghdad), and also the mound of Kuyunjik, site of ancient Nineveh, opposite Mosul. But, although he wrote valuable memoirs of his travels and investigations,[4] he was unable to carry out serious excavations. The climate ruined his health, and

---

[4] He also made a large and valuable collection of oriental manuscripts and antiquities which he gave to the British Museum.

he died of cholera in 1817, after refusing to leave the stricken city of Baghdad where, as his biographer writes:

> "He continued nobly to exert himself to quiet the alarm of the inhabitants, and to assist the sick and dying."

When Layard came to Mosul the situation was different. Great progress had been made in the decipherment of cuneiform. First in this field was the German scholar Grotefend, in 1802. In 1835 an English officer, Lieutenant (later Sir Henry) Rawlinson, set himself the task of copying the inscriptions on the great Behistun Rock in Persia, which were trilingual, i.e. in Old Persian, Elamite, and Babylonian. From this and similar inscriptions he and other scholars obtained enough comparative material to enable them to begin to understand the wedge-shaped characters. From now on, every inscribed brick or stone acquired potential value as a document. If only the language barrier had been broken, a whole new chapter might be written into the history of the human race. The ruins, mute for so long, would speak.

Layard's first visit to Mosul was brief, although he spent some time surveying and studying the great mound of Kuyunjik. Then he and Mitford moved on to Baghdad. At this time the British Resident was a certain Colonel Taylor, a distinguished orientalist with whom the young man became friendly. He also met some of Taylor's junior officers, Lieutenants Campbell, Selby and Jones, who he says, "employed themselves while engaged in their professional duties in geographical and archæological researches". Continuing their journey, they managed to see and study the cuneiform inscriptions at Behistun, which stimulated Layard's curiosity still more, so that, by the time the young travellers reached Hamadan, Henry had decided that he was *not* going to Ceylon. Mitford travelled on to India. Layard swung southward to explore the wild country of the Bakhtiyari tribes (whose costume he subsequently adopted and loved to wear). The Bakhtiyari were the most turbulent of the Persian tribes. But Layard's adventures among them, which fill a large part of his book, have no place here.

Eventually he returned to Baghdad, where, for reasons of economy, he lived in a mud-hut, but paid frequent visits to the Residency, where he was able to use Taylor's library. He became very friendly with Selby and Jones, men of his own age, and with them went on several expeditions in the two small armed steamers, the *Assyria* and the *Nitocris*. In 1842, when war between Persia and Turkey seemed imminent, Taylor asked Layard to go to Constantinople to report to the British Ambassador on the situation. On the way he again visited Mosul, where he had the opportunity of meeting Paul Emile Botta, the French Consular Agent, who in that year began excavations in the mound of Kuyunjik. This was the beginning of Mesopotamian excavation. The curtain was about to rise on the ancient Assyrian world.

When Rich's *Narrative of a journey to the site of Babylon* was published it caused a stir throughout European academic circles. The French Asiatic Society in particular was interested in the possibilities of excavation in the Mosul area. Botta, a naturalist and son of a historian, was appointed as French Consular Agent partly because of his diplomatic experience in the Middle East, but also because Jules Mohl, of the Asiatic Society, saw in him the potentialities of an archæologist. National prestige entered into this. The British profited from the fact that the British East India Company, when choosing their first Resident in Baghdad, had accidentally chosen a man who became a gifted amateur archæologist. There was no accident in the French Government's selection of Botta for the post at Mosul. The difference of the attitude of the two countries to archæology is typical, and can be observed throughout the years which followed, when Layard, who became an archæologist by chance, had to do his great work on a parsimonious grant from the British Museum, while Botta had liberal financial support from the French Government. It says much for the character of these two men that national differences and rivalries never interfered with their friendship.

Botta's first great discovery was at Khorsobad, a village some fourteen miles from Mosul. He had begun by making trial trenches at Kuyunjik, but with poor results; then, hearing by chance that sculptured stones had been seen in the vicinity of Khorsobad, he transferred his workmen to that site. It was March, 1843.

Hardly had the workmen begun to cut their trenches into the great mound when huge limestone slabs were revealed. On these slabs were vigorous sculptures in relief; scenes of battles and sieges, religious ceremonies with strange gods, and always the figure of an Assyrian King in a tall headdress and wearing a thick curled beard, watching the triumphs of his armies.

"Within a few days," writes Seton Lloyd, "it was clear that an astonishing and epoch-making discovery had been made, and Botta was able to dispatch to Mohl his famous message, 'I believe myself to be the first who has discovered sculptures which with some reason can be referred to the period when Nineveh was flourishing'." [5]

Botta had discovered the new capital of Assyria built by King Sargon II at the end of the eighth century B.C. At the time of the discovery, decipherment of the cuneiform inscriptions (with which the slabs were covered) had not progressed sufficiently far for the name of the king to be identified, but soon Henry Rawlinson, the young officer who had worked on the Behistun Rock inscriptions, was to become British Resident at Baghdad, where he continued his studies of the ancient language and gave benefit of his learning to such archæologists as Botta, Layard, and others working in the same field.

The effect of this discovery on the Victorian world was comparable to that of the Tomb of Tutankhamun on the "twenties" of this century. Assyria suddenly became news, and men studied their Bibles for any scraps of information which the Jewish chroniclers had given, and quoted with relish Byron's famous lines about the defeat of Sennacherib.

"The Assyrian came down like a wolf on the fold
And his cohorts were gleaming in purple and gold,

⁵ Lloyd, Seton. *Foundations in the Dust*. Pelican Books. London.

*And the sheen of his spears was like stars on the sea
Where the blue wave rolls nightly on deep Galilee."*

In France and England illustrated magazines were full of pictures showing in detail scenes from the wars and conquests, ceremonies and daily life of a people who, until then, had been known only by a few biblical references and the vague accounts of classical historians. At long last the British authorities were prodded into reluctant action. Between 1843 and 1845 Layard had managed to get himself a diplomatic post on the staff of the British Ambassador to Turkey, Sir Stratford Canning. When news of Botta's momentous discoveries came through Canning was as excited as Layard, and Botta was generous enough to allow them to see his confidential dispatches, which passed through Istanbul. Layard, whose impatience can be imagined, urged upon Canning the necessity of obtaining official support for a British excavation of some of the other mounds which he had seen; Kuyunjik for instance, or Nimrud. Canning, just as he was about to return to Britain on leave, delighted his young assistant by telling him that he himself would agree, temporarily, to finance an excavation at Nimrud. If the results were successful, then Canning hoped to persuade the British Government to finance further excavations. As soon as a *firman* (official permit) had been given by the Turkish Government, Henry Layard was hurrying eastwards across the mountains. . . .

"I crossed the mountains of Pontus and the great steppes of the Usun Yilak as fast as post-horses could carry me, descended the high lands into the valley of the Tigris, galloped over the vast plains of Assyria, and reached Mosul in twelve days."

CHAPTER TWO

City of the Winged Bulls (2)

Every visitor to the British Museum knows the huge, winged and human-headed bulls which stand sentinel at the entrance to the Assyrian section. Each weighs over ten tons. Of black basalt, glossy and sinister, they are overpowering in their brutal strength. They, and nearly all the Assyrian carved and sculptured reliefs in the gallery behind them, were prised from their foundations by crowbars, hauled by ropes till they toppled on to specially built platforms, moved on rollers across miles of desert under a burning sun, winched aboard ship and brought down the Persian Gulf to Bombay, then around the Cape of Good Hope to the Port of London; all under the supervision of Henry Layard over one hundred years ago. And he did it on what we would call "a shoe-string".

Arriving at Mosul he had audience with Turkish Governor, Mohammed Pasha, whom he did not trust. So, in order to conceal the real purpose of his visit, he pretended to be going on a hunting trip.

"On the eighth of November, having secretly procured a few tools, and engaged a mason at the moment of my departure, and carrying with me a variety of guns, spears and other formidable weapons, I declared that I was going to hunt wild boars in a neighbouring village, and floated down the Tigris on a small raft constructed for the journey. I was accompanied by Mr. Ross, a British merchant of Mosul, my Cawass, and a servant."

Layard's objective was Nimrud, one of the great mounds which lay on the west bank of the Tigris south of the mound of Kuyunjik, where Botta had been working. The name is a romantic one. According to the Book of Genesis, Nimrud was the son of Cush and the grandson of Ham, famous for his exploits as a hunter. That this legendary name should be attached to an ancient Assyrian mound intrigued Layard, and when, after five hours' journey, the great hill loomed up against the sunset his excitement was great.

"I had slept little during the night," he writes. "Hopes, long cherished, were now to be realized, or end in disappointment. Visions of palaces underground, of gigantic monsters, of sculptured figures, and endless inscriptions, floated before me."

In the morning when he left his tent:

". . . the lofty cone and broad mound of Nimrud broke like a distant mountain against the morning sky. But how changed was the scene of my former visit! The ruins were no longer clothed with verdure and many-coloured flowers; no signs of habitation, not even the black tents of the Arab, was seen across the plain. The eye wandered over a parched and barren waste, across which occasionally swept a whirlwind dragging with it a cloud of sand."

The last time Layard had seen Nimrud was in spring; the wonderful, fugitive spring of Iraq, when, for a few weeks, the rains fulfil the Biblical prophecy that "the desert shall blossom like the rose". But now it was November, and to the aridity of the landscape was added the silence and emptiness of a deserted land. Owing to the extortions and cruelty of the local Governor, Keritli Oglu, the villagers had deserted their homes, and even the Arab tribesmen had moved from the plain which they normally inhabited to the south of the Zab river. However, in one of the hovels the visitors managed to find a few Arabs, one of whom, Sheikh Awad, told Layard why the district had been deserted. On being told why the Englishman had come to Nimrud, Awad be-

came more cheerful, and offered to help obtain workmen. He also
told Layard an ancient tradition connected with the ruins.

> " 'The Palace,' said he, 'was built by Athur, the Kiayah,
> or lieutenant of Nimrud. Here the holy Abraham, peace
> upon him! cast down and broke in pieces the idols which
> were worshipped by the unbelievers. The impious Nim-
> rud, enraged by the destruction of his gods, sought to slay
> Abraham, and waged war against him. But the prophet
> prayed to God, and said, "Deliver me, O God, from this
> man. . . ." ' "

Abraham's prayer was answered.

> "He sent a gnat, which vexed Nimrud night and day, so
> that he built himself a room of glass in yonder palace,
> that he might dwell therein, and shut out the insect. But
> the gnat entered also, and passed by his ear into his brain,
> upon which it fed, and increased in size day by day, so
> that the servants of Nimrud beat his head with a hammer
> continually, that he might have some ease from his pain;
> but he died after suffering these torments for four hun-
> dred years."

And Layard adds:

> "Such are the tales to this day repeated by the Arabs who
> wander round the remains of a great city; which, by their
> traditions, they unwittingly help to identify."

One day's digging in the mound was enough to convince
Layard that it contained ruined buildings. His first trench revealed
the upper part of a large slab of alabaster. Working from this
point a second slab was uncovered, then a third, then a fourth, until by the end of the morning ten such slabs had been found, each
standing vertically and fixed to its neighbour, forming a square. In
the centre of each slab was an inscription in cuneiform. They then
attacked the side of the mound, at a place near which fragments of
alabaster had been seen, and once again, almost immediately, a
wall was revealed bearing similar inscriptions in the ancient writing.
But Layard noticed that "the slabs had evidently been exposed to

intense heat, were cracked in every part, and threatened to fall to pieces as soon as uncovered."

On the first day he had only six workmen, which he increased to eleven during the next few days. Scientific excavation was then unknown, and Layard's methods were extremely crude by modern standards. He had neither the time nor the labour force needed to excavate each chamber thoroughly. When he found walls he dug along them, revealing the inscriptions, but left the middle of each room unexcavated. Nevertheless, by sheer chance, he discovered, in that first day's work, the remains of two Assyrian palaces which had stood on the site, one of which had evidently been built partly with material taken from the earlier palace.

He also attacked the huge conical mound which stood at the north-west corner of the site, and found it was built of solid mud-brick. At the time he had no idea that it was the remains of a tiered tower, a typical feature of Assyrian cities, and those of Babylon and Sumeria which had preceded them. Botta had also encountered a similar structure at Khorsobad, without at first recognizing its function.

Within a few days, of course, the news of Layard's discovery had leaked back to Keritli Oglu in Mosul, and the Governor requested to see him. Like most Orientals, he could conceive of only one motive in digging—to find gold, and his suspicions were confirmed when a tiny fragment of gold leaf, which Layard had found in one of the chambers, came into his possession. Shortly afterwards Layard was politely informed by Da'ûd Agha, captain of the Turkish irregular troops in the area, that excavations must cease because the Governor had heard that there was a Moslem cemetery on the site, and that the Englishman was disturbing the graves of True Believers.

Layard again went to see Keritli Oglu, a fat Turk with a face as vile as his reputation. "Nature," writes Layard, "had placed hypocrisy beyond his reach. He had one eye and one ear; he was short and fat, deeply marked by smallpox and harsh in voice. . . . He had revived many good old customs, which the reforming spirit of the age had suffered to fall into decay. He particularly insisted on *dish-parassi;* [1] or a compensation in money levied upon all villages in which a man of such rank is entertained, for the wear and tear on his teeth in masticating the food he condescends to receive from the inhabitants."

Layard pointed out that there were no graves on the mound, to his knowledge, and also gently recalled an incident in the Governor's career, when, in his own words "at Siwas the Ulema tried to excite the people because I encroached upon a burying-ground. But I made them eat dirt! I took every gravestone and built up the castle walls with them."

But the old rascal was ready with an answer.

"Ah, but there I had Mussulmans to deal with . . . and here we have only Kurds and Arabs, and Wallah! they are beasts. No, I cannot allow you to proceed; you are my dearest and most intimate friend; if anything happens to you, what grief should I not suffer!"

On his return to Nimrud, Layard discovered that the Governor had been trying similar tactics to those he employed at Siwas, only this time in reverse. There he had destroyed a burying-ground. At Nimrud he was creating one. One day Da'ûd Agha came to Layard and admitted shamefacedly that, on the Governor's orders, he and his troops had, for two nights, been employed in bringing gravestones from distant villages and re-erecting them on the mound.

" 'We have destroyed more real tombs of True Believers,' said he, 'in making sham ones, than you could have defiled between the Zab and Selamiyah. We have killed our horses and ourselves in carrying those accursed stones.' "

Da'ûd Agha was a tough but friendly character, a free-booting soldier and a man after Layard's own heart. They soon came to an arrangement. While Layard returned to Constantinople to obtain

---

[1] Literally "tooth-money".

a more strongly worded *firman* which would prevent any further interference by the local authorities, Da'ûd Agha and Layard's agent (whom he left in charge of the excavations) carried out the Englishman's secret instructions. When, at the beginning of January, he returned to Nimrud he found that they had been obeyed almost too faithfully.

> "Not only were the counterfeit graves carefully removed, but even others, which possessed more claim to respect, had been routed out."

But as usual, Henry was equal to the situation, and entered into an elaborate theological discussion with the aggrieved Arabs—

> "in which I proved to them, as the bodies were not turned towards Mecca, they could not be those of True Believers. I ordered the remains, however, to be carefully reburied at the foot of the mound."

Layard and his workmen soon came upon treasures more exciting than slabs of inscribed cuneiform. Even before he departed for Constantinople two enormous bas-reliefs had been uncovered. One depicted a battle scene.

> "Two chariots, drawn by horses richly caparisoned, were each occupied by a group of three warriors; the principal person in both groups was beardless, and evidently a eunuch. He was clothed in a complete suit of mail, and wore a pointed helmet on his head, from the sides of which fell lappets covering the ears, the lower part of the face, and the neck. The left hand, the arm being fully extended, grasped a bow at full stretch; whilst the right, drawing the strings to the ear, held an arrow ready to be discharged. A second warrior urged, with reins and whip, to the utmost of their speed, three horses, which were galloping across the plain. A third, without helmet, and with flowing hair and beard, held a shield for the defence of the principal figure. Under the horses' feet, and scattered about the relief, were the conquered, wounded by the arrows of the conquerors."

The other sculptured relief depicted the siege of a castle of a walled city. From the turrets of the castle warriors fired arrows, slingers were shown in action, and "a female figure, known by her long hair . . . held her right hand raised as if in the act of asking for mercy." One of the defenders, with raised torch, was trying to burn a huge catapult or siege engine which had been brought against the wall along an inclined plane. One of the attackers was setting light to the gate of the castle, while another applied an iron instrument to the stones in an attempt to force the foundations.

Here, and at Khorsobad, where Botta was excavating a similar palace, men of the nineteenth century saw, for the first time, the terrible Assyrians in action; "a people delighting in war". No longer merely a name, they had stepped out of the pages of the Bible and become real again.

Some of these sculptured reliefs and inscriptions had been so badly damaged by fire as to be too fragile for removal. Evidently part of the palace had been set on fire when it was sacked. But later, exploring another part of the mound, Layard found intact sculpture and inscriptions, capable of being removed. The most dramatic discovery came one morning when Layard was returning to Nimrud after visiting the camp of a local Sheikh. Suddenly two Arabs came galloping towards him, urging their mares at the top of their speed.

> "On approaching me they stopped. 'Hasten, O Bey,' exclaimed one of them—'hasten to the diggers, for they have found Nimrud himself. Wallah, it is wonderful, but it is true! We have seen him with both our eyes. There is no God but God!' and both joining in this pious exclamation, they galloped off, without further words, in the direction of their tents."

On reaching the ruins Layard found the workmen at the foot of a deep trench.

> "Whilst Awad advanced and asked for a present to celebrate the occasion, the Arabs withdrew the screen they

had hastily constructed, and disclosed an enormous human head sculptured in full out of the alabaster of the country. They had uncovered the upper part of a figure, the remainder of which was still buried in the earth. I saw at once that the head must belong to a winged lion or bull, similar to those of Khorsobad and Persepolis."

It was a masterpiece of Assyrian art. As Layard had conjectured, it was the upper part of a huge human-headed bull, one of a pair which had stood on each side of a doorway. It was not surprising that the workmen had been so amazed and terrified by the apparition.

"The gigantic head, blanched with age, thus rising from the bowels of the earth, might well have belonged to one of those fearful beings which are pictured in the traditions of the country, as appearing to mortals slowly ascending from the regions below. One of the workmen, on catching the first glimpse of the monster, had thrown down his basket and run off towards Mosul, as fast as his legs would carry him. I learned this with regret, as I anticipated the consequences."

These were soon apparent. The report of the terrified Arab threw Mosul into commotion. The inhabitants poured out of the town and across the river to see the miracle. Other complications, both political and theological, soon arose. The Ulema (holy men) called together hurriedly to discuss the matter, were unable to decide whether Nimrud had been a true-believing prophet or an infidel, but in the meantime they sent a protest to the Governor, Ismail Pasha, who had replaced the detestable Kretli Oglu. He was a much more reasonable man than his predecessor, but was compelled to ask Layard to suspend operations until the matter was cleared up. He gave orders that "the remains should be treated with respect, and by no means be disturbed, but that excavations should be stopped at once".

Layard complied, dismissing all but a handful of workmen, until the disturbance had subsided. In the meantime he was able to study at leisure the remains of the palaces he had uncovered, and indulge in some typical nineteenth-century reflections on the ruins.

> "For twenty-five centuries they had been hidden from the eye of man, and they now stood forth once more in their ancient majesty. But how changed was the scene around them! The luxury and civilization of a mighty nation had given place to the wretchedness and ignorance of a few half-barbarous tribes. The wealth of temples, and riches of great cities, had been succeeded by ruins and shapeless heaps of earth. Above the spacious hall in which they stood the plough had passed, and the corn now waved . . . for now is 'Nineveh a desolation and dry like a wilderness, and flocks lie down in the midst of her; all the beasts of the nations, both the cormorant and the bittern lodge in the upper lintels of it; their voice sings in the windows; and desolation is in the thresholds.' " [2]

Nimrud, of course, was not Nineveh, but the quotation was apposite enough.

It had now become clear that if the work was to proceed two things were necessary, (*a*) firm authority from the Turkish Government, and (*b*) a grant from the British Treasury. Canning, in Constantinople, succeeded at last in obtaining the first, but when, at the end of his term as British Ambassador to the Porte, he returned to England and tried to enlist official support for Layard, he had little encouragement. It was only when he threatened, half in jest, to co-operate with Rawlinson (now installed in Baghdad) in a joint enterprise, that at last the British Museum advanced £2,000, a miserably inadequate sum in contrast with the generous allowance Botta had received from his Government. But even before official confirmation of the grant came through, Layard had returned to his self-appointed task.

His troubles were not over, even when the necessary *firman* was granted by the Porte. Botta had been temporarily replaced at Mosul by another Frenchman, Rouet, a mean-spirited and jealous

[2] Zephaniah, ii. 13 and 14.

man, who did his best, by private intrigue, to hinder Layard's work, and also sent his agents in all directions to stake claims on as many unexcavated mounds as possible. Thus began an undignified international scramble for portable Assyrian antiquities, with the Louvre and the British Museum cheering from the side-lines. Fortunately there were scholars who remained aloof from this sordid struggle, and gave generous and unstinted help to their colleagues of other nationalities. Rawlinson, for example, worked away steadily at the decipherment of the cuneiform, and, in order to enable him to continue working in the hot weather, built himself a little shelter at the bottom of the Residency garden overlooking the river. Over this shelter water was pumped perpetually, enabling the great man to work in tolerable comfort, even when the temperature of Baghdad rose to 120 degrees in the shade. In this water-cooled study both Botta and Layard were equally welcome.

When, in November, 1846, Layard's workmen once more drove their picks and spades into the mound of Nimrud, the discoveries he made more than fulfilled his dreams. The little boy who had lain "under the great Florentine table" absorbed in *The Arabian Nights* was able to tell the Victorian world a tale almost as fantastic—though true.

> "The six weeks following the commencement of excavations upon a large scale were among the most prosperous and fruitful in events, during my researches in Assyria. Every day produced some new discovery. . . ."

One by one the stone-lined chambers of the palaces of Ashurbanipal and Ezarhaddon revealed themselves after a darkness of nearly three thousand years. As hundreds of tons of earth were removed by the chanting workmen, the sculptured reliefs and inscriptions, the entrances guarded by winged bulls and lions, the procession of gods, gleamed in the sunlight. The brutal vigour of Assyrian art was equalled by the savagery of many of the scenes it depicted. For the Assyrians, as we know now, were essentially a warrior-race. Such culture as they possessed—the cuneiform system of writing, the sciences of mathematics, astronomy, medicine, were borrowed from the earlier peoples whom they overthrew, and whose documents they copied. The walls of the palaces in which the Assyrian kings feasted and held court were adorned, not with painted frescoes depicting gardens, flowers, trees and birds, as, for example, in Egypt, but either scenes of battle and conquest, or the triumphs and celebrations which followed. Here are a few brief extracts from Layard's description of these scenes.

> ". . . the king, the two warriors with their standards, and an eunuch are in chariots; and four warriors, amongst whom is also a eunuch, on horses. The enemy fight on foot, and discharge their arrows. . . . Eagles hover above the victors, and one is already feeding on a dead body. . . . Groups of men, fighting or slaying the enemy, are introduced in several places; and three headless bodies are the principal figures in the second bas-relief representing the dead. . . ."

Even grimmer were some of the reliefs discovered later; prisoners are shown as being impaled on spikes, or flayed alive, and the inscriptions, when they were eventually deciphered, contained such lines as:

> "I slew one of every two. I built a wall before the great gates of the city; I flayed the chief men of the rebels, and I covered the wall with their skins. Some of them were enclosed alive within the bricks of the wall, some of them were crucified with stakes along the wall; I caused a great multitude of them to be flayed in my presence, and I covered the wall with their skins."

With such scenes and words before our eyes, we can understand the exultation of the prophet Nahum at the thought of Nineveh's destruction.

> "Woe to the bloody city! it is all full of lies and robbery; the prey departeth not."

> "The noise of the whip, and the noise of the rattling wheels, and the prancing horses, and the jumping chariots."

". . . Thy shepherds slumber, O king of Assyria; they thy nobles shall dwell in the dust; thy people is scattered upon the mountains, and no man gathereth them."

"There is no healing of thy bruise; thy sound is grievous; all that hear the bruit of thee clap their hands over thee; for upon whom hath not thy wickedness passed continually?"

In the following year, 1847, before he returned to London, Layard took soundings in the mound of Nineveh (Kuyunjik) and located the palace of Sennacherib. But he was not to excavate it thoroughly until two years later. Meanwhile, back in England, he had the mortification of finding that when his precious cases of antiquities were opened in the British Museum, many of the objects were broken, a number were missing, and the whole collection had been disarranged and the cataloguing ruined.

The mischief was traced back to Bombay. There, while the cases were resting in the Customs House preparatory to shipment to England, the local British colony could not resist the temptation to open the cases and examine their contents. A local clergyman had even given a lecture on the most precious of Layard's finds, the famous Black Obelisk of Shalmaneser III—no doubt in support of some half-baked religious theory. For whereas, in France, interest in Assyrian antiquities was predominantly scientific and æsthetic, British scholarship was, at this period, bedevilled by cranky theologians determined to establish the literal truth of the Old Testament. When the Bombay clergyman and his friends had enjoyed themselves, they repacked Layard's finds so carelessly that many of them were injured or destroyed, and their archæological value impaired.

By contrast, Botta's discoveries were transported to France with the greatest care; the French Government provided a naval vessel for the purpose, and liberally financed the preparation and publication of Botta's *Monument de Ninivé* in five magnificent volumes with steel-engravings reproduced from the lovely drawings of Flandin.

"So appreciative were the French of the real value of his finds" writes Seton Lloyd, "that in fact the sum granted for this production equalled, if not exceeded, that which originally made the excavations possible." [3]

When Layard tried to obtain official financial support for the publication of his own drawings and plans, he was refused. Fortunately John Murray's publishing firm stepped in, and it is to them we owe the folio of drawings which eventually appeared. Layard also wrote a more popular account, *Nineveh and its Remains,* which aroused such interest among the general public that, in 1849, the British Museum was moved to offer him £4,000 to reopen his excavations. Later, after it had been accepted, the offer was reduced to £3,000.

In October, 1849, Layard returned to Mosul, and with Christian Rassam, the British vice-consul, recommenced his excavations. By this time Rawlinson and others had made such progress with the decipherment of the cuneiform writing that it was possible to read simple inscriptions. Attention now began to be centred on these, even more than on sculptured scenes, though these too acquired fresh interest, as they were often inscribed, and might reveal the names of the Assyrian kings and details of their campaigns.

Layard now turned his attention to the mound of Kuyunjik (Nineveh), and was rewarded by finding the palace of Sennacherib, the same king who is mentioned in the second Book of Kings (ch. 19).

"Now in the fourteenth year of King Hezekiah did Sennacherib king of the Assyrians come up against all the fenced cities of Judah and took them."

"And Hezekiah king of Judah sent to the king of Assyria to Lachish, saying; I have offended; return from me; that which thou puttest on me I will bear. And the king of Assyria appointed unto Hezekiah king of Judah three hundred talents of silver and thirty talents of gold."

[3] Lloyd, Seton. *Foundations in the Dust.* Pelican Books. London.

"And Hezekiah gave him all the silver that was found in the house of the Lord, and in the treasures of the king's house."

"At that time did Hezekiah cut off the gold from the doors of the temple of the Lord and from the pillars which Hezekiah king of Judah had overlaid, and gave it to the king of Assyria."

The Jews, like other petty tribes whose lands lay athwart the path of the Assyrian and Egyptian armies, had suffered the usual fate of such peoples when the two mighty empires were in conflict. Hezekiah had sided with the Egyptians, and his punishment was to see his "fenced cities" destroyed, and to pay heavy tribute to the Assyrian king.

When Layard dug into the mound of Kuyunjik, he found, on the inner walls of Sennacherib's palace, a sculptured relief showing the siege of the town of Lachish mentioned in the above passage. The whole violent scene is depicted with the usual vigour and realism of Assyrian sculpture—the attackers mining under the walls, the helmeted warriors climbing a steep ramp under the protection of their shields, and the showers of stones, torches and flaming arrows thrown down by the desperate but doomed defenders. Then follows the triumph, with Sennacherib, seated on his throne, receiving the throngs of captives, men and women, while the captured Jewish chieftains, pinioned to the ground, are being flayed alive by torturers armed with long knives.

One does not blame Hezekiah for stripping the gold from the House of the Lord to save himself and his people from such a fate.

But Layard's greatest triumph at Nineveh was the discovery of the Royal Library, two large chambers piled more than a foot deep in inscribed tablets; 26,000 of them, ranging from historical literature and diplomatic correspondence to business contracts, and scientific and medical documents.

"Science held high place; medicine proper (distinct from magic) is accorded due position on some five hundred tablets, which give good, honest, practical prescrip-

tions for every ill under the sun, from ear-ache to ophthalmia, to childbirth and the restoration of the apparently
drowned, showing a knowledge of some five hundred
drugs; botany had recorded some hundreds of names
of plants, with a vast display of knowledge of their properties; the chemist had already discovered the practical
use of a large number of minerals . . . and he has left
an invaluable treatise on the components of glass and the
glazes of pottery." [4]

But we owe this literature, not to the Assyrians, but to the peoples
of Babylonia and Sumeria, who developed a high civilization in
Lower Mesopotamia more than two thousand years before Sennacherib was born. In fact some of the folk-myths, epic poetry and
legend found in the Assyrian king's library was as remote from
Sennacherib as he is from us. The Assyrian scribes had copied and
adapted them.

Layard and the archæologists of 1849 did not know this, but,
like Schliemann when he excavated Troy and Mycenæ, they set
the feet of later generations of scholars on the path which led them
in time to the discovery of a much earlier and more attractive civilization. The work of these later archæologists, and the Sumerian
"Lost Cities" they discovered, will be discussed in the next chapter.

In April, 1851, Henry Layard returned once more to London.
His archæological work was over, and his diplomatic career had
begun. One hundred and twenty cases of his finds were shipped to
England, to find a resting-place in the British Museum, where they
occupy a great deal of wall-space. There, if you are so minded,
you may study the exploits of those grim warriors; bearded, like
the Victorians themselves, they suggest something of Victorian
ruthlessness and love of power. Seton Lloyd observes:

"These enormous Assyrian bulls had something in common with the ponderous conservative philosophy of the
mid-Victorian period, with its unshakable faith in the
best of all possible worlds, with its definite social castes

[4] R. Campbell-Thomson. *A Century of Exploration at Nineveh.* London,
1929.

duly prescribed by the Catechism, all doubtless to be maintained *in sæcula sæculorum.*"

To us who have had more intimate acquaintance with the realities of war and conquest, the savage power of the Assyrian reliefs has less appeal. To the writer at least, the interest lies more in the character and achievements of the man who found them.

To those who argue that these archæological treasures should have been left in Mesopotamia, there are two possible answers. First, if the mounds of Kuyunjik, Nimrud, could have been left undisturbed to be found by our own generation they would undoubtedly have been excavated with much greater care and skill, and much that was destroyed would have been saved. But from the moment that Europeans became interested in Ancient Assyria, it was inevitable that the ancient cities would be excavated. If Layard had not removed the sculptures and brought them to England, either they would have been taken to other European museums, or, left exposed, as many were, they would have been deliberately destroyed by the ignorant fanaticism of the Arabs, to whom every "graven image" was an abomination. So, taking the long view, perhaps both Britain and Iraq have reason to be grateful to Henry Layard.

CHAPTER THREE

Lost Cities of Babylonia

The Assyrian cities—Nineveh, Nimrud, Ashur and others—were built mainly along the upper reaches of the Tigris, in the hill country of northern Mesopotamia. Hundreds of miles to the south, where the two great rivers, the Tigris and Euphrates, crawl sluggishly across an endless, dun-coloured plain, lay the much more ancient land of Sumeria, later called Babylonia. To the authors of the Old Testament it was the "Land of Shinar" to which the descendants of Noah journeyed "from the east" and built themselves a city.

> "And the whole earth was of one language, and of one speech. And it came to pass, as they journeyed from the east, that they found a plain in the land of Shinar; and they dwelt there. And they said to one another 'Go to, let us make brick, and burn them thoroughly.' And they had brick for stone, and slime they had for mortar. And they said 'Go to, let us build a city and a tower, whose top may reach unto heaven; and let us make us a name, lest we be scattered abroad upon the face of the whole earth.' "

So begins the eleventh chapter of Genesis. The primitive ancestors of the Jews probably did settle in this area, but if so they were only one people among many. What is quite certain is that one of the two earliest civilizations on earth grew up in Lower Mesopotamia,[1] and among its cities was "Ur of the Chaldees", birthplace of Abraham.

[1] The other was Egypt.

40

Until the middle of the last century nothing was known of the Sumerians and their civilization, apart from a few references to Shinar in the Bible. The land itself did not attract travellers. Sir Leonard Woolley's description of it tells us why:

"Standing on the summit of this mound" (of Ur) "one can distinguish along the eastern skyline the dark tasselled fringe of the palm-gardens on the river's bank, but to north and west and south as far as the eye can see stretches a waste of unprofitable sand. To the south-west the flat line of the horizon is broken by a grey upstanding pinnacle, the ruins of the staged tower of the sacred city of Eridu which the Sumerians believed to be the oldest city on earth, and to the north-west a shadow thrown by the low sun may tell the whereabout of the low mound of al 'Ubaid; but otherwise nothing relieves the monotony of the vast plain over which the shimmering heat-waves dance and the mirage spreads its mockery of placid waters. It seems incredible that such a wilderness should ever have been habitable for man, and yet the weathered hillocks at one's feet cover the temples and houses of a very great city." [2]

Yet to anyone responsive to the appeal of the remote past, southern Mesopotamia has a compelling fascination. For just as, at sunset, sky and cloud, sea and land, form and reform in ever-changing patterns, so, in Iraq, Old Testament stories, Babylonian myths, written history and archæological revelations merge and mingle so that one hardly knows where one element ends and the next begins.

For example, we have already quoted the passage in Genesis which describes how the descendants of Noah built a city in the "Land of Shinar". But we can go back even further than that, to the story of the Deluge.

"And it came to pass after seven days that the waters of the flood were upon the earth. . . . And the flood was forty days upon the earth; and the waters increased,

[2] Woolley, Sir Leonard. *Ur of the Chaldees.* Pelican Books. London.

and bare up the ark, and it was lift up above the earth.
. . . And the waters prevailed, and were increased
greatly upon the earth, and the ark went upon the face of
the waters."

Among the 26,000 cuneiform tablets discovered by Layard in
the Royal Library of Ashurbanipal at Nineveh was an epic poem
called "Sa nagba imuru", which means "He who saw everything",
better known as the Epic of Gilgamesh. Tablet XI contains the
following lines:

> *"Man of Shuruppak, son of Ubar-Tutu,*
> *Tear down (this) house, build a ship!*
> *Give up possessions, seek thou life.*
> *Despise property and keep the soul alive!*
> *Aboard the ship take thou the seed of all living things.*
> *The ship that thou shalt build*
> *Her dimensions shall be to measure.*
> *Equal shall be her width and her length.*
> *Like the Apsu shalt thou seal her. . . ."*

Then the poem goes on to describe how Gilgamesh, the hero,
built his ship.

> *"Ten dozen cubits each edge of the square deck*
> *I laid out the shape of her sides and joined her together. . . .*
> *. . . I hammered water-plugs into her.*
> *I saw to the punting-poles and laid in supplies . . ."*

Then came the Deluge.

> *"Consternation over Adad reaches to the heavens,*
> *Turning to blackness all that has been light.*
> *(The wide) land is shattered like (a pot)*
> *For one day the south-storm (blew)*
> *Gathering speed as it blew (submerging the mountains)*
> *Overtaking the people like a battle.*
> *No one can see his fellow,*
> *Nor can the people be recognized from heaven. . . ."*

—until, on the seventh day—

> *"The flood-carrying south-storm subsided in the battle*
> *Which it had fought like an army.*

The sea grew quiet, the tempest was still, the flood ceased.
I looked at the weather; stillness had set in,
And all mankind had returned to clay.
The landscape was as level as a flat roof. . . ."

". . . On Mount Nisir the ship came to a halt.
Mount Nisir held the ship fast,
Allowing no motion. . . .
When the seventh day arrived,
I sent forth and set free a dove.
The dove came forth, but came back;
There was no resting place for it and she turned round.
Then I sent forth and set free a swallow.
The swallow went forth, but came back;
There was no resting place for it and she turned round. . . ." [3]

And so on, until at last "a raven went forth and, seeing that the waters had diminished, he eats, circles, caws, and turns not round". Nearly all the familiar elements of the Bible story are there (though the details are slightly different), but set down with far more energy, vividness and pace. Yet that Assyrian tablet, though probably inscribed in the eighth century B.C., was subsequently proved to be a copy of a much more ancient Sumerian poem, examples of which have been found dating from about 1500 B.C. And the poem itself is even older than that, probably dating from before the invention of writing (*circa* 3000 B.C.).

The Book of Genesis, in its present form, is not earlier than about 700 B.C., and it is certain that the compilers of the Old Testament were drawing on literary material older than the earliest traditions of their own race; and that material came from the Land of Shinar, the birthplace of their patriarch Abraham. How they inherited it is not certain; it may have come down to them from their remote ancestors who lived in Lower Mesopotamia, but other elements may have been acquired when they were exiled in Babylon, in the sixth century B.C.

In the first half of the nineteenth century European travellers in Lower Mesopotamia began to look for the biblical cities. Baby-

[3] *Ancient Near Eastern Texts.* Princeton University Press, 1950. (Translation of *The Epic of Gilgamesh*, by E. A. Speiser.)

lon was easy to identify. Its site had never been lost, and among
the tumbled mass of great mounds near the village of Hillah,
twenty-five miles south of Baghdad, was one prominent artificial
hill which still bore the name "Babil". In 1811, Claudius Rich,
whom we have already met, rode there with his young wife. He
was the first to make a thorough and intelligent examination of
the ruins, which he sketched and surveyed. He watched local workmen excavating and carrying away tons of ancient mud-bricks,
and was able to take away a few inscribed specimens (as noted by
Lord Byron). At this time the cuneiform script had not been
deciphered, and Rich had neither the resources nor the skill to
make a scientific investigation.

Nevertheless, his *Memoir on the Ruins of Babylon,* originally
published in Vienna, stirred the interest of European savants, and
gave the initial impetus to Mesopotamian archæology. Despite
the conventional piety of its introduction, which exhorts us to remember how unimportant Babylon was in the eyes of the Jewish
God, the *Memoir* breathes the true spirit of scientific enquiry. The
young Englishman went to Babylon not to sentimentalize over its
ruins, but to observe, measure, and record his findings for the benefit of future investigators. His book is well illustrated with his careful maps, drawings and plans. Armed with the works of Herodotus,
Strabo and other classical writers who described the city, he set
out to identify, if he could, the features they had mentioned.

"From the accounts of modern travellers," he wrote,
"I had expected to have found, on the site of Babylon,
more or less than I actually did. Less, because I could
have formed no conception of the prodigious extent of
the whole ruins, or of the size, solidity, and perfect state,
of some of the parts of them; and more, because I thought
that I should have distinguished some traces, however
imperfect, of many of the principal structures of Babylon.
I imagined I should have said 'here were the walls, and
such must have been the extent of the area. There stood
the palace, and this most assuredly was the tower of Belus.' I was completely deceived; instead of a few isolated

mounds, I found the whole face of the country covered with vestiges of building, in some places consisting of brick walls surprisingly fresh, in others, merely a vast succession of mounds of rubbish. . . ."

Hills and banks of earth and brick, broken by deep ravines and honeycombed with tunnels made by brick-quarriers, and, occasionally, substantial fragments of well-built brick walls, were all that Rich could see of "the mighty city" of the Old Testament, where Balshazzar the King had

"made a great feast to a thousand of his lords, and drank wine before the thousand".

And where was the great hall in which—

"came forth the fingers of a man's hand, and wrote over against the candlestick upon the plaster of the wall of the king's palace; and the king saw the part of the hand that wrote . . ."

If parts of it still existed, there was no means of identifying them. Nor did Rich manage to trace any remains of the mighty walls which Herodotus described in the fifth century B.C.

As for the legendary Tower of Babel, Rich finally narrowed down its possible site to two particularly high mounds, but without any strong conviction that either was correct. In fact, Babylon was altogether a puzzle and a disappointment. Though huge, the site had been so plundered and hacked about that it seemed impossible ever to establish layout or identify its buildings.

Forty years after Rich's visit, Henry Layard came to Babylon. The sight of the wide-spreading ruins of the once-proud capital of western Asia moved him deeply.

"I shall never forget the effect produced upon me by the long lines and vast masses of mounds, which mark the site of ancient Babylon, as they appeared in the distance one morning as the day broke behind them. The desolation, the solitude, those shapeless heaps, all that remains of a great and renowned city, are well calculated to impress and excite the imagination. As when I first beheld the mounds of Nineveh, a longing came over me to learn what was hidden within them, and a kind of presentiment that I should one day seek to clear up the mystery."

But in this case Layard's presentiment was false. He was no more successful than Rich in establishing the layout of the city, or in finding objects of intrinsic or artistic value. Such discoveries as he made were minor ones, the usual inscribed bricks (all bearing the name Nebuchadnezzar), some pottery and seal-cylinders, and a few late skeletons, probably dating from Seleucid times.

> "No relic or ornament had been buried with the bodies. The wood of the coffins was in the last stage of decay, and could only be taken out piecemeal. A foul and unbearable stench issued from these loathsome remains, and from the passages which had become the dens of wild animals, who had worked their way into them from above. . . ."

After a few weeks Layard had to admit defeat and disappointment. "The discoveries," he wrote, "were far less numerous and important than I could have anticipated, nor did they tend to prove that there were remains beneath the heaps of earth and rubbish which would reward more extensive excavations. . . . There will be nothing to be hoped for from the site of Babylon." But nearly half a century later the great man was proved to have been utterly wrong.

However, it would be unfair to blame Layard; because when he made his pessimistic forecast little was known about the ancient cities of Lower Mesopotamia. Many were known to exist; their dark mounds rose in scores along the banks of the two rivers, and on the wide-spreading plain between. Now that the ancient writing could be partially read, a few of these mounds had even been identified from inscribed bricks found on the sites. But it was still not realized that, unlike the Assyrians, who had near access to good building-stone, the peoples of ancient Babylonia and Sumeria had had to build their cities almost entirely of mud-brick, either sun-dried or burned; indeed often they did not even bother to make bricks but built their walls of solid mud. When such cities fall into ruin, it is almost impossible to distinguish between remains of walls and the surrounding earth and fallen debris. The archæological methods of 1850 were quite unequal to this task; Layard, when he began trenching in the mounds of Babylon, cut through mud-brick walls and rubbish alike, without realizing which was which. Botta had a similar puzzling experience at Ashur, the old capital of Assyria, which was also built of mud-brick. A new technique of excavation was needed, calling for minute observation, scrupulous care, and great patience; the touch of the watch-maker, rather than the blacksmith. The pioneers of this new "fine-comb" method in Mesopotamia were the German archæologists of the *Deutsch-Orient Gesellshaft*. Their leader was Dr. Robert Koldewey.

The romance of Koldewey's achievement was of a different kind from that of Layard and Botta. In March, 1899, he arrived in Babylon, which was still the same confused jumble of mounds, ditches and ravines which Rich and Layard had seen. Yet when, fifteen years later, the outbreak of the First World War stopped the excavations, the ruins had taken on a shape. The city which Herodotus had seen nearly twenty-five centuries before, with its Sacred Way, its Ishtar Gate flanked by huge towers, and almost every one of its principal buildings, even the remains of the great wall which Rich failed to find, could be identified with precision. Near the centre of the city they had identified E-temen-anki, with its high *ziggurat,* or staged tower, which was proved to have stood to a height of nearly two hundred and fifty feet—almost certainly this was the original "Tower of Babel" described in Genesis, although Birs Nimrud, further west of the city, is an alternative candidate.

Babylon was one of the most ancient cities of southern Mesopotamia. It was the capital of the great King Khammurabi (*circa* 1790 B.C.), but its origins go back even further, probably to about 3000 B.C. The city is mentioned in the tenth chapter of Genesis, which speaks of Nimrud, and adds, "and the beginning of his kingdom was Babel and Erech, and Accud, and Culneh in the land of Shinar".[4]

But the Babylon which Koldewey investigated was that of King Nebuchadnezzar (605–562 B.C.), who carried the Jews into captivity with "the princes of Judah and Jerusalem, and the carpenters, and the smiths", the time of which Jeremiah spoke, when

> "A voice was heard in Ramah, lamentations, and bitter weeping; Rachel weeping for her children, refused to be comforted for her children, because they were not . . ."

It was this city which Herodotus saw in the fifth century B.C. Until fifty years ago, when Koldewey laid bare the streets and temples, the Greek historian's description was still one of the main sources of information concerning Nebuchadnezzar's city. He says of it:

> "In addition to its size it surpasses in splendour any city in the known world."

And then goes on to describe the great wall, which, he says, covered a circuit of fifty-six miles and had a breadth of fifty cubits (about eighty feet). He estimated its height at 200 cubits (about 320 feet).

> "On the top of the wall they constructed, along each edge, a row of one-roomed buildings facing inwards with enough space between for a four-horse chariot to run. There are a hundred gates in the circuit of the wall, all of bronze with bronze uprights and lintels. . . . The great wall I have described is, so to speak, the breastplate or chief defence of the city; but there is a second one within it, not so thick but hardly less strong. There is a fortress in the middle of each half of the city; in one the royal palace surrounded by a wall of great strength, in the other the temple of Bel, the Babylonian Zeus. . . . It has a solid central tower, one furlong square, with a second erected on top of it and then a third, and so on up to

─────────────

[4] The sites of these cities have been identified.

eight. . . . On the summit of the topmost tower stands a great temple with a fine large couch in it, richly covered, and a golden table beside it. The shrine contains no image, and no one spends the night there except (if we may believe the Chaldeans who are the priests of Bel) one Assyrian woman, all alone, whoever it may be that the god had chosen. The Chaldeans also say—though I do not believe them—that the god enters the temple in person and rests upon the bed."

Herodotus also describes how the Euphrates divided Babylon into two districts, and that in earlier times citizens wishing to pass from one district to the other had to use boats. However, Nitocris, a Babylonian queen, temporarily diverted the river into a basin, and then

"as near as possible to the centre of the city she built a bridge over the river with the blocks of stone which she had prepared, using iron and lead to bind the blocks together. . . . Finally, when the basin had been filled and the bridge finished, the river was brought back into its original bed. . . ." [5]

Other classical authors, such as Pliny, Strabo and Ctesias, supplemented this information, and Diodorus the Sicilian wrote of the "hanging gardens" of Queen Semiramis. These were raised on a high platform on which grew grass, flowers, and large trees, perpetually watered by artificial streams fed by water pumped from the river. There had also been a great processional way, raised high above the ground-level of the city, which had straight streets set at right-angles, and temples and palaces, the magnificence of which had no parallel in the ancient world.

To disinter what survived of these glories, and to reconstruct on paper what had perished, would seem an impossible task. It is to the lasting credit of Koldewey and his assistants—both German and Iraqui—that they succeeded.

[5] Herodotus. *The Histories,* translated by Aubrey de Selincourt. Penguin Books. London, 1954.

"Presumably the following of baked-clay walls," writes Seton Lloyd, "which presents little difficulty, led imperceptibly to the mastery of the far more difficult task of tracing sun-dried brickwork. It is, in any case, certain that by the end of their second season they had equipped themselves with a gang of skilled Arab wall-tracers whose descendants and successors have formed the nucleus of the workmen employed on almost every excavation from that day to this . . . the recovery of architectural detail became a fine art, with the result that, by the time the work at Babylon was interrupted by the first rumours of war in Europe, the whole layout of the imperial city with its complicated fortifications, monumental gateways, procession street, and almost every one of its principal buildings had been excavated or sufficiently traced to make a convincing and reliable reconstruction." [6]

To attempt to summarize Koldewey's work in a few pages would be an impertinence, but here are a few examples. The German excavators found remains of the great girdle-wall which Herodotus describes, and which Rich and Layard failed to locate. In most respects the Greek historian had been right. There were, as he wrote, two walls, an inner and an outer, the space between being filled with rubble. The inner wall was of crude brick, the outer of burned brick, and at intervals of roughly 165 feet along the inner wall were towers, each about 27 feet wide and projecting beyond the wall on both its faces. The total width of the two walls, with the rubble filling, was approximately 80 feet, the dimensions given by Herodotus; a width sufficient, as Koldewey writes, "for a team of four horses abreast, and even for two such teams to pass each other."

"This broad roadway," he adds, "was of the greatest importance for the protection of the great city. It rendered possible the rapid shifting of defensive forces at any time to that part of the wall which was specially pressed by attack."

The main discrepancy between Herodotus' description and Koldewey's findings was in the length of the outer wall. Herodotus

*Lloyd, Seton. *Foundations in the Dust*. Penguin Books. London, 1947.

makes the total circuit fifty-six miles, Koldewey only thirteen miles. The figure given by Ctesias is approximately 42 miles— four times the correct measurement, which suggests that Ctesias mistook the figures representing the whole circumference for the measure of one side of the square. As for Herodotus, arithmetic was never his strong point.

Nebuchadnezzar himself mentions this work in a cuneiform inscription, quoted by the German scholar.

> "That no assault should reach Imgur-Bel, the wall of Babylon; I did, what no earlier king had done, for 4,000 ells of land on the side of Babylon, at a distance that it (the assault) did not come nigh, I caused a mighty wall to be built on the east side of Babylon. I dug out its moat, and I built a scarp, with bitumen [7] and bricks. A mighty wall I built on its edge, mountain-high. . . ."

Koldewey also found and excavated the great ceremonial roadway which passed north to south through the central area of the city. The central part of this road was laid with slabs of lime-stone more than three feet square, and on each side were "slabs of red breccia veined with white". The edge of each slab was inscribed with the words:

> "Nebuchadnezzar, King of Babylon, son of Nabopo-lassar, King of Babylon, am I. The Babel street I pave with blocks of shadu stone for the procession of the great Lord Marduk. Marduk, Lord, grant eternal life."

Marduk was one of the chief gods of Babylon.

This processional roadway was lined on each side with high defensive walls, 23 feet thick, and adorned with brilliantly coloured enamelled bricks, many of which were found on the site. These high walls led to the mighty Ishtar Gate, a double gateway still standing to a height of forty feet, and covered with enamelled brick reliefs of bulls and dragons in vivid colours. The effect of this grand

---

[7] Bitumen is common in Iraq. The translator of the passage from Genesis quoted at the beginning of this chapter uses the word "slime", but the correct translation of the Hebrew word is "cement", i.e. bitumen.

ceremonial approach, and massive walls and towering gate, must have been awe-inspiring. The lions, a glowing gold against a ground of blue enamelled bricks, marched in line on either side of the broad, paved road. As Koldewey writes:

> "The high defensive walls . . . guarded the approach to the gate. Manned by the defenders, the road was a real pathway of death to the foe who should attempt it. The impression of peril and horror was heightened for the enemy, and also for peaceful travellers, by the impressive decoration of long rows of lions advancing one behind the other with which the walls were adorned in low relief with brilliant enamels."

Within the southern citadel, called by the Arabs the Kasr, the archæologist excavated the lower part of a vaulted building with fourteen massive barrel-vaults which "could move as freely upwards or downwards within the enclosing quadrangle as the joint of a telescope". The Babylonians of 600 B.C. understood the function of that expanding joint. Koldewey continues: "In this respect the vaulted building is unique among the buildings of Babylon; and in another respect it is also exceptional. Stone was used in the building. . . . It is remarkable that in all the literature referring to Babylon, including the cuneiform inscriptions, stone is only mentioned as used in two places, in the north wall of the Kasr *and in the hanging gardens*. . . ." [8] (Our italics.)

In one of the western cells of this vaulted structure, the excavators came upon a curious well, unlike any found in Babylon or any other ancient city. It had three shafts, an oblong one in the centre with a square shaft on each side. "I can see no other explanation," writes Koldewey, "than that a mechanical hydraulic machine stood there, which worked on the same principle as our chain pump, where buckets attached to a chain work on a wheel placed over the wall."

There seems little doubt that this was the substructure of the

[8] Robert Koldewey. *The Excavations at Babylon*. Translated by Agnes S. Johns. Macmillan and Co. Ltd., 1914.

building which supported the famous Hanging Gardens, vainly sought for by former explorers. Probably the vaulted roof bore the layer of earth on which the trees were planted.

> "The roof is protected by an unusually deep layer of earth. The air that entered the chambers through the leaves of the trees must have been delightfully cooled by the continuous watering of the vegetation. Possibly the palace officials did a great part of their business in these cool chambers during the heat of the summer . . . the protection of the roof from the permeation of moisture, as described by Greek and Roman authors, agrees well with what we know of the practice of ancient architects."

The author adds "the expression 'hanging' has no doubt heightened the fame of the gardens, although the term *pensilis*" (from Curtis Rufus) "conveyed no such marvellous ideas to ancient scholars as they do to us. *Pensilia* are the balconies of the Romans, and were nothing out of the common for them. The reason that the hanging gardens were ranked among the seven wonders of the world was that they were laid out on the roof of an occupied building."

South of the principal court the excavators found the largest chamber in the citadel, the throne-room of the kings of Babylon, over 150 feet long and 60 feet wide. Opposite the main door was a double niche in which no doubt the throne stood, so that the king could be seen by those who stood outside the great court. Here, possibly, Belshazzar held feast on that fateful night when the Medes and Persians stormed the city.

> *"And in that night was Belshazzar the king slain, and his kingdom divided."*

One by one the principal buildings were revealed by the Germans' patient methods; the Temple of Nimach, the Moat Wall of Imgur-Bel, and the sacred precinct which enclosed the *Ziggurat* (Tower) Etemenanki, "the foundation stone of heaven and earth" —The Tower of Babylon itself. It consisted of a huge rectangular courtyard, surrounded by buildings, some perhaps intended to house pilgrims who came to the shrine of the god, others the rich and spacious homes of the high priests. This was, as Koldewey says, "the Vatican of Babylon", the place which Herodotus described as "The brazen-doored sanctuary of Zeus Belus". From one end of the courtyard rose the tower itself, in eight stages, though to what height it originally climbed we cannot be certain. Both Nebuchadnezzar and his father Nabopolassar have left inscriptions which emphasize its height. Nabopolassar says:

> "At this time Marduk commanded me . . . ; the tower of Babylon, which in time before me had become weak, and had been brought to ruin, to lay its foundations firm to the bosom of the underworld, while its top should stretch heavenwards" (trans. Delizsch).

And his son boasts that

> "To raise up the top of Etemenanki that it may rival heaven I laid my hand."

These great towers or *ziggurats,* the most characteristic feature of Sumerian, Babylonian and Assyrian cities, were a material expression of the plain-dwellers' yearning for height. From these lofty structures reared into the sky they could look down on what was then the most fertile land on earth, mile after mile of flat green fields, palm groves, and vineyards, criss-crossed by a network of irrigation canals, where now there is nothing but dull brown waste expanding to the horizon. At dawn and sunset the dried up troughs of the ancient canals still show as dark lines across the alluvial plain, the only memorials of the millions who created one of the first two civilizations on earth.

That civilization depended on the complex system of irrigation, developed and maintained over thousands of years, but when, in the thirteenth century, the Mongul hordes swept across Mesopotamia, burning, looting, and killing, the pumps ceased working, the channels silted up, the depopulated fields died.

Babylon itself, after a brief resurrection, has returned once more to the shapeless mass of ruins which Rich and Layard saw, for mud-brick walls, once exposed, soon crumble, and since the Germans left the Arab builders of Hillah have quarried away practically every brick of the Ziggurat of Etemenanki. It exists only in the pages of Koldewey's book, which one reads with a certain sadness.

"For what is written information in comparison with the clearness of the evidence we gain from the buildings themselves, ruined though they are? The colossal mass of the tower, which the Jews of the Old Testament regarded as the essence of human presumption, amidst the proud palaces of the priests, the spacious treasuries, the innumerable lodgings for strangers—white walls, bronze doors, mighty fortification walls set round with lofty portals and a forest of 1,000 towers—the whole must have conveyed an overwhelming sense of greatness, power and wealth, such as rarely could have been found elsewhere in the great Babylonian kingdom.

"I once beheld the great silver standing statue of the Virgin, over life-size, laden with votive offerings, rings, precious stones, gold and silver, borne on a litter by forty men, appear in the portal of the dome of Syracuse, high above the heads of the assembled crowds. . . . After the same fashion I picture to myself a procession of the god Marduk as he issued forth from Esagila, perhaps through the peribolos, to proceed on this triumphant way through the Procession Street of Babylon."

CHAPTER FOUR

Lost Cities of Babylonia (2)

During the latter half of the nineteenth century scholars gradually mastered the cuneiform writing so that more and more of the ancient inscriptions could be read. It should be emphasized that cuneiform itself is not a language, but a writing system. Like the Latin alphabet, which can be used to write in German, French, Italian, and other European tongues, so the little wedge-shaped characters were used by many peoples of Western Asia to write their own languages and dialects; Sumerian, Akkadian, Assyrian, Persian and so on. This had a direct and vital bearing on the search for the lost cities of Babylonia. Before the inscription could be deciphered, archæologists like Rich and Layard were interested mainly in material remains—buildings, sculpture, arms, furniture, and domestic objects—but once the inscriptions could be read a whole new chapter opened.

We have already mentioned the royal library of Sennacherib, discovered by Layard at Nineveh. In 1852 Layard's former assistant, Hormudz Rassan, re-opened the mound on behalf of the British Museum, and discovered yet another royal library, that of King Ashurbanipal; the floor of the chamber was stacked high with inscribed tablets, and on the walls were the famous "lion-hunt" reliefs now on view in the British Museum. At the time these could not be fully deciphered, but later, when they were, they revealed that there had existed a much older civilization in southern Mesopotamia, where, indeed, this system of writing appears to have been invented.

Already, however, thanks to the researches of Henry Rawlinson, who in 1851 had returned to his post as Resident in Baghdad, some names could be read. Two years earlier another young Englishman, William Kennet Loftus, a member of the Turco-Persian frontier commission, had made an adventurous trip on horseback across the desert and marshes of Chaldea from the Euphrates to the Tigris, accompanied by a young friend, H. A. Churchill. He was astounded and excited to find, in many places, great mounds marking the sites of long-dead cities, and evidences of an elaborate system of cultivation, canals and ditches which proved that once there had been green fields and orchards where now there was only desert. The head of the Mission, Colonel Williams, was so impressed by the young men's report that he agreed that Loftus should undertake an excavation at one of these cities, in company of two friends, Boutcher and Kerr Lynch. Loftus returned to the site and dug there for three months, but the place was so huge that he could make but little impression on it. However, from inscriptions found there Rawlinson was able to identify the ancient name of the town. It was *Erech*. And again men remembered the tenth chapter of Genesis, which describes the generations of the sons of Noah;

> "And Cush begat Nimrud; he began to be a mighty one in the earth. . . . And the beginning of his kingdom was Babel, and *Erech,* and Accad, and Calneh in the land of Shinar . . ."

Then Loftus moved to another site, Senkara, where his work was somewhat hindered by lions which hung about the camp at night and, one by one, devoured the archæologist's dogs.

> "Poor Toga was heard to give one stifled yelp, and all was over with our last guardian; he was carried off and demolished at a meal."

Soon Rawlinson received inscribed tablets found at Senkara, and once again he was able to identify its original name. It was Larsa, the "Ellasar" of the fourteenth chapter of Genesis.

While Loftus worked at Warka and Senkara, another amateur, J. E. Taylor, British Vice-consul, was investigating the mound of Tell Muquyyar near Nasiryah. It had well-preserved remains of a high *ziggurat*. Into this Taylor drove a tunnel and by accident came upon a small inscribed cylinder in the corner of the mud-brick masonry. He dug into the other corners and found similar cylinders, which he sent to Rawlinson for decipherment. The name was *Ur,* the city of the Chaldees, home of Abraham.

At this time none of the excavators who worked on these great mounds had any conception of their true age. Comparative dating by pottery, and the careful study of stratification, as an indication of age and comparative date, had yet to be developed. All that lay in the future, when a more scientific generation of archæ-ologists were able to prove that some of these mounds e.g. Warka, had been continuously occupied for more than four thousand years. In the meantime, as more hoards of baked clay tablets—palace archives—were found and read, it became possible to establish the names of the kings of these long-vanished civilizations, and to study their history, religion and folk-myths. And the mounds of Baby-lonia, which Layard and others thought would yield little or noth-ing, became of even greater interest than the stone-built palaces of the Assyrian kings, who, in comparison with the Sumerians, were mere newcomers.

A great impetus came when the tablets found in the Royal Libraries of Nineveh were properly deciphered, for many of these were found to be copies of much earlier documents. One of the pioneers in this field was George Smith, who, in the 'sixties', had been an apprentice to a firm of bank-note engravers. During his lunch-hours he used to frequent the British Museum, studying the Assyrian inscriptions which by this time were on exhibition. One of the Museum staff, impressed by the young man's enthusiasm and knowledge, gave him a small post on the staff, and encouraged him to study. This, of course, was what Smith wanted, and when he was given the task of sorting out and identifying the thousands of clay tablets from the Library of Ashurbanipal, he made a discovery which immediately brought him into the news. In his own words:

> "Commencing a steady search . . . I soon found half of a curious tablet which had evidently contained originally six columns . . . On looking down the third column, my eye caught the statement that the ship rested on the mountain of Nizir, followed by an account of the sending forth of the dove. . . . I saw at once that I had here discovered a portion at least of the Chaldean account of the deluge."

This was the passage part of which is quoted in the previous chapter. When Smith read a paper on the subject it caused such a stir, particularly among the theologians, that one of the London newspapers agreed to send Smith out to Nineveh at the head of an expedition, with a view to finding a portion of the story which was missing. The almost unbelievable fact is that, after cutting through the mounds of debris left by the previous excavators, he found, almost immediately, the precious missing fragment.

Smith, unhappily, died four years later, of dysentery contracted on a journey across the desert from Mosul to the Mediterranean, the first Assyriologist, as Seton Lloyd says, "to meet his death in the field".

The poem of which the "Deluge" story forms part is the "Epic of Gilgamesh", a legendary hero of Sumerian folktale. As a work of literature it has been compared with Homer's epic poems. It is not in the Assyrian language, which was Semitic, but in an unknown, non-Semitic tongue. A number of other inscribed tablets found in the royal libraries were also in this language, and fortunately there were bi-lingual texts and syllabaries which enabled them to be deciphered and read. It was discoveries such as these, and tablets found on southern Mesopotamian sites, which introduced to the world the mysterious Sumerians, who had occupied Lower Mesopotamia at some remote period before 3000 B.C. They share with the Ancient Egyptians the distinction of being the inventors of writing, and of creating the first civilizations on earth.

From the "seventies" to the present day, archæologists of several nations have helped to piece together the history of these people. By this time the trend of research had begun to change. Instead of pecking away at a large number of mounds in the hope of quickly finding portable loot for Museums, archæologists were sent out on organized expeditions, financed by their Governments, or by Universities or Museums, and concentrated on a thorough, leisurely exploration of a few selected cities. Such was the French expedition to the mound of Telloh (ancient Lagash) under Sarzec, and the American expedition under Peters, which dug for years at Nippur.

Ernest de Sarzec had been French vice-consul at Basra. Finding time hanging heavily on his hands he sought permission to excavate the extensive ruins of a then unknown city near the Shatt al Hai canal, about which he had been told by a certain Mr. J. Asfar, a dealer in antiquities. First shaking off the eager bloodhound of the British Museum, Homudz Rassam (who had also sniffed out the site), the Frenchman succeeded in getting exclusive permission to excavate, and a financial grant from his Government.[1] Then, season after season, for twenty-five years, he systematically examined the whole vast area. Although his excavating technique was almost brutal by modern standards, and his plans incomplete and sketchy, de Sarzec was the first man to dig out a large Sumerian city and to reveal its remarkable art to the world.

Although Sumerian art has many admirers, the writer must confess that he is not one of them. The archaic sculpture which de Sarzec found, the little, paunchy, pop-eyed men and gods, are certainly striking and vigorously executed. To a generation bored by the naturalism of Greek and Roman sculpture they provided a welcome stimulus, and when they were exhibited at the Louvre (where some of the finest examples are on view) they attracted

[1] If any readers think these sporting terms inappropriate, I recommend them to read Sir Wallis Budge's *By the Nile and Tigris*. There the pack can be heard in full cry.

wide interest among the great contemporary artists of the French school, and to some extent influenced their work. But compared with the Egyptian sculpture of the same period (*circa* 2500 B.C.), there is, in the writer's view, something perverted and repellent about Sumerian statuary. Like the Aztec or Maya art of North America, one either likes it or loathes it.

There are excellent examples in the British Museum, e.g. the famous "Governor of Lagash", and in leading American Art Galleries such as in New York and Pennsylvania. The reader must judge for himself.

Sumerian cities, such as Lagash, Eridu, Ur and Nippur, arose in the early part of the Third Millennium, though there were settlements on the sites in even earlier times. They were built of mud-brick, as described in Genesis, and contained palaces of their Governors or Kings (dependent on the status of the city) and one or more huge temples, of which the most prominent feature was a high tower or *ziggurat*. Their principal gods were nature-deities; such as Anu, god of the sky, Ki, the earth-goddess, Enlil, war-leader and storm-god, Enki, god of the waters on whom the Sumerians depended. For, as in Egypt, life in ancient Sumeria depended on the great river, the waters of which were canalized and channelled off to water the fields. Rainfall occurred only for a brief period each year, when the Euphrates flooded; the water, conserved behind dams, was fed to the fields during the long dry season by an elaborate system of canals and ditches.

It was this which enabled nomadic ancestors of the Sumerians to settle permanently in one place, to become agriculturalists and herdsmen, and to develop a civilization. The products of that civilization, their walled cities, their social organization with its legal and administrative systems, their science and art, all derived ultimately from the river beside which they lived. Writing, which they appear to have invented,[2] arose from the need to keep records of

[2] There is evidence to suggest that the ancient Egyptians, who also developed a writing system before 3000 B.C., were influenced by the Mesopotamian valley-civilization, perhaps by the immigration of peoples from the Euphrates valley.

crop-yields, heads of cattle, etc. Astronomy and mathematics, and the invention of the calendar, could develop in a country where the sky is clear for most of the year, and where the accurate observation of the seasons—the time to sow and the time to reap—was essential. The craft of metal-working, the production of bronze weapons and tools, would develop more rapidly and effectively within a social organization in which the itinerant craftsmen would be formed into guilds, protected and encouraged by the State. Architecture developed under the same stimulus, when a standardized system of measurement made possible the planning of monumental buildings.

The building material was mud, readily accessible in infinite quantities and easily moulded into bricks, which could be sun-dried or baked in kilns. Stone was rarely used; it was expensive and had to be brought from a great distance. As we have seen, the excavation of such buildings called for special delicacy and care, which was absent from the work of the earlier explorers, who often drove their tunnels carelessly through mud-brick walls which more painstaking workers would have detected. But gradually, thanks largely to the efforts of Koldewey and his associates at Babylon, the necessary techniques were evolved.

Next on the scene were the Americans, who in 1887 began to excavate Nippur under the auspices of the University of Pennsylvania. Their first season was disastrous. The Director of the expedition, Peters, had not lived in the East and was ignorant of Arab manners and customs. Instead of enlisting the help and protection of the local Sheikh, he put his workmen in the charge of a Turkish commissar. Tension arose, which was aggravated by Peters' nervousness and irritability. There was a little petty thieving which old hands like Layard or Botta would have taken in their stride, but, when a camp-guard killed a tribesman, Peters lost his head and sent for soldiers. The outcome is vividly described by Hilprecht, a member of the expedition who later became its leader. He gives a lively idea of the perils of Mesopotamian archæology in the "eighties".

"On Thursday, 18 April, long before the sun rose, the whole expedition was in readiness to vacate the mounds and force their way to Hilla, when, upon the treacherous orders of Mukota, an Arab secretly set fire to our huts of reeds and mats and laid the whole place in ashes in the short space of five minutes. For a while the utmost confusion prevailed; the *zabitye* got demoralized, and occupied a neighbouring hill; and while we were trying to save our effects, many of the Arabs commenced plundering. Half the horses perished in the flames, firearms and saddlebags and 1,000 dollars in gold fell into the hands of the marauders, but all the antiquities were saved. Under the war-dance and yells of the frantic Arabs the expedition finally withdrew." [3]

Three years later the American expedition returned to make a second attempt, this time more successful. In three seasons' digging they unearthed thirty thousand inscribed tablets, mostly business documents, but including over two thousand literary texts of high importance. In fact, of all the Sumerian literature known to exist, the majority was found at Nippur by the American excavators.[4] Among these tablets was one inscribed with a fragment of the "deluge" myth, in a different version to that found at Nineveh.

Another poem describes the death of Gilgamesh, the Sumerian hero; a third tells the story of how the goddess Inanna, queen of Heaven, visits the Underworld, a theme which has obvious parallels with the folk-myths of other ancient peoples; e.g. the Greek story of Persephone. It is an eerie tale, full of ghosts, and monsters, and demons with which the primitive imagination peopled the world of the dead, and reminiscent, in some ways, of the Ancient Egyptian *Book of what is in the Underworld*. The goddess, determined to visit the nether regions, against all prudent advice, adorns herself with her queenly jewels in preparation for the journey. The passage

[3] Hilprecht. *Exploration in the Bible Lands.*
[4] Although the scope of this book does not permit a description of all Mesopotamian excavations, honourable mention must be made of other important American excavations; at Bismayah, at Farah and elsewhere, and especially the work of J. H. Breasted's Oriental Institute of Chicago, at Tell Osmar, Khafajah and Tell Ajrab.

is interesting as a description of the toilet of a Sumerian queen five
thousand years ago.

"The sugurra, *the crown of the plain, she has put upon her head,*
The wig *of her forehead she has taken,*
The measuring rod (and) line of lapis lazuli she has gripped in
    her hand,
Small lapis stones she has fastened about her neck,
Sparkling *stones she has* fastened *to her breast.*
A gold ring she has put about *her hand,*
A breastplate which . . . *she has* tightened *about her breast,*
Kohl *which* . . . *she has daubed on her eyes,*
With the pala-garment, the garment of ladyship, she has covered
    her body. . . ."

When Inanna returns from the Underworld, she is accompanied by ghosts and demons.

"When Inanna ascends from the nether world
Verily the dead hasten ahead of her.
Inanna ascends from the nether world,
The small demons like the spear shafts,
The large demons like . . . . *s*
Walked at her side . . .
. . . *They who accompanied Inanna,*
(Were beings who) know not food, who know not water,
Who eat not sprinkled flour,
Who drink not libated (water)
Who take away the wife from the loins of man,
Who take away the child from the . . . *of the nursemaid* . . ."
    etc.

Reading this passage, one recalls Homer's description of the
Shades which Odysseus visited in search of news of his comrades
who fell at Troy. Perhaps all these myths have a common origin in
the remote prehistory of the human race.

Among the Nippur tablets was a rather lovely "Paradise-
myth" in which the idealized conception of Paradise is rooted in
the agricultural and pastoral economy of ancient Sumeria.

    "In Dilum" (Paradise) "the raven utters no cries,
    The ittdu-*bird utters not the cry of the* ittdu-*bird,*

The lion kills not,
Unknown is the kid-devouring wild dog,
Unknown is the grain-devouring. . . .
Unknown is the . . . widow,
The bird on high . . . s not its . . . ,
The dove droops not its head,
The sick-eyed (says) not 'I am sick-eyed',
The sick-headed (says) not 'I am sick-headed',
The old woman says not 'I am an old woman'
Its old man (says) not 'I am an old man'." . . .

Enki, the water-god, impregnates Ninhursag, the "mother of the land", though not before he has first brought her gifts of cucumbers, apples and grapes, and there is a reference to the dykes and ditches on which the Sumerians relied for the irrigation of their land.

"A second time he was filling with water,
He filled the dykes with water,
He filled the ditches with water,
He filled the uncultivated places with water,
The gardener in the dust in his joy
He embraces him. . . ."

The rich fertility symbolism of this is apparent, as it is in the passage in which the water-god "poured the semen in the womb of Ninhursag".

"She took the semen in the womb of Ninhursag,
She took the semen into the womb, the semen of Enki.
One day being her one month,
Two days being her two months,
Three days being her three months,
Four days being her four months,"

and so to the ninth day

"Nine days being her nine months, the months of womanhood,
Like fat, like good princely fat,
(Ninue), the mother of the land, like (. . . fat)
(Like fat, like good princely fat)

Gave birth to Nimmu
Nimmu . . . d at the bank of the river. . . ." [5]

Incidentally, although this has no direct bearing on Lost Cities, I cannot forbear from a mild protest against the exaggerated admiration sometimes given to these ancient poems. Surely respect for their age and historical value should not blind one to their literary defects! Some of them, for example "The Epic of Gilgamesh", are magnificent, and take their place alongside the heroic literature of the world, but too many, in my view, are marred by the irritating repetitive trick which one finds in a more modified form in Hebrew verse. At its best this effect can be intensely moving, as in the "Song of Deborah":

"At her feet he bowed, he fell, he lay down
At her feet he bowed, he fell;
Where he bowed, there he fell down dead."

And in:

"O my son Absalom, my son, my son Absalom!
would God I had died for thee, O Absalom,
my son, my son . . ."

But carried to excess it can become grotesque and even faintly comic, as in the passage quoted above:

"Like fat, like good princely fat,
Ninue, the mother of the land, like fat,
Like fat, like good princely fat,
Gave birth to Nimmu . . ." etc.

With the rapid progress of decipherment, these little tablets, which were found in thousands in the ruins of Sumerian cities, began to acquire commercial value. Shrewd Arab dealers employed workmen to carry on illicit digging on the sites after the archæologists had left. A flourishing trade developed; the tablets were crated in Baghdad and exported to Europe and America. At Telloh, for

[5] This, and other quotations from the Nippur tablets, are translated by S. N. Kramer and quoted from *Ancient Near Eastern Texts*, by kind permission of the University of Princeton Press. (1950.)

example, the illicit diggers struck a great hoard of tablets in the temporary absence of de Sarzec, covered them up so that he should not find them, and then, when he had gone, reopened the cache and sold the tablets to the Baghdad antiquity merchants. Sir Wallis Budge, of the British Museum, himself no mean exponent of this kind of legerdemain, was neatly tricked by a Baghdad official, who, hearing that the Englishman had applied for permission to dig at a certain site, sent out his own workmen in advance, and was rewarded by finding ten thousand tablets which he sold to the dealers.

One of the chief benefactors of this profitable deal sent Budge a delightful consolatory message, quoted by Mr. Seton Lloyd in his *Foundations in the Dust,* to which I am indebted for some of the material in this and preceding chapters. I cannot resist requoting it, for it sums up so charmingly the typical oriental attitude to archæology, particularly in Budge's time.

> "Be not sad of heart for such a thing has never happened to any seeker for antikat before. We have all the tablets in Baghdad, we are all your friends, and we have kept the tablets for you. You will buy them and they shall go out of the country quickly, and you will be able to live with your English friends in Baghdad and not be obliged to sit in the desert with the jackals and vultures, and burn by day and freeze by night. Besides, there are now many oranges in Baghdad." [6]

These written documents, and also the little cylinder seals with their engraved scene, helped archæologists to understand the purpose of some of the buildings they unearthed in the Sumerian towns, especially the temples. Both Layard and Botta had encountered ruins of high towers at Khorsobad, Nineveh, Nimrud and other Assyrian sites, without at first understanding their function. They always formed part of a large temple (as in Babylon), and practically every large Sumerian city had at least one; some had as many as three. From Sumerian religious inscriptions it seems certain that they were used in some religious ritual, as were the

---

[6] Budge, Wallis. *By Nile and Tigris.* Vol. II.

Mexican pyramids, and sacrificial rites were probably performed on them.

On New Year's Day a procession of priests and nobles went to the temples, which stood high above the rest of the city, to perform a fertility rite, of which the culmination was the ceremonial and probably physical union of a priest and priestess. On that same sacred morning, the smoke of sacrifice would be seen curling into the blue sky, from the roof-top of every lofty tower on the vast plain. The Sumerians were giving thanks to their gods for the wealth of their land, and invoking their aid for the future.

We do not know what happened to the chief celebrants after the ceremony; probably they were ritually sacrificed, as among the Indian peoples of America thousands of years later. Some support for this theory is provided by the so-called "royal" graves of Ur, found by Sir Leonard Woolley in 1926, the most dramatic archæological discovery in southern Mesopotamia. The expedition which Woolley led was jointly supported by the British Museum and the University Museum of Pennsylvania.

The mound of Tell Muquayer had been superficially examined by J. E. Taylor, when he found, in the corners of the *ziggurat,* the inscribed cylinders on which Rawlinson read the name "Ur". R. Campbell-Thomson had also made some soundings in 1918. Woolley began his excavations there three years later. During his early seasons he thoroughly excavated the great temple enclosure and the *ziggurat* with its triple staircase. Here, as in Babylon, there seem to have been "hanging gardens", for Woolley found evidence that quite large trees had been planted on its upper terraces. As other archæologists suspected, the Sumerian *ziggurat* was a kind of artificial mountain.

He also established that, at the time of its greatest glory— five thousand years ago—Ur had been a port. The head of the Persian Gulf, which is now some seventy miles to the south, then came nearly to the walls of the city, and quays ran deep into the maze of the streets. Most of the houses within the walled enclosure were almost exactly like those in which the Iraqui peasants live to-day, small-roomed, mud-brick dwellings with flat roofs; the system of agriculture, the crops grown, the food eaten and the cattle raised, were much the same in ancient Sumeria in 1957. The main difference was in the public buildings, the palaces of the kings, and the high-walled temples and towers.

Just outside the inner wall of Ur was an enormous rubbish tip, most valuable archæologically, since it contained the stratified debris left by scores of generations, and enabled Woolley to ascertain that Ur had been occupied more or less continuously for more than four thousand years. In 1926, when the workmen were digging deep shafts into the mound, they came upon the remains of a cemetery. The uppermost graves had been plundered, and the archæologist had every reason to suspect that all would have been ransacked in antiquity.

More than 1,400 of these simple "private graves" were dug or noted, half of which had been plundered by ancient tomb-robbers, probably the workmen engaged in digging the later graves. Then Woolley came upon deep shafts and tunnels, sometimes sunk deep and then driven horizontally, clearly the work of plunderers who were after bigger game. Tomb-robbing is an ancient and skilled profession. In Egypt, as I know from archæologists whose work I have watched, the presence of these robber's shafts usually arouses excitement. They indicate that thousands of years ago some enterprising and resourceful rogue knew that here was something worth finding, and there is always the remote possibility that he failed to find it.

"Near the end of the 1926 season the excavators at Ur came across a deep shaft, unlike the others, at the bottom of which was a hoard of copper weapons, and among them—overlooked by the robbers—a superb dagger of gold, with a hilt of lapis-lazuli and a gold sheath. Near it was a cone-shaped reticule ornamented with a spiral pattern and containing a set of little toilet instruments, tweezers, lancet, and pencil also of gold. Nothing like these things had ever before come from the soil of Mesopotamia; they revealed an art hitherto unsuspected and they gave promise of future discoveries outstripping all hopes." [7]

Woolley's next important find, though less sensational, was interesting enough. He found, deep down, slabs and blocks of lime-stone forming a kind of paving. On a Sumerian site, in which the buildings are of mud-brick, the finding of hewn stone was astonish-ing, as there is no stone in the Euphrates delta, and to find stone blocks at such a depth was puzzling. Could they be, perhaps, the roof of a tomb? Woolley had to wait until the next season's digging to find out.

It was a tomb, large, and built of stone, but apart from a few scattered fragments of a gold diadem—suggesting the richness of its original contents—it was empty. A long tunnel leading from the roof to ground level told the excavators why.

However, Woolley was not entirely disappointed. He had found a two-chambered tomb of stone, with a blocked doorway at one end leading to a slanting ramp cut down through the earth from ground-level. This was, at the time, unique, and caused much speculation. Perhaps there were other tombs in the vicinity, and it was just possible, though unlikely, that one of them had escaped the attention of the tomb-robbers. Woolley resolved to try again. During the 1928–29 season, two more sepulchres of similar con-struction were uncovered, but they, too, had been robbed.

Then came a discovery more strange and awe-inspiring than any archæological find of the past century, apart from the tomb of Tutankhamun, in Egypt. One day Woolley came upon five bodies lying side by side in a shallow sloping trench. This was not near the plundered tomb, but some distance away. Below them was a layer of matting. Tracing this along, Woolley found another group of bodies:

"Those of ten women carefully arranged in two rows:
they wore head-dresses of gold, lapis lazuli, and elaborate
bead necklaces, but they too possessed no regular tomb

[7] Woolley, Sir Leonard. *Ur of the Chaldees.* Penguin Books. London, 1954.

furnishings. At the end of the row lay the remains of a
wonderful harp, the wood of it decayed but its decoration
intact, making its reconstruction only a matter of care
. . . across the ruins of the harp lay the bones of the
gold-crowned harpist. . . ." [8]

A little further along the pit he made an even more curious
discovery; animal bones, with the remains of a wooden sledge-
chariot, which had been richly decorated with red, white and blue,
mosaic, and golden lions with manes of lapis lazuli and shell. The
bones were of asses which had drawn the chariot, and near them
lay two crushed human skeletons of the grooms who had led them
into the pit.

Yet these bodies, and those of the women, had not been enclosed in a built tomb, but lay on the sloping floor of a dug-out pit,
which had afterwards been refilled with earth. Among the objects
accompanying the bodies were an inlaid gaming board, a set of
chisels and a saw of gold, copper vessels, wooden chests adorned
with lapis, and lovely vessels of volcanic glass, alabaster, marble,
silver and gold.

". . . tall slender silver tumblers nested one inside another; a similar tumbler in gold, fluted and chased, with
fluted feeding-bowl, a chalice, and a plain oval bowl of
gold lay piled together, and two magnificent lion's heads
in silver, perhaps the ornament of a throne, were amongst
the treasures of the crowded pit. The perplexing thing
was that with all this wealth of objects we had found no
body so far distinguished from the rest to be that of the
person to whom all were dedicated; logically our discovery, however great, was incomplete."

Soon another pit was revealed, about six feet below the first,
and also approached by a long ramp, at the foot of which lay the
bodies of six soldiers, in two ranks, their spears beside them and
copper helmets on their crushed skulls. Beyond them, lower down
the ramp, were the remains of two wagons drawn by oxen, whose

[8] Woolley, Sir Leonard. *Ur of the Chaldees.* Penguin Books. London,
1954.

skeletons were found with those of the drivers beside them. Further down still the archæologists came upon a stone chamber, against the outer wall of which leaned the skeletons of nine women wearing magnificent gala head-dresses of lapis and carnelian. From these hung golden pendants shaped like beech-leaves, and the ladies had also worn large gold ear-rings, silver hair ornaments, and necklaces of gold and lapis lazuli.

> "... the whole space between them and the wagons was crowded with other dead, women and men, while the passage which led along the side of the stone (tomb) chamber was lined with soldiers carrying daggers, and with women. ... On top of the bodies of the 'court ladies' against the chamber wall had been placed a wooden harp ... by the side of the wall of the pit was a second harp, with a wonderful bull's head in gold, its eyes, beard and horn-tips of lapis lazuli, and a set of en-graved shell plaques not less wonderful; there are four of them with grotesque scenes of animals playing the parts of men, and while the most striking feature about them is that sense of humour which is so rare in ancient art, the grace and balance of the design and the fineness of the drawing make these plaques one of the most instructive documents we possess for the appreciation of the art of early Sumer." [9]

The stone chamber at the end of this lower pit had been plundered, although the robbers had left, among other things, an inscribed cylinder seal with the name of the tomb's owner, A-bar-gi, and two model boats, one of copper, the other of silver. But in the upper pit (in which the ass-drawn sledge-chariot was found) the tomb-chamber was intact, and contained the body of a lady named Shu-bad, resting on a bier, with a gold cup near her hand, and the upper part of her body covered by a mass of gold beads, silver, carnelian, agate, chalcedony and lapis lazuli. Her head-dress, of gold and semi-precious stones, was of the finest, and later Woolley

[9] Woolley, Sir Leonard. *Ur of the Chaldees.* Penguin Books. London, 1954.

was able to reconstruct it on a wax head modelled on a Sumerian skull.

Space forbids a complete description of this extraordinary discovery, which must be read in Sir Leonard Woolley's own account in *Ur of the Chaldees*. Several questions, however, require a brief answer here. First, who were these people, and when did they die? Woolley believes that they were royal persons who ruled in Ur round about 2700 B.C.

In his book he boldly describes the tombs as "the graves of the Kings of Ur". Many support his view, but there are other archæologists who have cast doubts on the theory. They might possibly be the bodies of glorified victims, priests and priestesses, who were sacrificed on the New Year's Day festival. The other, even more intriguing question is "whose were the bodies which lay outside the tomb; the soldiers, and the ladies in elaborate toilet with their elaborate head-dresses and rich jewellery"? And how did they come to die?

After a very careful investigation of the evidence, Woolley reached the conclusion that they had entered the burial-pit alive, together with the ox-wagons and the sledge-chariot, and then took poison, or a sleeping draught. The bodies lay in orderly rows; there were no signs of a struggle; the ladies' head ornaments were neatly in place, the soldiers with their arms beside them. The position of one of the harps, which lay on top of the bodies, indicates that someone entered the pit after the victims had lost consciousness and placed the instruments in position, probably also tidying the corpses before the pit was refilled. Clearly they were the attendants of the important personages buried in the stone-built chambers, who had followed him—or her—perhaps voluntarily—to the life beyond the grave. But whether A-bar-gi and Shubad were royal personages who had died natural deaths or sacrificial victims of high rank, will probably never be known.

Woolley found yet a third "death-pit", in which there had been a holocaust of victims, sixty-eight women and six men. The women's bodies lay in orderly rows, the heads of one row lying across the legs of the next. In this pit Woolley found a tiny piece of evidence which suggests that the victims entered the pit alive. Each of the "court ladies", as Woolley describes them, had evidently worn a silver head band. The silver had decayed, but remains of the decomposed metal showed near the skulls. But one lady had no head band. This puzzled Woolley for a time, until he found, near the body but not on the skull, a discoloured piece of metal, which on examination proved to be a silver head band *rolled up*. Probably its owner was late in dressing, and either forgot, or did not have time to put on her head band with the rest. She left it in a pocket of her robe, which protected it from corrosion, so that it survived to tell what is surely one of the strangest and most touching human stories revealed by archæology.

CHAPTER FIVE

A Forgotten Empire

Now we move from the featureless plain of Lower Mesopotamia to the high mountain plateau of Central Turkey (or Asia Minor). Even to modern travelled Europeans, Turkey is still a less familiar country than Egypt, Iraq, Syria and the Lebanon, homes of the earliest civilizations. The western and south-western portion, where the Greek colonists settled in about 700 B.C., is probably the best known, but the mountainous interior was *terra incognita* until about eighty years ago.

The western half of the country is a huge tongue-shaped peninsula with the Mediterranean to the south, the Ægean to the west, and the Black Sea to the north. It presents almost every conceivable variety of landscape and climate; alpine in the east, semi-tropical on the north-east coast, with a high central plateau; while the extreme western shores, facing the Ægean, have a typical Mediterranean landscape of olive-groves and vineyards, and a warm, dry climate like Italy or southern France. The southern coastal plains fronting on the Mediterranean grow citrus-fruit and cotton. In fact if you were a Swiss, a Scotsman, an African, Italian or Russian, you would find some part of Asia Minor where you were at home.

But such is the evocative power of a name that "Turkey" still summons up, in the minds of many people, a picture of an oriental land peopled by turbanned men and veiled ladies, despite the fact that Kemal Ataturk abolished the veil and instituted European dress more than thirty years ago. Turkey is a rich and lovely land, and, if travel became cheaper, would probably be as popular among western visitors as any southern European country.

The Ægean and Mediterranean provinces were occupied from very early times; the Greeks founded their earliest colonies there, and such kings as Crœsus of Lydia and the legendary Midas of Phrygia [1] are well known. But until fairly recently practically nothing was known concerning the interior and the eastern provinces in early historic and prehistoric times. A glance at the map will show that the south-eastern part of the country is not far from the ancient kingdom of Assyria, on the upper Tigris, yet it is a curious fact that, though excavations in northern Mesopotamia have revealed traces of human occupation going back more than seven thousand years, there is, at present, no evidence to show that southern Mesopotamia and Asia Minor were known to human beings earlier than 3000 B.C., or indeed, that the central plateau was occupied for some time after that. In fact there seems to have been a kind of "barrier" which, says Lloyd, "seems to correspond with surprising accuracy to the contour line at which the southern slopes of the mountains reached or exceeded a height of 2,000 feet. The 'barrier', therefore, though oriented approximately east and west, follows an irregular line with deep indentations where, for instance, the valleys of the Tigris and Euphrates penetrate far into the highlands, and a notable extension northwards into the Cilician Plain." [2]

Below that line there had been human occupation for perhaps several thousand years. Above, until the end of the Fourth Millennium, there appears to have been only animal and plant life. Some archæologists suggest as an explanation the fact that wheat and cereals, on which the first agricultural communities depended, could be grown on the Syrian plain, but not above the 2,000 feet level. The harsh winters of Anatolia may also have had much to do with it.

Yet, in 1500 B.C., a high civilization existed on the mountain plateau, a fact which was only discovered during the past century. The first clues leading to its discovery were found, not in the

[1] The famous "Phrygian cap" became one of the symbols of the French.
[2] Lloyd, Seton. *Early Anatolia,* Penguin Books. London, 1956.

mountains of Asia Minor, but in the pages of the Bible, and in the inscriptions of the older civilizations of Assyria, Babylonia and Egypt.

In the Old Testament there are a number of references to a people called the Hittites. Abraham, seeking a burial place for Sarah his wife, bought the cave of Macphelah, in Hebron, from "the sons of Heth". Esau married Hittite wives, and in the Book of Numbers there is a reference to the part of Palestine which the Hittites are said to have occupied.

> "Amalek dwelleth in the land of the south; and the Hittite, and the Jebusite, and the Amorite, dwell in the mountains; and the Canaanite" (i.e. Phœnicians) "dwelleth by the sea, and along by the side of Jordan."

The best known of the Biblical Hittites is of course Uriah, who was sent to his death when King David coveted Uriah's wife, Bathsheba. Incidentally, Mary, the mother of Jesus Christ, was of the "house of David", and Jesus himself may have been a remote descendant of Bathsheba. These Old Testament Hittites seem to have been dwellers in Palestine and Syria; they were neighbours of the Jews, and early nineteenth-century students of the Old Testament considered them of equal, not inferior, political importance. In fact, as Sayce points out, a distinguished Bible critic of the mid-nineteenth century questioned the authenticity of a passage in the Second Book of Kings (vii. 6), which states that when the Assyrians were camped about Samaria the panic-stricken Samarians said:

> "Lo, the king of Israel hath hired against us the kings of the Hittites, and the kings of the Egyptians, to come upon us."

The ancient Egyptians, the critic knew, were a mighty power at this time, and to him it seemed absurd to equate them with the Hittites, a tribe of no greater power than the Jews. "No Hittite kings," he wrote, "can have compared in power with the King of

Judah, the real and near ally, who is not named at all . . . nor is there a single mark of acquaintance with contemporary history."

However, as we shall see, there was nothing wrong with the Bible historian's "acquaintance with contemporaneous history". It was the critic who was wrong, though one cannot blame him, since the truth about the Hittites was not revealed until the decipherment of Egyptian, Babylonian and Assyrian inscriptions put archæologists on the right track.

The Egyptian writings, the first to be deciphered, gave historians the first clue. On a number of Egyptian temples there are records of wars waged by the Egyptian Pharaohs against the peoples of western Asia. Long lists of these enemies appear, usually with vigorous sculptured reliefs depicting the Pharaoh clutching the hair of a captured Asiatic, and joyously smashing his skull. Tuthmosis III, of the Eighteenth Dynasty (1555–1350 B.C.) is shown doing this. So are Sethi I, Ramesses II and Ramesses III, who reigned roughly between 1300 and 1200 B.C. Among these enemies one race is singled out for special hatred, the "abominable Kheta". Egyptologists noted the resemblance between this word and the Hebrew name for the Hittites, "Khatti". The Egyptians of the Eighteenth and Nineteenth Dynasties were often at war with these people, who were evidently formidable foes. On one of the temples of Ramesses II (*circa* 1250 B.C.) is an enormous carved relief which shows the defeat of the Kheta at the Battle of Kadesh, a town on the Orontes, in Syria. The enemy are depicted with singularly unpleasant faces, long-nosed and slit-eyed, with prognathous jaws, and wearing heavy woollen clothing. It was presumed that the details of dress were probably accurate, but that the faces were caricatures.

Yet, argued scholars, if the Kheta were the Biblical Hittites, how was it that, apart from the above quoted passage in Kings and one other, the Jewish writers had seemed to regard the Hittites as a small and usually friendly tribe, no more powerful than themselves? Yet the Egyptians, who, in the fifteenth century B.C., were the great power in the world, were so pleased with the victory over the "abominable Kheta" that they devoted much wall-space to a description of their defeat. Perhaps even more striking evidence of Egyptian respect for these unattractive but powerful people was a treaty between King Ramesses II and the Hittite king Hattusilis, the terms of which were inscribed on a stone stela found at Thebes, the Egyptian capital. In this carefully worded diplomatic document the two monarchs agree not to encroach on each other's territory, and to give aid if either is attacked. To strengthen the bond Ramesses II married one of the Hittite king's daughters, and the two queens of "Kheta" and Egypt exchanged congratulatory letters.

The Hebrews are not even mentioned on the Egyptian inscriptions, unless the word "Habiru", which occurs in a long list of conquered minor tribes, refers to them.

Another important clue came from Assyrian inscriptions; the finding and decipherment are described in the preceding chapter. Among these was an inscription from the reign of Tiglath-Pileser I (1100 B.C.) referring to a town called Milid in Syria, where the Assyrian king came into contact with a kingdom called "Great Hatti"; later, when returning from a campaign which took him to the shores of the Mediterranean, Tiglath-Pileser received homage from another king of "Great Hatti"; this probably occurred at Carchemish, on the upper Euphrates. Egyptian "Kheta", Hebrew "Khatti", Assyrian "Hatti" . . . surely these must be one and the same people? They were known in Palestine, they fought the Egyptian armies at Kadesh, well to the south, and they had kings who had apparently ruled in northern Mesopotamia. But who were they? What had they looked like? Were the Egyptian portraits true ones, or were they caricatures? And such a powerful kingdom must surely have had a capital. Where was it? For a long time these questions remained unanswered.

In some ways archæology is not unlike a jig-saw puzzle, one finds a piece, then another which seems to fit it, and then another isolated bit which seems to have no connection with the first two pieces. So one puts it aside, hoping to find a place for it later. The jig-saw may be put together in half an hour or less. The archæological picture may take centuries to form, and may never be completed.

In the search for the mysterious Hittite civilization, a few odd clues turned up at Hamath and Aleppo, in Syria. In each of these places were blocks of basalt inscribed in an unknown form of pictographic writing. One of the Hamath stones had been noted as early as 1812 by the traveller Burckhardt. It was not Egyptian, nor Phœnician, and certainly wasn't the well-known cuneiform of Babylonia and Assyria. In Aleppo, the inscribed stone had been let into the wall of a mosque, and had been worn smooth by sufferers from ophthalmia, who rubbed their eyes against it, believing it to have magical properties. When European scholars showed interest, the local people took away the block and hid it. Then, when these inscriptions had been copied and circulated among scholars, reports began to come in of other inscriptions in the same writing, but this time not in Mesopotamia, but far to the north in the Taurus Mountains of Asia Minor.

In 1876 Professor A. H. Sayce read a paper to the Society of Biblical Archæology, mentioning the blocks found at Aleppo and Hamath, and putting forward the theory that they were Hittite inscriptions. His reasons for believing this would take too long to explain here, but the theory aroused great interest, which was increased when still more inscriptions were found, on the hills above Smyrna, at Laja Huyük, and at a remote village called Boghaz Köy, which lies in a bend of the Halys river on the high tableland of central Asia Minor.

These facts are dramatic enough in themselves. They are much more so when considered in relation to the little-known country in which the inscriptions had been discovered. The trend of archæological research was carrying the explorers ever northward. The first ancient civilization they had revealed was that of Egypt, south of the Mediterranean. Next they had explored valleys of the Euphrates and Tigris, in Mesopotamia. Now they stood on the plains of northern Syria, to the north of which rose the forbidding range of the Taurus Mountains, which to the Romans marked the limits of the Inner (i.e. the southern) and the Outer Worlds, a barrier beyond which even they had not dared to pass. The civilization of Egypt and Babylonia had been valley-cultures, where men had grown their crops and pastured their flocks beside the banks of great rivers. Was it credible that a prehistoric civilization had existed in the inhospitable mountains of Asia Minor?

Between 1880 and 1900 a succession of European investigators made long and arduous journeys into the remoter parts of Turkey; the Germans Hummann and Puchstein, and the Frenchman Chantre, the Englishmen Hogarth, Headlam, Anderson, and Crowfoot. Each brought back reports of inscriptions, sculptures and even ruined cities, particularly in the Taurus and anti-Taurus mountains. At Boghaz Köy they confirmed earlier reports of massive walls built on a steep escarpment, and, two miles away, a cleft in the hill-side, on the natural walls of which was carved a double procession of figures in high relief. In the centre of what had been the city-area of Boghaz Köy was a great weathered slab of stone, the Nishan Tash, covered with hieroglyphs like those found at Hamath, Aleppo and many other places.

> "At Alaja Huyük was a gateway flanked by huge sphinxes leading to a mound of debris which clearly covered an ancient city or large building. Farther west were the rock-reliefs at Gavur (Giaour) Kalesi ('Unbelievers Fortress') and in the hills above Smyrna, were other rock-sculptures known since the time of Herodotus, who had described them as representing the nymph Niobe and the Egyptian king Sesostris." [3]

But at this time it was impossible to tell how old those inscriptions, buildings, and sculpture were.

Meanwhile, in far-off Egypt, a peasant-woman digging for fertilizer at Tell el Amarna had come upon a hoard of baked-clay tablets in cuneiform, which, when at last scholars pronounced them genuine, proved to be part of the archives of the Egyptian Pharaoh Akhnaten (*circa* 1400 B.C.), and contained diplomatic

[3] Gurney, O. R. *The Hittites*. Penguin Books. London, 1954.

correspondence between the King of Egypt and the rulers of Babylon, Assyria, Mittani, and other great kingdoms. And among them
again, there were references to the *Kheta*. At this period, following
a long interval of peace, the Hittites were apparently again thrusting southward into Syria, and threatening the Pharaoh's vassal-
states in Palestine.

Under pressure from the advancing Hittite king, the governors of some of the Pharaoh's Palestinian provinces had turned
traitor, and were attacking their still-loyal neighbours. The governors of these beleaguered towns wrote desperately to Akhnaten
for help which never came. One of the Amarna letters reads:

> "Behold Aziru" (a disloyal vassal) "has fought my
> chiefs, and the chiefs whom I dispatched to the city of
> Simyra he caused to be seized in the city. Both the city
> Beruta (Beirut) and the city Ziouna are sending ships to
> the city. All who are in the land of the Amorites have
> gathered themselves. . . . I need men to save the rebel-
> lion of this land. . . . Give me soldiers!"

But the wily Hittite king, Shubbililuma, always keeping in
the background and professing continued friendship to the Pharaoh, moved his pieces on the board, and Simyra fell to Aziru. The
still loyal governor, Ribbadi, wrote again:

> "Grievous is to say what he has done, the dog Aziru.
> Behold what has fallen the lands of the king on account
> of him, and now behold what has befallen the city of
> Simyra—a station of my Lord, a fortress . . . and they
> spoil our fortress . . . ah, the cries of the place . . . a
> violent man and a dog. . . ." [4]

These and other documents stimulated still greater interest
in the origins of the Hittites, but, although a slender thread of
evidence had led the investigators to Asia Minor, there was as
yet no written proof that this was indeed the home of the Khatti.

By the end of the century the now numerous inscriptions in
the undeciphered "Hittite" hieroglyphs were published by a Ger-

* Translated by Professor Sayce.

man scholar, Messerschmidt, and from then on a succession of scholars, mainly German, concentrated on solving the mystery. The conclusive discovery was made by Dr. Hugo Winckler, who decided to make extensive excavations at Boghaz Köy, in many ways the most impressive site.

When Winckler and the earlier travellers went to Boghaz Köy they had to approach it along a narrow mountain track from Alaja Huyük. To-day one can drive all the way by car along a well-surfaced road; yet the approach is still dramatic. First there is a wide fertile valley, but gradually as one nears the site the hills close in on either side until one reaches a point at which two mountain streams break into the plain through deep, narrow gorges. Where the streams meet is the modern village, but beyond and above it rises a rocky spur, flanked on each side by the precipitous cliffs below which the mountain torrents foam and thunder. On that spur, high above the flat roofs of the modern village, lie the ruins of the ancient city.

On the lower slopes, immediately above the village, are the ruins of what we now know to be the older settlement, with its citadel built on a flat-topped rock. Higher still, however, some of the rock outcrops were crowned with massive masonry, and, girdling the whole area, which covers about three hundred acres, are substantial remains of a great wall, built of ponderous stone blocks. A modern archæologist, Mr. Seton Lloyd, writes:

"The first thing which strikes the visitor . . . is its immense size compared with most other Bronze Age cities, for it takes the greater part of a morning to make the complete circuit of the walls at a comfortable pace. Next, one is impressed by the formidable strength of the fortifications, particularly the southern enclosure wall of the extended city, and imagines the Herculean task which their construction must have represented. . . . A huge rampart of earth, of which the outer slope is sometimes faced with glacis of dressed stones, raises the foundations to a consistent level. Above this is the main wall, built in the form of a double shell, with rubble-filled chambers between and punctuated by projecting towers. In the more vulnerable sectors there is a lower 'apron' wall, also with towers, and this would have to be breached before the main wall could be approached." [5]

These towers were pierced by gateways ornamented with the extraordinary sculptured reliefs on which so many travellers had commented, and which, by the time of Winckler's arrival in 1906, had been widely published. One gate was flanked by crude sphinxes, faintly reminiscent of the Egyptian sphinxes but coarser and uglier. On the wall of another gateway was the carved figure of a warrior striding foward, dressed in a short tunic, wearing a plumed helmet, and grasping a battle-axe in his right hand. Flanking a third portal were sculptured lions. The Assyrians, as we have seen, ornamented their gateways with carved lions and bulls, but the lions at Boghaz Köy had not the supple, feline strength of the Assyrian animals; they were squat, broad and heavy, as were the figures of men and gods carved on the walls of the sanctuary Yazilikaya, not far away. The heavy, bulky strength is the most characteristic feature of Hittite sculpture. It has nothing of the suavity and grace of Egyptian or Babylonian art. Yet it is impressive in a different way. The stocky, broad-shouldered men in their heavy clothing and tall, conical hats were clearly a mountain people accustomed to a harsh climate; and their strong boots with turned-up toes—surely they were snow shoes?

When Winckler and his staff of the Deutsche-Orient Gesellschaft began their excavations the existence of a powerful Hittite kingdom had been accepted, and all the indications pointed to its homeland having been in Asia Minor. But still there was no written evidence to prove this. In 1879, when Professor A. H. Sayce published his book *The Hittites,* he had to admit that:

"Of the history of the 'White Syrians' or Hittites who lived in the land of Pteria, near the Halys, we know nothing at present beyond what we can gather from the ruins

[5] Lloyd, Seton. *Early Anatolia.* Penguin Books. London, 1956.

of their stronghold at Boghaz Köy and their palace at Eyuk."

And the "Hittite hieroglyphs", of which numerous examples had been found, still defied all efforts to decipher them.

But all doubts were at an end when Winckler unearthed at Boghaz Köy a cache of more than ten thousand inscribed tablets. The little baked-clay tablets, which had enabled archæologists to breathe life into the dead cities of Assyria and Babylonia, were now to do the same for the forgotten Hittite Empire. Of those found at Boghaz Köy, which had evidently formed part of the palace archives, the majority were in an unknown language. But some years before a Norwegian scholar, Knudtzon, noticed that among the famous "Amarna" tablets found by the Egyptian peasant woman were two in an unknown language, which Knudtzon suggested was of Indo-European origin. Here, at Boghaz Köy, Winckler found thousands of tablets *in the same language*. Because the two Amarna tablets seemed to refer to a district called *Arzawa,* the locality of which was then unknown, scholars gave the provincial name *Arzawan* to the unknown language.

But not for long; for when the Boghaz Köy tablets could be exhaustively studied, it was discovered that among them there were a number written in the now familiar Akkadian language of Babylonia. And these revealed that without any doubt the theories of Sayce and others were correct. This part of Asia Minor was indeed the territory of the mysterious Hatti, and Boghaz Köy or Hattusas (its original name) had been their capital. The Hittites had been traced at last to their Anatolian homeland. Final confirmation came with the discovery, at Boghaz Köy, of the Hittite version of the famous treaty between Ramesses II, King of Egypt, and the Hittite king Hattusilis. The Egyptian inscription, in the hieroglyphic script of the Nile Valley people, was inscribed on the wall of the Temple of Karnak in Thebes, the Egyptian capital. The Boghaz Köy tablet was in Babylonian cuneiform, which was evidently the language used by the Egyptian and Asiatic kings for diplomatic correspondence. And since the Treaty could be precisely dated on the 21st regnal year of Ramesses II, i.e., in the second half of the thirteenth century B.C., this gave a firm date for some of the Boghaz Köy tablets. As for the unknown language written in cuneiform—in which most of the newly found tablets were inscribed, there could now be no doubt that this was the actual language of the Hittites; the name Arwazan was dropped, and the language was called Hittite. The next task was to decipher it.

In an abbreviated account such as this must necessarily be, much fascinating detail has to be left out, and readers who wish to follow the full story of the uncovering of Hittite civilization should read Professor Garstang's attractively written book *The Land of the Hittites* (1910). Garstang visited Dr. Winckler when he was working at Boghaz Köy, and also conducted excavations himself at Sakeje-gozii in North Syria. The most up-to-date and authoritative account in English is by Professor Garstang's nephew, Dr. Gurney, whose book *The Hittites* was published in 1952.

To sum up briefly, the position in 1906, after Winckler's discovery at Boghaz Köy, was that cuneiform tablets in the Akkadian language, found on that site, indicated that this was Hattusas, the Hittite capital from the fifteenth to near the end of the thirteenth century B.C.—roughly two hundred years. Winckler gave a list of Hittite kings from Shubbililiuma (who had given so much trouble to the Egyptian Kings of the Eighteenth Dynasty) to Arnuwandas, who reigned near the end of the thirteenth century B.C. After that the records ended. During this period the Hittites ruled, from Asia Minor, a confederacy of subject states, some in Asia Minor and others in Northern Syria. But the mass of the tablets, which were in the Hittite language, could not then be read; neither could the Hittite hieroglyphs, the "picture-writing" which had already been detected at Hamath, Aleppo and other places in Syria, and also on numerous rock-inscriptions in Asia Minor.

It is also clear that the many other ruined towns and settlements on the high tableland and in the eastern mountains, with their similar sculpture and inscriptions, formed part of a common civilization, and that that civilization was Hittite. Equally certain was that that civilization extended southward, deep into Syria, and that such cities as Carchemish, on the Upper Euphrates, Milid, and Hamath, had also once been Hittite. Just before the outbreak of the First World War the British Museum sent out Dr. D. G. Hogarth to excavate at Carchemish. His assistant was a young Oxford graduate making his first acquaintance with a land in which he was later to become famous as a guerilla leader. His name was T. E. Lawrence.

Another member of this expedition was Leonard (now Sir Leonard) Woolley. They brought back to the British Museum more examples of Hittite sculpture and more inscriptions in Hittite hieroglyphs.

With the outbreak of the First World War, when Turkey fought on the side of Germany, British and German "Hittitologists" took separate paths; the Germans concentrated on the decipher-ment of the Hittite cuneiform tablets found at Boghaz Köy and other places; while British scholars attempted to decipher the hieroglyphs. This division continued, to a large extent, in the inter-war years, and until the Hittite cuneiform writing had been deciphered, mainly by German scholars: F. Sommer, F. Friedrich, H. Ehelolf and A. Gotz. Other scholars who made notable contri-butions were the Czech Hrozny, the Swiss Forrer, the Frenchman Délaporte, and the American Sturtevant, who published a *Com-parative Grammar of the Hittite Language,* summarizing the work of the German savants.

Although this book is concerned mainly with the physical remains of lost cities, some readers may be curious to know how the Hittite cuneiform tablets were deciphered. Very broadly speaking it was a matter of proceeding from the known to the unknown. The Akkadian and Sumerian languages of Babylonia were known, and it happened that the Hittite scribes, who natu-rally knew both languages, sometimes used Sumerian or Akkadian words as abbreviations even in the inscriptions written in their own language. Sometimes there were duplicate texts, each of which occasionally used Sumerian or Akkadian words, *but not necessarily in the same places.* To give a very rough parallel, imagine duplicate copies of a sentence in English, in which French words had occasionally been used. One version might read:

> "John is suffering from a *malaise* of the spirit. He complains constantly of *ennui.* He has lost all his former *joie de vivre.* Even his delight in fine *cuisine* has vanished. At the Splendide last night the *maître d'hôtel* failed to tempt him even with his famous *bouillabaisse.* Also he seems to have lost his old dexterity. He has become *maladroit.*"

Imagine that, in the above passage, the English words are Hittite, an unknown language, and that the French words are Sumerian, which is known. If, later, another inscription was found which obviously bore the same text, but in which the French words had been replaced by English, you might get this:

> "John is suffering from a (sickness) of the spirit. He complains constantly of (boredom). He has lost all his former (joy of life). Even his delight in fine (cooking) has vanished. At the Splendide last night the (head waiter) failed to tempt him even with his famous (fish-soup). Also he seems to have lost his old dexterity. He has become (clumsy)."

A scholar comparing the second passage with the first, would be able to recognize the meaning of the bracketed words. Later when he encountered the same words in another inscription, their position in relation to other parts of the text might give him a clue to the meaning of the still undeciphered passages.

This very crude and inexact illustration may serve to demonstrate one of the methods used by philologists in attempting to decipher an unknown language. It was a very long, laborious and painstaking task, involving the strictest discipline. It could only be accomplished by studying a vast mass of material, proceeding by slow stages, never indulging in guesswork, and never assigning a meaning to a word unless it could be positively proved. But, by using such methods, German and other scholars had, by 1933, succeeded in deciphering passages of the Hittite cuneiform texts. A few passages apparently referring to religious ritual and worship remain obscure.

The British were less fortunate with the hieroglyphs; until quite recently they had only one small and inadequate bilingual clue, the "Boss of Tarkondemos", which had only nine cuneiform and six hieroglyphic signs. There were also place-names and a few personal names known from Assyrian inscriptions.

> "Starting from these," writes Gurney, "five scholars —Bossert (German), Forrer (Swiss), Gelb (American), Hrozny (Czech), and Meriggi (Italian), working independently, have now reached a considerable measure of agreement on the values of most of the signs so far as they are used phonetically, and have determined the general structure of the language. But in spite of this the inscriptions remain largely unintelligible, for the ideograms and vocabulary in general still present an insuperable obstacle." [6]

Meanwhile, from 1920 onwards, a succession of archæologists have continued to excavate Hittite sites in Asia Minor and in Syria, including of course Boghaz Köy itself. The excavator in the field was helped by the philologist working in his study, and vice versa. The result is, to-day, that the lost cities of Asia Minor are no longer mysterious ruins for travellers to wonder at. We know a great deal about the people who built them, the names of their rulers, their military and social organization, their religion and daily life.

We still know very little concerning the so-called "Syrian Hittites" mentioned in the Bible, though their relationship with the Hittites of the northern mountains is now recognized to have

[6] However, *see* page 105.

been much closer than was formerly admitted. "Hieroglyphic Hittite" and "Cuneiform Hittite", though not the same languages, are closely related.

Men of many nations have contributed to our present knowledge; German, Swiss, Czech, Danish, French, British, American and, not least, the Turkish archæologists who, since the war, have excavated several important sites in Anatolia.

CHAPTER SIX

A Forgotten Empire (2)

The historical Hittites were not the first people to occupy Asia Minor. The name Hatti was given to the country by the indigenous people of the land, whom we call Hattians.

The Hittites of the Egyptian and Assyrian records, the people who ruled from Hattusas and whose language we call Hittite, were invaders who seem to have been established in the country as early as 1900 B.C., and who made war on the local princes. They brought with them their own language, which philologists tell us was of Indo-European origin, i.e. it stems from the same root from which grew nearly all European languages, including our own, unlike the languages of Ancient Egypt, Babylon and Assyria, which had a different origin. This Indo-European or "Aryan" group of languages seems to have originated in very remote prehistory somewhere in northern India and Afghanistan.

But when the invaders had established themselves in Hatti they adopted the name of the land they had occupied, and were thus known to their neighbours as the Kheta, the Khatti, or the Hittites. In the same way the inhabitants of Britain, most of whom are descended from Anglo-Saxon and Scandinavian invaders, still call their island by its original name of Britain.

According to the historical records found at Boghaz Köy, the land was first divided into separate states, but eventually one king, Labarnas, conquered the neighbouring petty kingdoms and brought them under his control.

> "And the land was small," says the record, "but wherever he marched to battle, he subdued the lands of his

enemies with his might. He destroyed the lands and made them powerless, and he made the seas his frontiers. And when he returned from battle, his sons went to every part of the land, to Hupsina, to Nenessa, to Landa, to Zallara, to Parsuhanda and to Lusna, and governed the land, and the great cities of the land were assigned to them."

The successor of Labarnas was Hattusilis I, in whose reign the capital was evidently transferred to Hattusas (Borghaz Köy), and during his reign and that of his successor the Hittites began to move out of their mountain fortress and advance southwards into the plains of northern Syria, no doubt attracted by the riches of the older civilization established there. Hattusilis I conquered Halap (Aleppo), and his son, Mursilis, even conquered Babylon, an event recorded in the Babylonian chronicle:

"Against Samuditana the men of Hatti marched, against the land of Akkad."

Scholars usually put this date at about 1600 B.C.

Internal struggles within the Hittite kingdom followed; there was the usual story of palace intrigue, assassination and murder, and an invasion of the Hittite domains by another Aryan people, the Hurrians. After about 1525 B.C. Telepinus, a usurper, consolidated his position and his reign was composed:

"an elaborate edict, in which a brief survey of Hittite history" (from which the Labarnas episode is quoted) "illustrating the dangers of discord and disunity in high quarters, led up to a proclamation of other rules for the conduct of the king and nobles. The laws thus promulgated seem to have been observed down to the last days of the Hittite Empire." [1]

The period which historians call the "Old Kingdom" of the Hittites seems to have ended with Telepinus. The Imperial period, that of the Hittites' greatest expansion, began with Tudhaliyas II, founder of a new dynasty. During his reign the Hittites' old en-

[1] Gurney. *The Hittites*. Penguin Books, 1954.

emies, the Hurrians, were destroyed by the great Egyptian warrior-king Tuthmosis III, who made the Egyptians supreme in northern Syria for thirty years. Then a new Hurrian power arose, the state of Mittani, on the "Great Bend" of the Euphrates. For a time Mittani was the most powerful state in Western Asia and a great source of trouble to both Egyptians and the Hittites. Round about 1457 B.C., when Tudhaliyas II sacked Aleppo, the Hittites and the Egyptians were probably allies, as the Amarna tablets record gifts to the Pharaoh from the king of "Great Khatti".

With the accession of King Shubbililiuma another piece of the archæological jig-saw slips into place, for this king was, of course, the wily general whose intrigues caused the defection of Egypt's allies during the reign of Amenophis III and his successor Akhnaten. He has every claim to be the hero-figure of Hittite history, for, not only did he destroy the once-formidable state of Mittani, but his armies, thrusting down into Syria, came into conflict with the King of Kadesh—an ally of the Egyptians—and destroyed his army. This was in about 1370 B.C.

Among the records found at Boghaz Köy was an account of an incident in the life of Shubbililiuma which seems directly connected with a dramatic episode in the annals of the Egyptian kings. The Hittite chronicler tells how, when Shubbililiuma was camped outside Carchemish, a messenger arrived with a letter from the Queen of Egypt, which read:

"My husband has died and I have no son, but of you it is said that you have many sons. If you would send me one of your sons, he could become my husband. I will on no account take one of my subjects as my husband. I am very much afraid."

Puzzled and perhaps suspicious, the Hittite king sent a personal envoy to the Egyptian court for details. Back came another letter from the Queen.

"Why do you say 'They are deceiving me?' If I had a son, would I write to a foreigner to publish my distress and that of my country? You have insulted me by speaking thus. He who was my husband is dead and I have no son. I will never take one of my subjects and marry him. I have written to no one but you. Everyone says you have many sons; give me one of them that he may become my husband."

When Winckler discovered this astonishing document, it was not known who was the Egyptian Queen who sent the message. But since that time Egyptologists have been able to provide what is almost certainly the true answer, and it unfolds one of the most touching stories which has ever been disinterred from the lost cities of the ancient world. The "husband who had died" was almost certainly the boy-king Tutankhamun, whose wonderful tomb was discovered by Mr. Howard Carter and Lord Carnarvon. His Queen, Ankhesnamun, whose delightful portrait can be seen on the famous golden throne of the king, was probably no older than Tutankhamun. In Egypt succession to the throne was always through the heiress; therefore whoever married the widowed queen would become Pharaoh. A powerful courtier, Ay, who had been Vizier (Prime Minister) to Akhnaten, was intriguing for power. But marriage could not take place until after the prescribed ninety days required for the embalming and burial of the royal body. It looks very much as if Ankhesnamun saw in this her only chance of avoiding marriage to the old courtier, a man much older than herself. So she sent her desperate message to the Hittite King.

The end of the story is a sad one. Shubbililiuma eventually sent one of his sons, but he was put to death on his arrival in Egypt, presumably at Ay's order. And Ay, who became the next king of Egypt, appears to have married Ankhesnamun, thus legitimizing his accession.

This three thousand year old tragedy is not a romantic tale lifted from an old fable, but the result of careful piecing together of historical evidence found at Thebes, in Egypt, and Boghaz Köy, in Asia Minor; cities which are some distance apart, and one of which was only identified fifty years ago.

Even to summarize the political history of the Hittite Empire would require more space than this book allows, and I shall not attempt it. But, from the chronicles of the successive kings which were found at Boghaz Köy, and from those of the neighbouring states with which the Hittites were often at war, a general pattern can be traced. It is a story of a hardy, warlike people, first establishing a united kingdom in their mountain home, but having to fight almost continually to keep it. Sometimes vassal states break away, and have to be reconquered. Sometimes there were struggles within the Hittite homeland itself. Shubbililiuma seems to have laid out the line of the great fortress wall which girdles Hattusas, with its ponderous gates—no doubt with good cause. But whenever they were powerful enough, the Hittites emerged from their mountains and thrust down into the richer lands to the south. In 1370 B.C. Halap (Aleppo) and Alakh (Atchana) in Syria became Hittite dependencies. So did Nuhassi in central Syria and Amurra, which included the Lebanon region and the coastal areas. Carchemish held out for a time but was taken in 1340 B.C., when the whole vast land between the Euphrates and the sea became part of the Hittite Empire.

Mursilis, son of Shubbililiuma, reconquered the neighbour-state of Arwaza, which, as we know from the Amarna tablets, had asserted its independence and been in friendly communication with Egypt. There was also trouble with the hostile tribes beyond the mountains to the north, and the rise of Assyria, on the upper Tigris, became a menace to the Hittite dominions. Then, in about 1300 B.C. the Egyptians, having regained their strength and unity under a new and powerful dynasty, began to move out of their valley and reassert their old dominion over Syria. In such kings as Sethi I and Ramesses II the Hittites must have seen the reincarnation of the formidable Tuthmosis III, who had thrown them out of North Syria. Conflict was inevitable, and in 1286/5 B.C., at Kadesh on the Orontes, the two Empires met in a battle of which the outcome was indecisive,[2] but the Hittites retained their hold on

[2] In spite of the boasts of Ramesses II in his temple inscription, the general opinion is that the Hittite king's superior strategy won the day.

North Syria. Eventually peace was restored, and, as we have seen, the Egyptian and Hittite kings signed a treaty of peace, copies of which were kept at both capitals. Assyria was rapidly becoming a threat to both Empires, so that, towards the end of the thirteenth century B.C., they became increasingly friendly, and, thirteen years after the signing of the treaty between Ramesses II and Hattusilis III, the Pharaoh married the daughter of the Hittite king.

The son of Hattusilis III, Tudhaliyas IV, ordered the carving of the great reliefs on the rock-walls of Yazilikaya, near Boghaz Köy. His name appears on them, and it is he who is represented in the famous sculpture showing the king in the arms of his god. During the latter part of this king's reign the Hittites began to have trouble in their westerly dominions. The records refer to the king of *Ahhiyawa* and to a certain *Attarissiyas,* a citizen of that country, who had apparently driven one of the Hittite king's vassals from his kingdom in the west of Asia Minor. Forrer, the Swiss scholar, even went so far as to suggest that *Ahhiyawa* was the land of the Achaeans (mentioned by Homer), and that *Attarissiyas* may have been Atreus, father of Agamemnon. The dates seem to fit, for we know that at this time the Greek sea-rovers, the Myceneans, were active in western Asia Minor. It is a fascinating possibility, but unless further written records turn up it must remain a theory. The main difficulty is that we cannot yet tell whether the mysterious kingdom of Ahhiyawa was across the sea, or on the mainland of Asia Minor.

Another familiar name crops up in Hittite records of this period, that of *Mitas*. The famous Phrygian king Midas (whose touch turned everything to gold) was probably the king of Muschki who lived in the eighth century, long after the Hittites had been driven out of Anatolia. But, as Gurney suggests, "it is possible that the Muschki (classical Moschi) were already in this region and that Mitas was a dynastic name". But here we reach a point where classical myth and archæological fact begin to mingle, and one can only speculate.

Not all the Hittite records were historical chronicles or religious texts. There was a code of laws, the details of which show that the Hittites were primarily an agricultural people. It contains such lines as:

> "If anyone borrows and yokes an ox, a horse, a mule, or an ass, and it dies, or a wolf devours it, or it goes astray, he shall pay in full value; but if he say 'By the hand of God it died' then he shall take the oath. . . ."

> ". . . If a pig goes upon a threshing floor or a field or a garden and the owner of the meadow, of the field, or the garden smites it so that it die, he shall give it back to its owner; but if he does not give it back he becomes a thief."

> ". . . If anyone steals bees in a swarm, formerly they used to give one mina of silver (but) now he shall give five shekels of silver." [3]

which suggests that the Hittites had inflation problems too.

What were the Hittites like as people? The only means by which we can judge them are their written documents, which tell us something of their minds, and their sculpture, which shows us what they looked like. On the whole they come out rather well by comparison with other contemporary civilizations. The harsh climate of their mountain homeland made them tough; they had no fertile valley to nurture them, as had the Egyptians and the Sumerians, and their geographical position subjected them to the pressure of neighbouring peoples. They never enjoyed, as did the people of the Nile Valley, long periods of settled peace, free from the threat of invasion.

In order to survive they had to be a military people, and their strong-walled cities and frontier fortresses indicate a state of martial preparedness. Their art and culture seems to have been borrowed from the older civilizations with which they came in contact; Egypt and Assyria influenced their sculpture; their hieroglyphic writing may have been derived from that of Egypt, and they also utilized the Babylonian cuneiform to write their own language.

[3] Translated by O. R. Gurney.

Judging from their documents they seem to have been at least as humane as the Egyptians in their conduct of war, and in their laws. And in both respects they were more civilized than the Assyrians, and did not share their lust for blood and torture. If they laid siege to an enemy city, and it surrendered, the people were spared provided due tribute was paid. The ruler of the city became a Hittite vassal, ruling on behalf of the Hittite king and supporting him in the event of war. If the city resisted and was taken, it was usually looted and its inhabitants taken as slaves. But they were not mutilated or tortured.

In common with all the ancient civilizations they made a clear distinction between slave and freeman, and the laws governing a freeman were more liberal than those governing a slave. A master could punish a slave as he wished, but, on the other hand, a Hittite religious document contains this passage:

> "If a servant is in any way in trouble, he makes a petition to his master; and his master hears him and is (kindly disposed) towards him, and puts right what is troubling him. Or if the servant is in any way at fault, and confesses his fault before his master, then whatever his master wants to do with him he will do. But because he has confessed his fault before his master, his master's spirit is soothed and the master will not call that servant to account."

Instructions from the king to his garrison-commanders include these orders:

> "Into whatsoever city you return, summon forth all the people of the city. Whoever has a suit, decide it for him and satisfy it. If the slave of a man, or the maidservant of a woman, has a suit, decide it for them and satisfy them."

> "Do not make the better case the worse or the worse case the better. Do what is just."

In judging such cases the King's officer was expected to co-operate with the civil authorities.

"Now the commander of the garrison, the mayor, and the elders shall administer justice fairly, and the people shall bring their cases." [4]

For the freemen, the only capital offences were rape, defiance of the State, and sexual intercourse with animals. Homicide, black magic, theft, assault resulting in death, could all be compounded by a money payment, or by restitution of property.

The marriage laws were patriarchal. A woman was given by her father in marriage; the bridegroom could become betrothed by making a present to his intended bride. But if she changed her mind before marriage took place she could break the contract, provided her father returned the present. The marriage was accompanied by a symbolic gift from the bridegroom to the bride's family, and the bride's father provided a dowry. In this, Hittite marriage customs followed those of Babylonia.

The walled cities, as in Mycenean Greece, were citadels for defence against enemy attack, when the population would withdraw within the fortifications, but in time of peace most of the population lived outside the walls, cultivating their fields and vineyards, and tending their herds. Within the city was the palace of the ruler, and usually several temples. There would also be quarters for the garrison, and among the Hittite documents one was found which gives the standing orders for the officer commanding the frontier defences. He had to post sentries to guard the roads, see to the closing of the gates at night, provide for the maintenance of the fortifications, and provide food, water and other stores. Frontier garrisons were mainly in the mountainous north and southwest, fronting on the lands occupied by wild tribesmen. In the south and west, where they faced the lands of their civilized neighbours, the Hittites preferred to use their vassal-kingdoms as "buffer states".

In warfare they were formidable foes, nimble strategists whose aim was to manœuvre the enemy into the open and expose him to their mobile arm—that swift and terrifying Hittite chariotry which

[4] Gurney. *The Hittites*. Penguin Books. London, 1954.

was renowned throughout Western Asia. The infantry were armed with axes, and wore short tunics as shown in the famous "Warrior" relief at Boghaz Köy. However, on the Egyptian sculptures depicting the Battle of Kadesh they are shown wearing long, short-sleeved robes and carrying spears. These, however, may be auxiliaries drawn from the vassal states.

Agriculture and stock-raising seem to have been their main source of wealth, but they also mined copper, iron, and exported these and other minerals to neighbouring countries in return for textiles and other manufactured goods. Here is a translation from a letter from King Hattusilis III to a neighbouring monarch, possibly the King of Assyria:

> "As for the good iron which you wrote about to me, good iron is not available in my seal-house in Kizzuwatna. That is a bad time for producing iron I have written. They will produce good iron, but as yet they will not have finished. When they have finished I shall send it to you. To-day now I am despatching an iron dagger-blade to you." [5]

Even before the Hittites had established themselves in Asia Minor there was a thriving trade between that country and Assyria. Not long ago, at Kültepe, some twenty miles north of Kayseri, archæologists found remains of a settlement of Assyrian merchants. The story of how the site was discovered, and the valuable information it eventually yielded, is one of the romances of Hittite archæology. Even as far back as 1880, tablets inscribed in the Akkadian language, commonly used for commercial correspondence, appeared in the hands of antique dealers of Ankara. In 1893 the source of some of these had been traced to Boghaz Köy (which is why Winckler went there in 1906), but others were eventually traced to the tiny village of Kültepe, near which was a prominent mound called Karahuyuk.

[5] In the fourteenth century B.C. iron was a precious metal in Egypt and Babylonia. In the tomb of Tutankhamun Carter found an iron-bladed dagger, probably one of the King's most precious possessions, more valuable than gold, which in Egypt was "as dust".

In 1906 the French archæologist, Chantre, made a few soundings in the mound but found little. Yet tablets from Kültepe continued to come on the market. Then Winckler tried, but without
result, and it began to be doubted if Kültepe really was the source
of the tablets. After the First World War a third attempt was made,
this time by a Czecho-Slovak expedition led by Hrozny. The story
of what followed is amusingly told by Mr. Seton Lloyd:

> "Hrozny, like his predecessors, cut his first trenches
> in the summit of the main mound, and spent several weeks
> excavating what he considered to be a 'Hittite Fortress'
> without coming upon any trace of tablets. It is a remark-
> able tribute to the purposeful reticence of the Kültepe
> villagers that they were now for the third time in succes-
> sion able to watch a party of foreigners engaged in this
> particular form of wild goose chase. Since the sale of the
> tablets had recently proved a reliable source of income,
> there could be little point in revealing their whereabouts.
> This time, however, the peasants' luck did not hold."

Hrozny was an excellent linguist and spoke good Turkish.
Two of his workmen came from the nearby town of Kayseri, where
the situation at Kültepe had been a long-standing joke.

> "By cross-questioning them he eventually arrived at
> the truth. The meadow to which they led him was hardly
> more than 100 yards from the foot of the main mound,
> but screened from it by a line of trees, and he could im-
> mediately see that its surface was disturbed by traces,
> only half-heartedly concealed, of amateur excavations
> on a considerable scale."

Hrozny directed his workers to the site, and in a short time
came upon more than one thousand tablets. The main mound, in
fact, represented the remains of a walled city or citadel, not Hittite,
but built by the indigenous inhabitants of Anatolia before the Hittites had become the ruling power. But near the city there had been
a settlement, a foreign commercial colony occupied by Assyrian
merchants domiciled in Asia Minor. It was called Kanesh, and
Hrozny and his successors found the remains of the Assyrian mer-

chants' dwellings, with their personal belongings and commercial documents still *in situ;* evidently they had had to leave hurriedly.

Dating presented no difficulties, as some of the documents had attached to them the names of contemporary Assyrian kings; not the more famous Assyrian monarchs of the seventh and eighth centuries B.C., whose palaces Layard had found, but those who had ruled the land of the Upper Tigris more than one thousand years earlier.

Finally, in 1948, twenty-two years after Hrozny had left Kültepe, a Turkish expedition under Tahsin and Nimet Ozguc returned to the site and made exhaustive excavations. They identified five separate building periods, dating from between about 2000 to 1700 B.C. Apart from the discovery of the merchants' houses, whose contents had been preserved almost undamaged, fresh stores of inscribed tablets have continued to turn up—about a thousand per season.

> "To select at random from among the tablets is like opening a new volume by some familiar author of our own time," writes Lloyd. "A few sentences are sufficient to evoke the atmosphere in which his characters live and revive one's interest in them. A Kanesh merchant, for instance, called Pushukin, has a letter from Asur-immitti, his business contact at home:
>
> " 'I have received your instruction and the day of the import of your tablets was made known to me. I provided your agents with three minas of silver for the purchase of lead. Now if you are still my brother, let me have my money by courier. . . .'
>
> "At once one is beside him in the upper room of his Anatolian house, as the envelope is broken from the letter and he smiles at the urgency of the request for payment, seeing perhaps in his mind the face of his correspondent and feeling once more the heat of the Mesopotamian sun. . . ."

The goods were evidently carried on the backs of donkeys. Transport factors were employed who were responsible for the safe transport of the goods imported; cloths and fabrics, "famous tissues called by exotic names" (no doubt for the Anatolian ladies); and in return, exports of lead, iron, carnelian, and other minerals from Asia Minor. The names of the factors exist, and so do their expense accounts.

Such is the picture we now possess of a people who, three thousand years ago, rivalled Egypt as the greatest power on earth. Yet, eighty years ago nothing was known of them, or their cities, save for a few references in the Bible and in Egyptian and Assyrian inscriptions. Less than fifty years ago they were still mute, but to-day we know almost as much about their language, customs, social organization, law and religious beliefs, as we do of their neighbours in Mesopotamia. And that knowledge increases every year as fresh discoveries are made.

A full description of all the Hittite and pre-Hittite sites which have been excavated during the past thirty years would fill many volumes. Among the most dramatic was a discovery made by Turkish archæologists, at Alaja Huyük, which lies about twenty miles north-east of Boghaz Köy. The site was known to nineteenth-century travellers as "Eyuk"; they described a large mound, near which stood two huge stone sphinxes which had evidently flanked some monumental gateway. Sporadic excavations were carried on in 1861, 1863 and 1906, and some large stone buildings and fine sculptured reliefs were uncovered. Then, in 1935, a Turkish expedition under Kosay and Arik went to Alaja Huyük, intending to penetrate to the deeper levels of the mound and look for evidence of the earliest inhabitants of the settlement. After examining and recording the Hittite remains near the surface, Kosay and Arik sank a deep shaft into the mound. Twenty feet down they were astonished to find remains of lavishly furnished tombs dating from the Early Bronze Age (*circa* 2500 B.C.).

"These tombs," writes Seton Lloyd, "were obviously those of priests or royalty, buried with considerable ritual among the valuable offerings and rich appointments of contemporary convention. Women were accompanied by their jewellery and toilet articles; men by their personal

ornaments and weapons. In each grave the body was surrounded by elaborately wrought 'solar discs' and animal
symbols, which had perhaps been carried as standards in
the funeral processions, and a profusion of images, liba-
tion vessels and other cult-objects. A very large propor-
tion of these were of gold and silver, beautifully wrought
in a technique which in some ways rivalled even the craft
of the Sumerian metal-smiths of Ur. Other objects were
of bronze, occasionally inlaid with more precious metals.
There were dagger blades of iron."

Thirteen of these tombs have been excavated at Alaja Huyük
between 1935 and 1939. They belonged, of course, to the pre-
Hittite people whom the Indo-European invaders overcame when
they entered Anatolia more than five hundred years later. When
the Hittite Empire was at its height, when Muttawalis was fighting
Ramesses II at Kadesh, those royal or priestly bodies had been
lying in their sumptuously furnished graves for over a thousand
years. The people whom the Hittites conquered were not barbarians.

The most important Hittite discovery of recent years was
made at Karatepe, in Cilicia, in 1947. This was a true "lost city"
set in remote and unusually beautiful surroundings. Karatepe is in
south-eastern Asia Minor, only about fifty miles north of the
"corner" at which the southern coast of Turkey, running east to
west, joins the north-south line of the Syrian coast. In ancient times
this land was called Cilicia. Just where the Cilician coastal plain
begins to rise into the foothills of the Taurus mountains is a recess
in the hill-side in which stands a wooded knoll known locally as
"the Black Mound". In this thinly-populated country antiquities
can sometimes remain unknown for centuries, and probably no one
save an occasional charcoal-burner ever visited this lonely place.

"Few, in fact, could have suspected that, in times almost beyond the horizon of historical memory, a king
had chosen it as his residence, and that beneath the
brambles and scrub-oak the symbols of his authority still
lay buried beneath the ruins of his castle. Yet such was

indeed the case, and in the revelation of the discovery, something of his dignity could be restored. For here, before the excavator's eyes, were carefully worded sentences which he had composed in two languages, and the crudely drawn images of the world in which he lived. Among these tumbled galleries of small stone pictures, his people also were to be seen; a graceless folk with sloping foreheads and receding chins, such as are known to have inhabited large areas of Anatolia in his time. Pausing in their various activities, they regard each other as though in wonder at the strange turn of fortune which had disrupted the tranquil obscurity of their long interment." [6]

So writes Mr. Seton Lloyd in his delightful book on *Early Anatolia*. The discovery was made in the autumn of 1945 by a group of Turkish archæologists led by H. T. Bossert and H. Cambel. A local schoolmaster, an enthusiastic amateur archæologist, told them of the site. It could be reached, he said, by five hours on horse-back from the little market-town of Kadirli. They made a preliminary visit to the site, found, among other things, a human statue lying on its face, and some sculptured lions with a standing human figure, and other pieces of sculptured reliefs. The rest was buried under the scrub. Two years later they returned and made a thorough investigation, and their finds created a sensation among students of Hittite archæology. For here, at long last, was the long-sought "bilingual clue" to the Hittite hieroglyphs. The remains of the city were of late date, about 800 B.C., long after the end of the Hittite Empire. On the crown of the hill were the remains of defensive walls laid out on a polygonal plan, with twenty-eight rectangular towers and an upper and lower gateway. On entering one of these gate chambers the archæologists found, on each side, inscribed and sculptured slabs. One slab was inscribed in Hittite hieroglyphs and the other in Phœnician. Accompanying the inscriptions were crudely carved reliefs showing, among other scenes, a sea-battle, an orchestra, various sporting activities, religious ritual,

Lloyd, Seton. *Early Anatolia*. Penguin Books. London, 1956.

and simple scenes of domestic life. The art is greatly inferior to the great period of Hittite sculpture, but archæologically the reliefs are of high importance.

Even more important, of course, were the bilingual inscriptions. Already philologists had mastered the main elements of the language's grammatical structure, and could guess at the general meaning of the inscription. But now they could understand the meaning of individual words, without which a full translation is not possible. As a result of this discovery the Hittite hieroglyphic inscriptions in Asia Minor, and scattered throughout the museums of the world, are at last beginning to speak. Philologists who for more than fifty years had to content themselves with the little "Boss of Tarkondemos" with its nine characters, must have smiled wryly on hearing that there had existed, throughout all that time, a full-length bilingual lying unknown on a remote Cilician hill-side.

The name of the king was Asitawad, an Anatolian name (not, as originally thought, Phœnician). The inscriptions record the building of the fortress to which he gave his own name, and then add the interesting information that he was also the ruler of the *Danuna*. These could only be the "Dananians", a tribe listed on the temple of Ramesses III as a member of the coalition of "sea-peoples" which the Egyptians fought and defeated in the twelfth century B.C. They may also possibly be identified with Homer's "Danaoi".

It will be remembered that the "hunt for the Hittites" began, in the lowlands of Syria, with the discovery of the hieroglyphic writing at Aleppo and Hamath. The quest eventually led the explorers to the mountains of Asia Minor and to Boghaz Köy, from which the Hittites ruled an Empire which stretched far southward into Syria. With the recent discovery of the bilingual inscription at Karatepe the wheel appears to have come full circle. Now, perhaps we shall be able to learn more of the "neo-Hittites" of Syria, the people whom the Hebrews knew, and who are mentioned frequently in the Old Testament.

Did the Hebrews know of the mountain Hittites of Anatolia?

It seems extremely doubtful. When King David married the widow of Uriah the Hittite, in about 1000 B.C., the Hittites had long been driven out of their mountain homeland by later invaders. The problem is a difficult one. What appears to have happened is that, towards the end of the thirteenth century B.C., the Hittite Empire broke under the onslaught of foreign invaders accompanied perhaps by a revolt of their vassal states. We know that in the reign of Arnuwandas III, the mysterious *Ahhiyawa,* who may have been Homer's Achaeans, were causing trouble in the province of Arzawa, which had been a Hittite dependency. A certain Madduwattas (whose name has been compared with the Lydian kings, Alyattes and Sadyattes), made common cause with the king of Ahhiyawa, whose name (in Hittite) was Attarissiyas (Greek Atreus?). Together they "took the whole land of Arzawa", and round about this time the Hittite inscriptions also refer to one Mitas who was beginning to give trouble in the eastern provinces.

Then, the temple inscriptions of Ramesses III tell us, there came a troubled period when a vast migration of peoples, moving down the coast of Palestine with their women and baggage wagons, threatened Egypt; these peoples included the "Achaiwasha", the "Danuna", and the "Peoples of the Sea". "The Isles," say the inscription, "were in tumult." Some of the invaders reached Egypt and were eventually defeated by the Pharaoh in a series of land and sea-battles. This migration of peoples occurred towards the latter part of the thirteenth century B.C., and is associated with wide-spread movements of population. It was at this time that the Philistines settled on the coast of Palestine, when the Mycenean Greeks were colonizing in Asia Minor and elsewhere. And it was at this time, historians believe, that the Hittites were swept out of Asia Minor. The Boghaz Köy "king-lists" came to an end, and, to judge from Homeric legends, the Phrygians became the leading power in Anatolia.

But, for more than five hundred years after this date, the Hittites continued to survive in Syria. Assyrian records of the eighth century B.C. still speak of "The Land of Hatti", and give the names of Hittite kings. The Old Testament "Book of Kings" and "Chronicles" also refer to the "King of the Hittites"; but he ruled in Syria, not Asia Minor. On the other hand, as Gurney writes:

> ". . . the language and the religion of these Neo-Hittites were not those of the Hittites of Hattusas" (Boghaz Köy) "nor were they those of the common people who had inhabited Syria under the Hittite Empire (for they were Hurrians). It seems that Syria must have been over-run by another people coming from one of the Hittite provinces, who had adopted the Hittite civilization."

These, evidently, were the Hittites mentioned in the "Book of Kings" and in the "Chronicles". Even so, a mystery remains. Who were the "Sons of Heth": from whom Abraham bought the cave of Macpelah? Abraham seems to have lived round about 1700 B.C., long before the Hittites had entered Syria, nor is there any evidence that their Empire extended as far south as Palestine.

Then there is the reference in the "Book of Numbers", quoted at the beginning of Chapter Five of this book, which describes the travels of the Israelites after the Exodus from Egypt. The date cannot be later than about 1250 B.C., yet it is clearly stated that "Amalek dwelleth in the land of the south; and the Hittite, and the Jebusite, and the Amorite, dwell in the mountains (i.e. of Judea). One ingenious explanation put forward by Professor Gurney is that in about 1330 B.C. a number of Hittites from Asia Minor, from the "city of Kurustamma", entered Palestine and settled there. He sites a Hittite document which describes how "the weather-god of Hatti brought the men of Kurustamma into the land of Egypt . . . and my father sent infantry and chariotry, and they invaded *the border land of Egypt, the land of Amka*. . . ." (Our italics.)

Now at this period, the "land of Amka", which is the B'ka Valley in the Lebanon, *was* "the border land of Egypt", since this part of Palestine was then an Egyptian province. But it seems highly unlikely that a tribe from a north-easterly province of Asia Minor would have penetrated so far south. If they did, this would account for the presence of Hittites in the Judean Hills in the fourteenth century before Christ, when the Israelites were entering "a land flowing with milk and honey".

The quest which began with the discovery of the Hamath and Aleppo stones is still far from being finished. The decipherment of the hieroglyphic writing of the "neo-Hittites" may carry us much further. Already it has led to the rediscovery of the lost cities of an almost forgotten race. Perhaps it will lead us to still more, not only in Asia Minor, but in Syria, where elements of Hittite civilization still survived when David ruled from Jerusalem.

CHAPTER SEVEN

"1984"-B.C.

The vast sub-continent of India-Pakistan contains many once-great cities now in ruins, but the majority of these were built in historical times, far later than those of Egypt and Mesopotamia. In fact, until comparatively recently, nowhere on earth, save China, was there conclusive evidence of any ancient civilization of comparable age to those of Egypt and Sumeria.

But in India, as in ancient Greece, there were traditions. According to Hindu chronicles, the history of India goes back to some three thousand years before the beginning of the Christian era, but there is no archæological evidence to support this. We know, however, that the first invasion of India was that of the Aryans. They came from the northwest and lived for a time on the southern slopes of the Himalayas before they invaded the great Indo-Gangetic plain and drove back the earlier Dravidian population into the southern part of the sub-continent. Most of our knowledge of them is derived from the *Rig Veda,* a collection of Hindu hymns which established the antiquity of their origin. They were a civilized people with an established and highly complex religious tradition, and were acquainted with the various arts. They worshipped innumerable deities, who are still venerated to-day; there must be few people who are not vaguely familiar with some of them—the god Indra, the god Vishnu, the god Shiva and her consort Parvati, and others.

Yet until just over thirty years ago all this information was traditional, based on Hindu myths and legends. Hindu civilization was obviously extremely old, but how old? Whereas in Egypt and

Mesopotamia there were cities, monuments and tombs, which, with their contents, could be positively dated by archæological evidence, in India there was no city which could be proved to have existed before about 500 B.C. In fact, Sir John Marshall, writing in 1922 of the monuments of ancient India commented that:

> "Before the rise of the Maurya Empire a well developed and flourishing civilization had existed in India for at least a thousand years; yet, of the structural monuments erected during those ages not one example survived save the Cyclopean walls of Rajagriha."

The Maurya Dynasty began in 321 B.C., and Rajagriha dates from the sixth century B.C.

And yet, a year before those words were published, one of Sir John's staff, Rai Bahadur Daya Sahni, had already made them out of date. For in 1921 he had made trial excavations in the ancient city-mound of Harappa, in the Punjab, where seal-stones with animal designs and a strange, undeciphered form of picture-writing had been found. These excavations quickly established that, beneath the mound of Harappa, were unmistakable evidences of an earlier city which had been occupied by a people who had lived during the *chalcolithic* period. Archæologists used this word to indicate an intermediate stage between the New Stone Age (neolithic) and the Bronze Age. In Asia Minor *chalcolithic* cultures begin roughly at about 2500 B.C., and in Mesopotamia somewhat earlier; but, of course, it did not follow that the Indus Valley peoples had reached a comparable state of civilization at the same time. Sir Mortimer Wheeler, in his book *The Indus Age,* writes:

> "What that implied in terms of absolute chronology was still undetermined, but it was clear enough that an urban culture appreciably earlier than the Maurya Empire, or indeed than Rajagriha, had now been identified. And in 1922 another member of Sir John's staff, Mr. R. D. Banerji, was already finding similar remains beneath a Buddhist stupa which crowned the highest of a large group of mounds known as *Mohenjo-daro* (possibly = 'the hill of the dead') nearly 400 miles away in the

Larkarna district of Sind. Within a few weeks of publication it was abundantly clear that a new chapter would have to be added to the prehistory of India and to the record of civilization." [1]

Within the past thirty years, as Sir Mortimer's "new chapter" has begun to be written, it has been established that there existed, in this part of India, a prehistoric civilization almost as old as that of Sumeria. The frontiers of Indian prehistory have been pushed back more than two thousand years.

Before we describe the two principal cities which have been excavated, and the vast area they controlled, it is worthwhile to consider the most ancient sacred literature of India, the Vedic Hymns. There are about one thousand of them, and they are addressed to the greatest gods of the Hindu pantheon, extolling their deeds and entreating them to accept the sacrifice of their worshippers. The hymns are in Sanskrit, the literary language of ancient India, a branch of the Indo-European family of languages from which our own is descended. Parts of the *Rig Veda* may refer to the time before the Aryan invaders entered India, though this cannot be proved, but many appear to belong to a time of strife and conflict, when the invaders from the north were moving into the land to which they have given their name, a time when they called upon their greatest god, Indra, to help them in battle. Indra was "the ruler of the bright firmament". Like Zeus in Greek mythology he stands at the head of heaven as king of gods, and in Vedic poetry he is represented as performing wonderful deeds for the benefit of good men, while possessing at the same time the attributes of a war-god.

In some of the hymns Indra is *puramdara:* "fort-destroyer". To assist his protégé, Divadasa, he destroys "ninety forts". These are evidently walled cities of some sort; the word *pur* occurs, meaning "rampart" or "stronghold"; some are of stone (*asmamayi*), others probably of mud-brick (*ama*—"raw", "unbaked"). He also

[1] Wheeler, Sir Mortimer. *The Indus Age.* Cambridge University Press, 1953.

destroys one hundred "ancient castles" and "rend forts as age con-
sumes a garment".[2]

Until recently it was assumed that these citadels were mythi-
l, or, as Macdonnell and Keith suggested, "were merely places
refuge against attack, ramparts of hardened earth with pallisades
d a ditch". But, just as in the case of the Homeric stories of
cient Greece, which used to be regarded as mere myths, the
ents described in the *Rig Veda* appear to have an historical basis.

In fact it can now be proved that when the Aryans entered
India they had to encounter not mere untutored barbarians but a
highly civilized people who had occupied the Indus Valley for at
least a thousand years before the invasion.

The evidence for this has been obtained mainly from the excavation of two "lost cities". One is Harappa, already mentioned,
a small town in the Montgomery district of the Punjab. The other is
Mohenjo-daro, more than three hundred and fifty miles to the
south-west. Mohenjo-daro is on the Indus; Harappa is on one of
its tributaries, the Ravi. Between and beyond these two large
cities, each three miles in circumference, archæologists have identified sixty smaller settlements on the Indus Plain and more in the
hills to the west, all of which have yielded evidence of a common
civilization, though uniformity was greatest among the valley settlements. The total area covers more than one thousand miles
from Rupar, at the foot of the Simla hills, to Sutkagendor, which
lies close to the coast of the Arabian sea. This area is much greater
than that of either Ancient Egypt or Sumeria; in fact almost twice
as large.

Anyone who has driven from Karachi across the Sind Desert
will agree that this is not the most attractive area of the earth's
surface. Where the Indus wanders slowly across the plain, it is
bordered by a wide green band of vegetation, and here and there
are areas which man has reclaimed from the desert by artificial
irrigation; apart from these the eye has no rest from the monoto-

[2] For these allusions to the *Rig Veda* I am indebted to Sir Mortimer
Wheeler's book *The Indus Age*.

nous, dun-coloured desert, on which only the tough desert scrub
and small bushy trees are able to survive. Throughout the long
summer it grills under an unrelenting sun; on windless days the
heat-waves dance and eddy above the tamarisk trees; when there
is a wind the blown dust stings the eyes. As the sun sucks from
the earth the last vestiges of winter rain, a scum of salt rises to the
surface, looking as one writer has expressed it, "like a satanic mockery of snow". Creaking bullock-carts move slowly along the dusty
roads, linking the dusty villages from which, occasionally, the tall
stupa of a Buddhist temple breaks the skyline. As in Babylonia,
the modern traveller finds it hard to believe that such an apparently sterile land could have supported a numerous population.

As the traveller moves northward, following the great river,
he sees, far away to his left, the hills of Baluchistan. Some three
hundred miles from Karachi a tributary flows into the Indus. Following this for another hundred miles he reaches a point where
another river, the Ravi, flows into it from the east, and fifty miles
farther on, on the right bank, rises the extensive village of Harappa, overlaying part of a complex of mud-coloured mounds. It
was here, in 1921, that Sahni dug into the mounds and discovered
evidences of a civilization which had existed for at least a thousand
years before the Aryans entered the Indus Valley; we call it *Harappan,* after the site at which it was first found.

Harappa was a difficult and somewhat unrewarding site to
excavate; difficult because the modern village occupies part of
the mound, unrewarding because it had been largely wrecked by
brick robbers who, in the nineteenth century, had extracted huge
quantities of dried mud-bricks for use as ballast on the Lahore-
Multan railway. Nevertheless, from the remains which survived,
the excavators were able to establish that the city had a circuit of
not less than three miles, and that its main features were a strongly-
walled citadel on the west and a "lower city" to the east and south-
east. The citadel, a rough parallelogram 460 yards long by 215
yards wide, was surrounded by a huge defensive wall of mud-
brick, 45 feet wide, with an external revetment of baked-brick 4

feet wide. Bastions projected at intervals to strengthen the defences and there were ramps and terraces approached by gates, and supervised from guard-rooms. The citadel stood on a brick platform, high above the plain, from which it was probably approached by flights of steps. The buildings which had stood within these defensive walls were too badly damaged to be identified.

When the archæologists began to examine the mounds north of the citadel they were luckier. Here, close to the old river-bed (the river is now six miles away) three important groups of buildings were uncovered.

"Towards the south, close to the citadel, is a double range of barrack-like dwellings. Further north are remains of five rows of circular working-platforms; and beyond these is a double range of granaries on a revetted platform. The ensemble shows co-ordinated planning, and, although the methods of the excavators were not such as to yield stratigraphical evidence of the requisite intricacy, it may be supposed that the whole layout is of approximately one date." [3]

The two lines of barrack-like dwellings were incomplete, but sufficient survived to show that each dwelling consisted of two rooms, with floors partially paved with mud-brick, fronted and backed by narrow lanes, the whole being enclosed within a wall. "It is evident," writes Wheeler, "that the original scheme was both distinctive and uniform, and was in fact a piece of government planning. . . . It may here be added that on and about the site of these coolie-lines, but at higher levels, sixteen furnaces were found. . . . The precise function of these furnaces is doubtful, but a crucible used for melting bronze was found in the vicinity."

The seventeen circular brick "working-platforms" were evidently used for pounding grain. One had held a wooden mortar, and round the central hole where this had stood were fragments of straw or husk. Burned wheat and husked barley were found in another. It seems clear that on these platforms, arranged in regi-

[3] Wheeler, Sir Mortimer. *The Indus Age.* Cambridge University Press.

mented rows, all overlooked by the frowning walls of the citadel, labourers had wielded long wooden pestles, pounding the grain in mortars. A similar system is used in Kashmir to-day, but the sinister significance of the Harappa platforms was the evidence they provided of supervised and regimented labour.

About one hundred yards to the north of these platforms was a system of granaries, each 50 feet by 20 feet, also arranged symmetrically in rows, with a passage between them. The floor of each granary was supported clear of the ground by low walls, to allow the circulation of air. There were small projecting air vents, and the total floor space of all the granaries was over 9,000 square feet.

Somewhat later, archæologists began to investigate the great mounds of Mohenjo-daro, nearly five hundred miles to the southwest in the Sind Province. Here there were few overlying modern buildings, save for a Buddhist *stupa* which rose above the highest mound.

When, after thousands of tons of earth had been removed, and the tangle of foundations, pavements and mighty walls stood naked to the sun, the least imaginative visitor was stirred to wonder. Throughout the world archæologists recognized the discovery as a new landmark in prehistoric research; a new road had opened into the remote past of mankind. For here was a great city almost, if not as old, as the Pyramids or Ur of the Chaldees. The Nile, the Tigris, and Euphrates could no longer be regarded as the only begetters of the earliest riverine cultures. The Indus, now, could take her place beside them.

It soon became clear that Mohenjo-daro was a product of the same civilization which had created Harappa. Like that city, it consisted of two main elements, a powerful walled citadel to the east and a lower city to the west. The citadel was built on a platform of mud-bricks and mud, resting on an artificial mound. There were remains of defensive bastions at the south-east corner; two of them apparently guarded a postern gate, but at a later stage in the city's development this gate had been blocked and replaced by a platform, which had collapsed. Among its debris the excavators found "about a hundred baked-clay missiles, each approximately six ounces in weight".

Within the citadel the diggers came upon a huge bath or tank, 39 feet long, 23 feet broad, and sunk eight feet below the level of the courtyard, which was surrounded by a corridor separated from the courtyard by ranges of brick piers. Flights of steps led down into the bath, which had been rendered water-tight; the floor was of bricks set on edge with gypsum mortar between, and the walls were treated in the same way. The outlet from the bath led through "a high and corbel-arched drain which wound down the western side of the citadel-mound". There were ranges of subsidiary rooms, one containing a well which supplied water for the bath, and there was a staircase leading up to the now-vanished upper storey or flat roof.

Other suites of rooms, each including eight small bathrooms, were found north of the Great Bath, carefully and solidly built. Their well-made brick floors were drained by runnels communicating with a drain, and every room had a small brick staircase which presumably led to an upper storey.

Even more remarkable than the Great Bath was a building lying to its west. It had first been detected by Mr. Ernest Mackay in the thirties; he had noted solid blocks of brickwork, each about five feet high, divided each from the other by narrow passages. Mackay thought that these might be the remains of a *hammam* or hot-air bath, but when the building was more or less completely cleared by Wheeler in 1950, its real purpose was revealed. It was the substructure of an enormous granary, which originally had been 150 feet long and 75 feet wide, built, like the rest of the city, of mud-brick. When fully revealed some of the walls were found standing to a height of more than 20 feet. The outer walls of the massive platform were sloped, giving the building a grim, fortress-like appearance, and at the northern end was a brick platform, the walls

of which were similarly sloped, save at one point where they were
vertical, "evidently to facilitate the hauling up of bales deposited
underneath".

The criss-cross arrangement of supporting walls was probably
intended to assist air-circulation, and there were vertical air-shafts
let into the outer walls. The granary itself, of which only the platform remained, had been built of timber. In area it was approximately the same as the group of granaries found at Harappa.

North-east of the Great Bath was another large building,
substantially built, with a large open court and a number of small
barrack-like rooms, some of which are carefully paved with bricks,
and have staircases. It has been suggested that this was a "collegi-
ate" building for priests, but this has yet to be proved. The buildings which lie underneath the Buddhist *stupa* and monastery cannot be touched at present; there are those who believe that there
may be found the temple of the deity or deities worshipped by the
Harappans. The arrangement of the citadels of Harappa and
Mohenjo-daro recall the theocratic administrations of ancient Sumeria; at Ur for instance, the priests of the moon-god administered
cloth-factories, breweries, bakeries and blacksmiths, on behalf of
the god, and, of course, the state. For the present this must remain
pure speculation, since the written inscriptions found on Harappan
sites cannot yet be deciphered.

For the time being, therefore, the lives of the ancient Harappans remain shadowy for us; all we can now know of them is derived from such of their buildings as have survived, and the objects
found in them. But quite a lot can be learned. For instance, we
know that they understood town-planning. The "lower city" of
Mohenjo-daro (see Plan in picture insert) was laid out in a
criss-cross pattern of streets which were evidently planned from the
start, unlike those of Ur, in Sumeria, which seem to wander incon-
sequentially. There is, however, something depressing and a little
sinister in this huddle of lanes and streets, all built of mud-brick and,
as far as can be ascertained, unornamented. Few windows opened
on those streets, though there may have been grilles for ventilation.

Within, the chambers opened on to courtyards, and partitions were probably of matting, to assist in the circulation of air.

The most astonishing feature, which makes the Harappan cities almost unique in the pre-classical world of the ancient East, is the elaborate system of drainage and sanitation. Bathrooms are very much in evidence; there are latrines with waste-channels leading to cess-pits, which were evidently regularly cleared by municipal workmen.

> "The noteworthy and recurrent features," writes Wheeler, "are the insistence on water-supply, bathing and drainage, together with a substantial stairway to the upper floor. In some houses a built seat-latrine of Western type is included on the ground or first floor, with a sloping and sometimes stepped channel through the wall to a pottery receptacle or brick drain in the street outside." And of the general layout of the Lower City he says, "The main streets are about 30 feet wide, and major *insulæ* or blocks are subdivided by lanes which are not infrequently dog-legged, as though (like the side-streets of Avignon, for example) to break the impact of the prevailing winds."

Besides private dwelling there were larger buildings which may have been industrial or commercial premises, and one, with conical pots sunk in the floor to take large jars, may have been a restaurant. Religious buildings have not been definitely identified, though the archæologists discovered, in the Lower City, a complex of thick-walled buildings with a ceremonial approach leading to a central space which may have contained a sacred tree, or perhaps the statue of a deity. Near this building was found a piece of statuary representing a seated or possibly squatting man, bearded, with a shaven upper lip, and a fillet round his brow, which was sub-naturally low. Like the other rare human figures found on Harappan sites, the face is prognathous and receding-chinned.

Up to date no examples of Harappan art have been found comparable in beauty and vitality to those of Babylonia or Egypt.

A large number of terra-cotta and faience figurines have been found, mostly of animals. The human figure is rarely represented, and when it is, the work is often crude and carelessly executed, as if human beings mattered very little. Among the numerous statuettes of animals are the elephant, rhinoceros, bison, monkey, turtle, sheep, dog, pig, and various unidentified birds. These give some idea of the variety of wild animals which thronged the Indus Valley in these remote times, and suggest that four thousand years ago the area enjoyed a moister climate encouraging a marshy or jungle type of vegetation. A considerable number of small clay statuettes representing a female figure have been found; probably a goddess. Sometimes she is represented with a large, wide-spreading head-dress and prominent breasts. Some of these figures have children at the breast; others have a pannier at each side, which, from the smoke stains sometimes found, were probably used for burning incense. She may have been the Harappan version of the "Mother Goddess" who was worshipped in many forms throughout the prehistoric world.

Some of the models are more skillfully made, such as tiny figurines made of *faience* (glazed paste) representing sheep, dogs, squirrels, and monkeys. Buttons, studs, finger-rings and bracelets have been found, made of this attractive green-blue substance. Gold beads have been found in a hoard of jewellery, probably the property of a goldsmith. Other stones used were carnelian and lapis-lazuli; steatite is used in quantity for such objects as beads and "pieces" for use on a games-board. Harappan parents made toys for their children, and there may have been professional toymakers. There are model oxen with movable heads, model carts with terra-cotta wheels, figures of women kneading flour, whistles made in the shape of a hollow bird, pottery rattles with clay pellets inside.

The commercial aspect of Harappan life is emphasized by the numerous weights and measures which have been found on city-sites. The weights range from very large types, with lifting-rings attached, to small weights probably used by jewellers. They show consistent accuracy, and fall into a well-defined system. A decimal system was used for the higher weights; measures of length also followed a decimal system. A fragment of shell "rightly interpreted as part of a scale," was divided accurately into units of 0.264 ins., with "a mean error of 0.003 ins."

Irrigation was practised, and remains of dams have been found to hold back the water of the river after the annual flooding. The Harappans grew, among other crops, wheat and barley, peas, melons, and on some of the seals there are representations of what may have been banana-trees. They were also stock-farmers, raising sheep and cattle, pigs and goats. The camel appears to have been known, also the buffalo, the Indian bison, the bear, and spotted deer. They also kept domestic dogs and cats. At one Harappan site, Caanhu Daru, a brick was found over which a cat and a dog had run while the clay was still wet. The paw-marks were easily distinguishable, and, says Mackay, "the deep impression of the pads and their spread indicated the speed of both animals".[4] The dog, as usual, was in pursuit.

Few noteworthy examples of Harappan art have been found; in general the better-finished statues, in alabaster, steatite and bronze, are stiff and formalized. Occasionally there are exceptions. One of the most interesting is a little figure of a dancing girl in bronze, found six feet below the surface-level of a house in Mohenjo-daro. It is nude; the head is provocatively thrown back, and the left arm is covered almost entirely from shoulder to wrist with bangles. She is of the aboriginal type, perhaps from Baluchistan, with a flat nose, curly hair and large eyes. The resemblance to Indian art of historical times is remarkable.

Other interesting similarities occur in the human or divine figures depicted on the tiny seals found on Harappan sites. One of these shows a figure seated on a low stool. The figure has three heads and is crowned by a tall head-dress. The left arm is covered with bangles; on one side stands a buffalo, on the other a rhinoceros,

[4] Mackay, Ernest. *The Indus Civilization*. Loval, Dickson & Thompson, Ltd. 1953.

and below the stool are two antelopes or goats. Sir John Marshall recognized in this figure the prototype of the Indian god Shiva, in his aspect as Pasupati, Lord of Beasts.

Occasionally one detects an affinity with the culture of Sumeria, with which the Harappans evidently had contact. For example, another seal has a representation of a figure with outstretched arms holding back lions. On another seal, which appears to have Sumerian affinities, a horned tiger is being attacked by a bull-man or "minotaur" reminiscent of the Sumerian Eabani created by the goddess Aruru to fight Gilgamesh.

No baked-clay tablets have been found, such as have revealed so much of the civilizations of Babylonia, Assyria and the Hittite Empire. Some of the seals are inscribed in a pictographic form of writing which cannot be read, as it bears no resemblance to any known script, and no bilingual clue has yet been discovered. (I was informed that Mr. Michael Ventris, the brilliant young scholar who succeeded in deciphering the Minoan "Linear B" script of Crete—without a bilingual—was about to set about this equally difficult task. Unhappily, Ventris was tragically killed in a motor accident a few weeks before these lines were written.)

The problem of dating has still not been completely solved, but from objects of other known cultures found on Harappan sites archæologists cautiously infer that the earliest date of the developed Harappan civilization (as represented by the cities) is not earlier than about 2500 B.C. However, both at Harappa and Mohenjo-daro there are still lower occupation levels which have not yet been examined. The rivers have risen considerably since these cities were built, and below a certain depth it is impossible to proceed without elaborate pumping-gear.

Did the Indus Valley civilization develop independently or was it in any way related to the earlier valley-cultures of Lower Mesopotamia? Informed opinion seems to be that while the Harappans, whose civilization apparently developed after that of Sumeria, may have received the *idea* from that area, they developed their own distinctive culture pattern independently of Mesopotamia.

"Evidence for contact with the West before 2300 B.C.," writes Wheeler, "is not impressive." [5]

As for the closing dates, the Indus civilization appears to have continued well into the first half of the second millennium B.C., i.e. the time of the Aryan invasion of about 1500 B.C. The traditions recorded in the *Rig Veda* have taken on a new aspect since the discovery of Harappa and Mohenjo-daro. It now seems very possible that the "forts" and "castles" which the god Indra "rent as age consumed a garment" were the walled cities of the Harappans; not only Mohenjo-daro and Harappa itself but other fortified towns and villages of the same period which archæologists have discovered along the river banks between and beyond the two principal cities. "Literary (or rather oral) tradition and archæological inference have apparently more in common with each other than had previously been suspected." [5]

The reasons for the decline of the Indus Valley civilization are not entirely clear. Some authorities suggest that climatic changes, a reduction in rainfall, may have altered the character of the land so that it could no longer support the abundance of plant and animal life on which the Harappan economic structure depended. This is a debatable point; if there were climatic changes, were they brought about through natural causes, or man-made ones; or both? The millions of kiln-dried bricks used in the construction of Mohenjo-daro, Harappa and other towns imply a large consumption of fuel for firing, and that certainly meant timber. Wood was also used extensively in Harappan buildings. Extensive felling of forests can alter a climate by reducing rainfall and encouraging soil erosion. It has happened in other parts of the world, and may have happened in the Indus Valley.

These at the moment can only be speculations, but it is certain, from an examination of the upper levels of Harappan cities, that in later years there was deterioration. The older, larger buildings were cut up into smaller rooms by partitions; the wide streets were encroached upon, lanes were choked with mean dwellings; clear

[5] Wheeler, Sir Mortimer. *The Indus Age.*

evidence of political and economic decay. Yet the final blow which felled the tottering structure undoubtedly came from without. Dramatic evidence of armed attack was found at Mohenjo-daro and elsewhere.

In one room at Mohenjo-daro the excavators came upon the skeletons of thirteen women with a child, some wearing bracelets, beads and rings, in attitudes suggesting sudden death. One of the skulls had a sword-cut, and another showed signs of violence. Elsewhere in the city nine skeletons lay in strangely contorted attitudes in a shallow pit with two elephant tusks. It has been suggested that they are the remains of a family, possibly of ivory-workers, who in attempting to escape had been cut down by the attackers. The raiders may have looted the bodies but left the tusks, which would be of no value to them. One of the public "well-rooms" disclosed a scene of grim tragedy. "On the stairs were the skeletons of two persons, evidently lying where they died in a vain endeavour to use their last remaining strength to climb the stairs to the street. Remains of a third and fourth body were found close outside. There seems no doubt that these people were murdered." In other parts of the town skeletons had been buried in tumbled heaps, without the funerary equipment which would have accompanied them had they been formally buried. In other places the bodies had been left where they lay.

In the light of such evidence, which appears to date from about the middle of the second millennium—the traditional date of the Aryan invasion—there seems little doubt of the identity of the attackers. "Indra," as Sir Mortimer Wheeler comments, "stands accused."

The founders of Hindu civilization brought with them the cultural traditions of their Aryan homeland, but, even from the few examples of Harappan art which have been found to date, there seems no doubt that the elements of the civilization of the conquered were absorbed by the conquerors, though some were ignored, e.g. Harappan sanitary engineering. Eventually a time came when even the traditions of the ancient peoples were lost, their language forgotten, and their cities disappeared under mounds of earth and debris left by later occupiers. But from evidence accumulated by archæologists during the past thirty years, more and more is being learned concerning this lost civilization. From a study of pottery styles, it has been possible to trace the beginnings of Harappan culture in the hill-villages of the upland valleys, where the remote ancestors of the city-builders of Harappa and Mohenjo-daro lived before descending to the plain. At one site, Jarmo, in the foot-hills of northern Iraq, radio-carbon datings have given 5000 B.C. or a little later as an approximate date.

Eventually, settlements grew up along the banks of the Indus and its tributaries, and gradually, an integrated society developed, apparently dominated by Mohenjo-daro and Harappa, twin capitals linked by the great rivers. In the absence of any written records, one can only speculate as to the type of society represented by those two cities, but they suggest a highly-disciplined state, drawing its tribute of grain on which the community depended, and storing it in the great granaries under the shadow of the citadels. The regimented rows of barrack-like buildings, the rows of platforms where the corn was ground under supervision, all suggest a powerful state organization, probably governed, as in Sumeria, by priests or priest-kings.

On the whole the picture is a grim one. While admiring the efficiency of Harappan planning and sanitary engineering, one's general impression of Harappan culture is unattractive. There is a drab, inhuman—almost sub-human—atmosphere about their cities; streets of plain, undecorated, mud-brick buildings, which, as Wheeler remarks, "however impressive quantitatively, and significant sociologically, are æsthetically miles of monotony".

One imagines those warrens of streets, baking under the fierce sun of the Punjab, as human ant-heaps, full of disciplined, energetic activity, supervised and controlled by a powerful, centralized state machine; a civilization in which there was little joy, much labour, and a strong emphasis on material things. Modern parallels are not difficult to find. Was this, perhaps "1984"—B.C.?

CHAPTER EIGHT

The Land without Sorrow

"This booke was wrote by me Robert Knox (the sonn of Robert Knox who died on the Iland of Zelone) when I was about 39 years of Age. I was taken prisoner on Zelone, 4th April, 1660. I was borne on Tower Hill in London, 8th Feb; 1641. My age when taken was 19 years; 1 month and 27 dayes. Continewed prisoner there 19 year 6 months 14 days So that I was prisoner there 4 month 17 days longer than I had lived in the world before, and on the 18th October 1679 God set me free from that Captivity, being then with the Hollanders at Arepa fort to whome be all Glory and prayse.

Robert Knox, 1696 in London."

In the year 1681 there appeared in the bookshops of London a work entitled *An Historical Relation of Ceylon, together with Somewhat Concerning Remarkable Passages of my Life,* by Robert Knox. It began with the above words.

Very few copies survive of Knox's book, and until 1910 practically nothing was known concerning its author, save what he tells us in *An Historical Relation,* etc. But in that year Mr. Donald Ferguson discovered, in the Bodleian Library at Oxford, some autobiographical notes and additional manuscripts. These, with the book, constitute the earliest account we possess, in English, of the island of Ceylon and its Lost Cities. Knox's father, born in 1581 at Nacton in Suffolk, was a sea-captain, "a Commander of a ship that traded in the Mediterranean Seas", and his son tells us:

"When I was aboute 14 years of Age, my father had built him a new ship (the same I was taken in) and my inclination was strongly bent for the Seas, but my father much avarce to make me a Seaman, it hapned some Sea Capts coming to see him, amoung other discourse, I standing by, asked my father if I was not to goe with him to Sea. Noe, saith my father, I intend my Sonn to be a tradesman, they put the question to me, I answered, to goe to Sea was my whole desire, at which they soone turned to my father, saying this new ship, when you have done going to sea, will be as good as a plentifull estate to your Sonn, and it is pitty to crosse his good inclination, since commondly younge men doe best in that Calling they have most mind to be in."

The result was that young Robert Knox did "goe to Sea", but not for long, for only three years after making his first voyage, he sailed in the *Ann,* his father's vessel, "on that fatall voyage in which I lost my father and myselfe and the prime of my time for businesse and preferment for 23 years tell Anno 1680". In 1659 the *Ann* was dismasted in a cyclone off the coast of southern India, and the crew had to go to Cottiar, in Ceylon, to buy a new mast. And that was the end of Robert's nautical career, and that of his father. With sixteen members of the crew they were taken prisoner by the Sinhalese, and taken to the court of their King, Rajah Singho. The elder man died in captivity, and Robert Knox remained the King's prisoner for nearly twenty years.

> "The causes of their detention," writes James Ryan in his introduction to the 1911 reprint of Knox's book, "were; (i) a quaint whim of King Rajah Singho to make a sort of menagerie of European captives; (ii) the jealousy of the Dutch at the possibility of English intervention; (iii) the disinclination of the captives themselves to make a determined effort to escape."

This speaks highly for the physical attractions of Ceylon, for, from his own account, Knox and his father did not have a happy time at the hands of Rajah Singho, whose cruelty, both to his own people and to captives, was horrifying. Yet, behind Knox's animadversions on the Sinhalese and their king, and in spite of his complaints that he "lost my father and myselfe and the prime of my time for businesse and preferment", the island held an enchantment for him. He was an intelligent man, an acute observer, interested in everything. In spite of his Puritan upbringing (his mother, he says, was "a woman of extraordinary piety; God was in all her thoughts") he studied the habits and customs of the islanders with a clear and unprejudiced eye. Occasionally, remembering his background, he trots out the usual Old Testament admonitions against "whoredom" and "idolatry", but on the whole he observes the life around him with a frankness and objectivity which would have done credit to a modern anthropologist.

Like Henry Layard and the Victorian adventurers of two centuries later, I suspect that Knox fell half in love with the strange, foreign civilization in which he found himself, and his twenty-year sojourn among the Sinhalese may have been due less to compulsion than a reluctance to return to a land of overclothed bodies, shut minds, and the Puritan intolerance.

"Ceylon" is a comparatively modern name for the island. The Ancient Greeks knew it as "Taprobane" (Copper-leaf), the Arabs as "Serendib", which the Portuguese changed, in the sixteenth century, to "Ceilao". But the most beautiful name is that given it by the Chinese—"The Land without Sorrow". It rises from the Indian Ocean, south of the most southerly tip of the subcontinent, a moist, green, tropical island, mountainous in the south, where the highest peak reaches 8,000 feet, but in the north expanding into a wide green plain, much of which is covered by impenetrable jungle. In that fecund green mass, swarming with animal life—elephants, leopards, panthers, monkeys—lie the ruins of great and beautiful buildings—cities which were lost for centuries.

In the sixth century B.C., a thousand years after the Aryan invaders had destroyed the civilization of the Indus Valley, Indian colonists from the Ganges Valley crossed the sea and invaded Ceylon. These were the ancestors of the modern Sinhalese, who are the dominant race in the island.

For more than 2,000 years they were ruled by Sinhalese kings.

Layard sketching the archive
chamber at Kuyunjik

The Bulls revealed at Nimrud

Human-headed Lion of Ashurbanipal

Lowering the great Winged Bull

Assyrian relief showing a colossus transported on a sledge, with workmen

Aerial view of Babylon

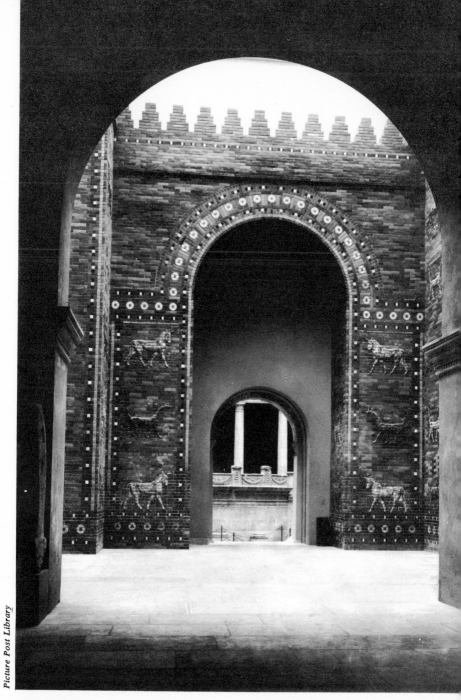

Reconstruction of the Ishtar Gate of Babylon from original materials

Carved lion, part of the decoration of the Ishtar Gate, Babylon

Carved dragon from the sculptured relief of the Ishtar Gate

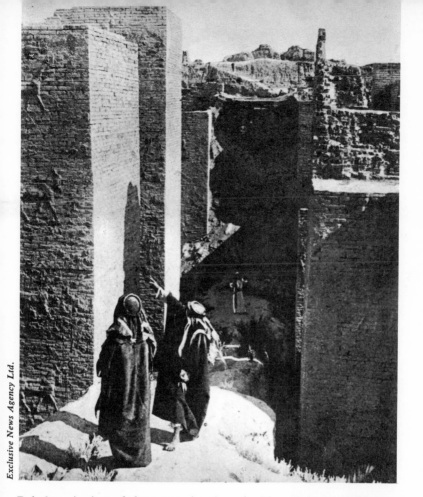

Babylon. A view of the processional road with sculptured reliefs

Babylonian tablet in
"cuneiform" writing

Hittite relief at Ivriz, Turkey

Hittite sculptured relief; hunting scene with "Hittite hieroglyphs" above

Hittite Sphinx at Alaja Huyük, Turkey

The Lion Gate of Hattusas (Boghaz Köy), capital of the Hittite Empire

Yasilikaya; Hittite reliefs showing Hittite soldiers

Postern Gate under the
walls of Hattusas

Three great statues of Hittite gods from Tell Halaf, Syria

Mohenjo-daro. A general view of the excavations

Brick platform in a building at Mohenjo-daro with recesses for dyeing, or possibly for grinding corn with pestles

Cambridge University Press

MOHENJO-DARO
HR AREA
A&B SECTIONS

Scale in feet

Plan of Mohenjo-daro

Ceylon. One of the oldest *dagobas* in the city of Anuradhapura

Ceylon; Polunnawara. Standing Buddha guarding reclining Buddha

Ceylon; Polunnawara. Section of the Lankatilika with the Kiri Vehera on right—one of the best preserved *dagobas* in Ceylon

View from the summit of the fortress of Sigri, Ceylon, showing council chamber and bath hewn out of rock

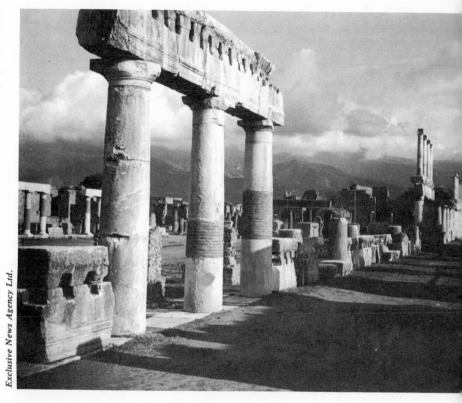

Exclusive News Agency Ltd.

Pompeii. The Forum, with Vesuvius in the distance

Paul Popper Ltd.

A reconstructed Pompeian garden

A wine-shop, or public house at Pompeii, showing flasks and money tills

Exclusive News Agency Ltd.

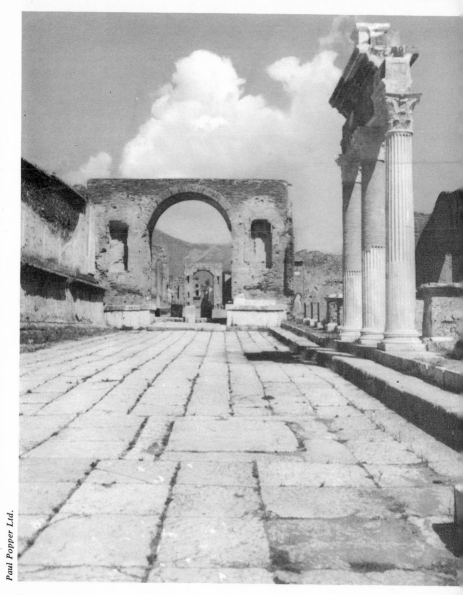

Pompeii. Triumphal arch and Macellum

Chichen-Itza. The Chichanchob, or Red House; the best-preserved example of Mayan architecture extant

Chichen-Itza. The Temple Building at the end of the Thaxtli, or hand-ball palace of the Mayas

Chichen-Itza. View of the ruins, showing in foreground the Caracol, with the Castillo, or Temple of the Plumed Serpent, in left background

The great canyon of the Urubamba, with precipices 2,500 feet high. The ruins of Vilcabamba lie on the top of the ridge between the two peaks. The city is invisible at the distance from which photograph was taken, but see next page

Bingham

Macchu Picchu, the "Lost City of the Incas" with temples and palaces of white granite, in the most inaccessible part of the grand canyon of the Urubamba

The first began his reign in 543 B.C.—about twenty years after the death of Nebuchadnezzar. The last ended his reign in A.D. 1815 —the year of Waterloo. Of these Sinhalese monarchs, Rajah Singho, who kept Knox a prisoner, was one.

But while the Sinhalese predominate in the south, the northern part of Ceylon was occupied by the Tamils, a Dravidian people from southern India, who established themselves there after generations of fighting. The Tamils are mainly Hindu, but the Sinhalese were converted to Buddhism in the third century B.C. —about two centuries after their first invasion of the island. There are also Moslem and Christian minorities.

The Sinhalese had been established in Ceylon more than two thousand years before the first Europeans settled in the island. These were Portuguese merchant adventurers who founded commercial settlements there in about A.D. 1505. A century and a half later the Dutch, who were then founding their colonies in the East Indies, drove out the Portuguese settlers, but Sinhalese kings still continued to rule from their capital, Kandy; as they did when, in 1785, the island became a British possession. But in 1815, as one authority discreetly puts it, "The Kandyan kings disappeared voluntarily".

It is as well, perhaps, to approach Ceylon through Knox's wondering eyes, since he saw the island when it was still a strange land, ruled by its native dynasty, when most of the jungle "lost cities" had not been discovered. And Knox had plenty of time to study it.

After describing the five principal cities occupied in his time, including Kandy, the then capital, Knox goes on to say:

> "There are besides these already mentioned, several other ruinous places that do still retain the name of cities, where Kings have reigned, tho now little Foot-steps remaining of them. At the North end of this King's Dominions is one of these Ruinous Cities, called Anurodgburro" (Anuradhapura) "where they say Ninety Kings have Reigned, the Spirits of whom they hold now to be Saints in Glory, having merited it by making Pagolda's and

stone Pillars and Images to the honour of their Gods,
whereof there are many yet remaining; which the Chin-
gulayes" (Sinhalese) "count very meritorious to worship,
and the next way to Heaven. . . . At this city of
Anurodgburro is a Watch kept, beyond which are no
more people that yield obedience to the King of Candy.
This place is above Ninety miles to the Northward of the
City of Candy."

And of the smaller occupied Sinhalese towns Knox says:

"The best are those that do belong to their Idols,
wherein stand their Dewals or Temples. They do not care
to make Streets by building their houses together in
rowes, but each man lives by himself in his own plantation, having an hedg it may be and a ditch round about
him to keep out Cattel. Their Towns are always placed
some distance from the Highways, for they care not that
their Towns should be a thorough-fair for all people, but
only for those that have business with them."

Knox's observations on the system of government, the religion, occupation, manners and customs of the people are valuable because at this time, when European influence was relatively
slight, they are probably characteristic of Ceylon in much earlier
centuries, when the Lost Cities were built. Of the King he says:

"As to the manner of his Government; it is Tyrannical
and Arbitrary in the highest degree; For he ruleth Abso-
lute and after his own Will and Pleasure; his own Head
being only his Counsellor. The Land all at his Disposal,
and all the People from the highest to the lowest Slaves;
both in Body and Goods wholly at his Command. Neither
wants He those three Virtues of a Tyrant, Jealousie, Dis-
simulation, and Cruelty."

The system seems to have been broadly feudal; "the King
Farms out his Land, not for Money, but Service." He ruled through
his great officers, called "Adigars, I may term them chief judges;
under whom is the Government of the Cities". Under these high
officials were others, whom Knox calls "Dissauvas" who were pro-

vincial governors; generals with a number of soldiers under them.
These officials seem to have been drawn mainly from the heredi-
tary aristocracy for, says Knox, "The King . . . regards not their
ability or sufficiency to perform (their office) only they must be
persons of good rank, and gentile extraction". They had a staff of
junior officials, secretaries, tax-gatherers, etc., in whom, perhaps,
we can see the pattern of all the ancient oriental despotisms such
as those of Assyria, Babylon and Harappa.

> "The next Officer under the Governor is the Lian-
> nah, The Writer. Who reads Letters brought, and takes
> account of all Business. . . . He also keeps registers.
> . . . Next to him is the Undia. He is a Person that gath-
> ers the King's Money; After him is the Monnananah, The
> Measurer. His Place is to go and measure the Corn that
> grows upon the King's Land. Or what other Corn belong-
> eth to him."

These officers were appointed and dismissed at the whim of
the King; none was appointed for life. When in power, the higher
officers enjoyed considerable wealth, often gained by bribery and
extortion, and Knox describes how "When they go abroad into
the Countries about the King's business, they go attended with a
number of Soldiers armed both before and behind them. . . .
These Grandees whensoever they walk abroad, their manner is in
State to lean upon the arm of some Man or Boy. And the Adigar
besides this piece of State, wheresoever he goes, there is one with a
great Whip like a Coach-whip before him slashing it, that all People may have notice that the Adigar is coming."

The peasants grew corn and rice, and, in the dry northern
part of the island especially, practised irrigation "casting up great
Banks in convenient places to stop and contain the Rains". They
grew vegetables and cultivated fruit-trees, including coconut-palms,
plantains and banana-trees, pineapples, pomegranates and vines.
But one tree they especially revered though it bore no fruit:

> "This they call Bo-gahah; we the God-Tree. It is very
> great and spreading, the Leaves always shake like an

Asp. They have a very great veneration for these Trees,
worshipping them; upon a tradition, That the Buddo"
(Buddha), "a great God among them, when he was upon
the Earth, did use to sit under this kind of Trees."

Buddhism came to Ceylon in about 300 B.C. from India.
Siddhartha, or, as he is sometimes called Gautama, was a Hindu
prince from northern India, who in the fifth century B.C. became
preoccupied with the problem of pain in human life. In an endeavour to cure him of this obsession, Siddhartha's father married
him to a beautiful princess, Yasodhara. ("The thoughts ye cannot stay with brazen chains A girl's hair lightly binds.") For
twelve years they were happy, and Yasodhara bore him a son.
Then, at the age of thirty, he broke away, and became for a time
an ascetic, after the manner of the Brahmins. This path too, he
rejected in the end, unconvinced that spiritual release could be
attained by mortifying the body. The doctrine which he finally pro-
pounded, and which is now the religion of one-third of the world's
population, is one of renunciation, freedom from attachment which
alone causes existence. He returned to his wife, who became one
of his first converts. Buddha ("The Awakened") as he came to
be called, was doubtful of the existence of gods, and never claimed
to be one himself. Yet, among the great mass of his followers he is
worshipped as a god, and the "idols" which Knox saw in the temples of Ceylon, were, and are of course, images of the Buddha
himself; it is strange that Buddhism, which is almost extinct in the
country of its origin, took such a hold of the peoples outside India that it is now the most widely held religion in Asia.

The Lost Cities of Ceylon were essentially the products of
religious enthusiasm. Among the Ancient Sinhalese the impulse to
create, latent in all human beings, went into the building of magnificent temples, sanctuaries, shrines, monasteries, and palaces for
the kings who raised them to the glory of the Buddha. The auto-
cratic power of these monarchs enabled them to concentrate the
man-power and resources of their kingdom on the creation of stu-

pendous monuments and public works, such as huge artificial lakes for irrigation, storage tanks, and canals which transformed what had been jungle into rich, fertile land. They employed armies of craftsmen—architects, builders, masons, sculptors, gardeners, goldsmiths, gem-cutters—in the enrichment and adornment of their cities.

The greatest of these, Anuradhapura, was begun at a time roughly contemporary with the conquest of Alexander the Great and his successors, and continued throughout the period of the Roman Empire. Yet even the greatest architectural achievements of the Roman Emperors cannot compare in size with the finest works of the Sinhalese kings who were their contemporaries. The area of Anuradhapura, for instance, was 250 square miles; the palaces of such monarchs as Tissa and Dutthagamini, as described by the ancient Sinhalese writers, would have made Diocletian's palace seem a poor thing by comparison; their great *dagobas,* artificial hills of masonry supporting shrines and reliquaries, were sometimes over three hundred feet high, and can be compared with the pyramids of Egypt. Their hydraulic engineering has no parallel save in the nineteenth and twentieth centuries; for example the artificial lake of Mineria, created in the third century A.D., by Maha Sen, had a circumference of twenty miles, and the masonry and earthwork dams which were made to divert the waters of the stream which fills it extend for eighty miles; their average height is eighty feet.

Centuries of warfare, between the Sinhalese and the invading Tamils (who were Brahmins) and between the Sinhalese themselves, eventually weakened the kingdom; the elaborate irrigation system was destroyed or impaired by neglect; and the jungle flowed back remorselessly over the gardened cities. Some, such as Anuradhapura and Polunnawara, were remembered as religious shrines, though they ceased to be capitals. Others were lost altogether until rediscovered by Europeans in the nineteenth and twentieth centuries. Until comparatively recent times a visit even to

Anuradhapura and Polunnawara, the best-known, involved great difficulty. Henry Cave, writing in 1897, advises intending travellers that

> "it is advisable to requisition a pair of horses and a spring wagon, two bullock-carts to carry provisions, beds, and camp furniture; three pairs of bullocks, one as a reserve in case of lameness or accident to the others; two horse-keepers; three bullock-drivers; a cook and a cook's mate; and about fifteen coolies. This somewhat formidable array is necessary because many of the places we intend to visit lie far from the roads that have recently been made through the province, and are only reached by jungle tracks of the roughest description." [1]

Fortunately, the problem of interpreting the ancient Sinhalese cities is made easier by the existence of writings in Sanskrit telling the story of their foundation, and giving the histories of the kings who built them. There are also many carved inscriptions which can be read. The earliest written chronicles are known under the title of the *Mahawamsa,* the name of the first or Greater Dynasty. Much of it is obviously mythical and legendary—though none the less delightful for that—but it contains a substantial amount of verifiable fact. A brief summary of some of the more important episodes will help towards a better understanding of the monuments themselves. For some of this information I am indebted to Lord Holden's *Ceylon* [2]—one of the most attractively written of recent books on the island.

Legend relates that the first king of Ceylon, Vijaya I, was the grandson of a lion. About 600 B.C., according to this traditional account, the King of Bengal had a daughter who seems to have shared some of the peculiarities of the Greek queen Pasiphae. "Maddened by lust," the legend states, "she descended privily at night from the upper storey" of her father's palace and seduced a pass-

[1] Cave, Henry W. *The Ruined Cities of Ceylon.* Sampson Low, Marston and Co. 1900.
[2] Lord Holden. *Ceylon.* George Allen and Unwin Ltd. 1938.

ing lion. The beast "roused to the fiercest passion by her touch took
her upon his back and bore her with all speed to his cave. There he
united with her, and from this union with him the princess bore
in time twin children, a son and a daughter."

Lord Holden continues:

"The hands and feet of this son, named Sihabahu,
were formed like those of a lion, and having reached the
age of sixteen, he inquired, without much sense of observation, 'Wherefore are you and our father so different, dear
mother?'"

On being told the boy was so shocked that he fled and took
refuge with the uncle of the princess. The lion, meanwhile, naturally incensed, ravaged the countryside until the King offered a
reward to anyone who would kill the animal. Most unfilially Sihabahu slew his father, and was rewarded by the kingdom of Bengal.
One of Sihabahu's sixteen sons, Vijaya, "after many intolerable
deeds of violence", was exiled from India and became the first
king of Ceylon.

Here we are on firmer ground, for it is known that Vijaya did
invade Ceylon round about 500 B.C., presumably with a large
force. He landed in the north-west and gradually brought the island under his control. He and his followers were Brahmins, the
religion of the Aryan invaders who destroyed the old civilization
of the Indus Valley, and subsequently conquered southern India.
Ceylon is called *Lanka* in the ancient Hindu chronicles and legends.

Who the original inhabitants were we do not know. The
ancient writings refer to them contemptuously as "Yakkas"—
devil-worshippers; they were half-savage races in various stages
of barbarism, of whom, wrote Cave in 1897, "a few scattered tribes
even still remain. Shunning every opportunity of contact with other
races, they still dwell in the forest, where they live on the products
of the chase, display the most elementary notions of religion in the
form of snake and demon worship, and exercise powers of reason
very little superior to those of the lower animals. . . ."

Vijaya and his successors brought with them the highly-developed civilization of their Aryan forbears, and, once established, built roads and cities, felled forests, created irrigation works, and transplanted to Ceylon the culture of their homeland, though modified to suit local conditions. But in the beginning their religion was Brahmin; they worshipped many gods.

Then, in the latter part of the third century B.C., came the conversion to Buddhism already mentioned. The story of how this was accomplished is related in the *Mahawamsa*. Devanampiyatissa (247–207 B.C.)—sometimes shortened to Tissa—was then King of Lanka. His fame had become known to the Emperor Asoka in India, who, though he had come to the throne after killing ninety-nine of his half-brothers (all born of different mothers), was an extremely devout Buddhist. His son, Mahinda, was a Buddhist priest, and the King decided to send Mahinda to Lanka to convert the Sinhalese monarch to the new faith. The meeting took place on the mountain of Mihintale, which has since become the holiest place in the island. Mahinda, who, according to the *Mahawamsa,* arrived by air, encountered the king while the latter was on a hunting expedition near Mihintale. Without further ado he set about interrogating Tissa to see if he was ripe for conversion.

"Tell me," Mahinda asked, "what is this tree called?"

"A mango," replied the king.

"Besides this are there any other mango trees?"

"There are many."

"Besides this mango and those other mangoes, are there any other trees in the world?"

"Yes, there are many others, but they are not mangoes."

"Besides the other mango trees and the trees that are not mangoes, is there any other?"

"Yes," replied the king. "This mango."

"Ruler of men," rejoiced Mahinda, "thou art wise." [3]

After this intelligence test, Mahinda proceeded to instruct Tissa in the Buddhist doctrine, with such success, says the chron-

[3] Cave, Henry. *Ruined Cities of Ceylon.* Sampson Low and Marston Ltd. 1900.

icle, that in a short time the king and his followers were converted to the new faith.

To commemorate the event Tissa and his followers, and their successors, erected many sacred buildings on the mountain of Mihintale; a *vihara,* or monastery, large numbers of monastic dwellings in the rocks, huge *dagobas,* artificial hills containing sacred relics, and a great granite staircase which ascends from the foot of the mountain to a height of more than one thousand feet.

Before leaving Ceylon, Mahinda promised to send the king several sacred relics of the Buddha; his right eye-tooth, his right collar-bone, his alms-bowl, and a branch of the sacred bo-tree under which he was sitting when he attained "Buddhahood". All these, says the *Mahawamsa,* duly arrived, accompanied by miracles. For instance, when the sacred urn containing some of the relics was brought before the king, he said:

> "If this is a relic of the Sage, then shall my parasol bow down of itself, my elephant shall sink to its knees, this relic-urn . . . shall descend on my head."

All of which, of course, happened, and the king, removing the urn from his head, placed it on the elephant's back. The elephant immediately trumpeted with joy, and the earth shook. Later, when the relics were being enshrined, the urn once more shot into the air and rested on the king's head.

The branch of the sacred bo-tree behaved just as dramatically. It was brought from India to Ceylon in a golden vase, and taken to the capital of Anuradhapura, where a rich shrine had been built to receive it.

> "At the hour when shadows are most extended the procession entered the Mahemegha garden, and there the king himself assisted to deposit the vase. In an instant the branch extricated itself, and, springing eighty cubits into the air, self-poised and resplendent, it cast forth a halo of rays of six colours. . . . Afterwards the branch re-entered the vase on the ground, and its roots, shooting downwards, forced it into the earth."

Naïve and charming though these legends are, it is important to remember that they, and the faith which they symbolized, provided the impetus which built the great cities of Ceylon. One may still see, at Anuradhapura, the great bo-tree, which, because of the self-reproductive powers of the species, may well be the descendant of that planted by Tissa more than two thousand years ago. Here, and at other places, one may also see the enormous *dagobas* or shrines, monuments to the piety of successive generations of kings who built them to enshrine the sacred relics. And the innumerable buildings which accompanied them, now buried under many square miles of jungle, were all ancillary to this main purpose, to honour the Buddha; the monasteries in which lived thousands of saffron-robed *thera,* or priests,[4] the rich palaces of the kings with their flowered gardens and acres of parkland, the homes of the workmen who hewed stone, and carved the statuary, the workers in gold and silver and ivory, the jewellers who cut the gems which sparkled in the shrines and temples—all served a religious function, as did the thousands who laboured in the corn and ricefields, producing the food which supported the legions of officials, priests, and devotees.

And yet, in spite of the austere faith of the Buddha, with its emphasis on "right action and right thought", its insistence on purity and the sanctity of life, human and animal, the history of the Sinhalese kings is not less bloodstained than that of most oriental monarchies. It is the familiar chronicle of tyranny, cruelty, bloodshed, murder and assassination. Punishments included impaling on stakes, being crushed beneath the feet of elephants, and being walled up alive. It is true that some of the kings seem to have been benevolent and humane, noble and chivalrous, but a great many were vile and depraved. But so, of course, were some Christian and Moslem rulers.

For fifty years after the death of Tissa, the Buddhist influence

---

[4] Though Thera is usually translated priest, preacher would be a better word. They have no sacramental functions.

continued and increased; Anuradhapura flourished in magnificence and beauty. Then, in about 145 B.C., a Tamil from southern India, one Elara, conquered Ceylon, and as he was a Hindu and therefore anti-Buddhist, much of Tissa's city was neglected or destroyed. The bo-tree, however, survived, as it happened to be equally sacred to the Brahmins. Meanwhile the descendents of the defeated Sinhalese kings, now living in the hill-country at Rohuna, plotted to regain their old kingdom, and among these were two brothers, Prince Gamani and another Tissa, who were to have great influence on the future of Ceylon.

Gamani, a hot-tempered youth, was so incensed by his father's unwillingness to let him wage war on Elara, that he sent his parent a woman's gown, with the words "if my father were a man, he would not speak thus to me; therefore he should put this on". For his insolent behaviour the young man was temporarily banished to Malay, while the Sinhalese, who probably secretly admired him, gave him the nickname *Duttha*—"angry". Thus he became known as Dutthagamani, and it was in this name that he reconquered Anuradhapura, mounted on a great elephant called Kandula, "foremost in strength, beauty, shape and in the qualities of swiftness and in mighty size".

Here the story becomes Homeric. Like Achilles and Hector in the *Iliad,* Dutthagamani and Elara met in single combat; not, however, on foot, but on elephants. Outside the south gate of Anuradhapura the two kings met, after the Tamils had been routed in furious battle. Shouting "None but myself shall slay Elara", the Sinhalese prince drove his elephant at his enemy, dodging the javelin that Elara flung at him. Kandula rent Elara's elephant with his tusks, so that it fell. Dutthagamani then leapt down and despatched his opponent with his dagger.

Afterwards the victorious king buried Elara's body with honour and solemnity, and afterwards the Kings of Ceylon, when passing Elara's monument, would alight to pay their respects to a brave enemy. Two thousand years later, when the last claimant to

the Sinhalese throne was defeated by the British, he got down from
his litter at the traditional place of Elara's death and made rever-
ence. This was in 1818.

King Tissa, who succeeded Dutthagamani, carried on great
building schemes at Anuradhapura, until, thirty years later, the
Tamils again reconquered the city. More plundering and devasta-
tion followed, until, in 27 B.C., the Sinhalese king, Vatthagamani,
reconquered it. His son, Coranga, who reigned at the beginning of
the Christian era, rates only a small mention in the *Mahawamsa,*
but Coranga's wife Anula, receives much more attention, for reasons which will become apparent.

She murdered six kings, five of whom were her husbands.

She first disposed of Coranga after becoming enamoured of
one of the palace guards, Siva. Coranga's legitimate successor was
Tissa, so Anula poisoned him too, in order to make Siva king.
Tiring of him after a year and two months, she poisoned him in
order to marry a carpenter who had pleased her. This man, Vatuka,
reigned only for one year and two months, when he in his turn
was murdered in order to make way for a woodsman named Tissa.
He also lasted one year and two months. Then followed Niliya, a
palace priest, who was, as the *Mahawamsa* relates, the last to meet
the same fate, for:

> "When the Princess Anula (who desired to take her
> pleasure, even as she listed, with thirty-two of the palace
> guards) had put to death Niliya also with poison, the
> Queen Anula reigned for four months."

At this point Kutankannatissa, a nephew of Anula's first victim, evidently decided that things had gone far enough. He put
the queen to death and assumed the throne. His successors reigned
for a further two centuries, during which, at one period, there
seems to have been a struggle between the monarchy and the
powerful priesthood. One of the later kings, Mahesena, pulled
down the "Brazen Palace"—the centre of Buddhist orthodoxy in
Lanka, and for a time supported an heretical minority. But in the
end he recanted, and built on behalf of the orthodox *bhikkhus* one

of the most splendid *dagobas* in Anuradhapura, the Jetavanarama Dagoba, and the great "tanks" (which are really huge artificial lakes) of Mineriya and Kantalai.

After the death of this king a weaker line of kings ruled, the *Sulawamsa* ("Lesser Dynasty"), who were less able to withstand the repeated Tamil invasions. The state grew weaker, Ceylon began to lose her wealth and independence, and during the eighth century A.D. the kings were forced to leave the ancient capital and build a new one at Polonnaruwa. This then became the leading city of Sinhalese Ceylon, while Anuradhapura was occupied and pillaged by the Tamils.

In A.D. 1000 Polonnaruwa also fell. There was one brief moment of revived glory for the Sinhalese kings, when in 1065 Vijaya Bahu I defeated the ancient enemy, and was crowned King of Lanka. His even more remarkable grandson, Parakrama Bahu I, assembled an army of over two millions, invaded India, overcame the King of Kandy, and forced him to pay tribute to Ceylon. Returning, he rebuilt Polonnaruwa, "erected a chain of ramparts round the city, a theatre for dance and song and 'a charming place, supported on one column, which seemed to have sprung up, as it were with the bursting of the earth. Its floor was of gold and was lighted by only one chandelier.' " [5] He also restored many of the buildings of the former capital, which by this time had become choked by undergrowth "where lurked tigers and bears" (as the *Mahawamsa* states), and established such peace and security in the island that "even a woman might traverse the island with a precious jewel, and not be asked what it was".

It was the last flicker of the flame. With the death of Parakrama Bahu the glory of the ancient Sinhalese culture went into its final decline. Plundering invasions by the Tamils; weak, selfish Sinhalese kings; all contributed to bring about the downfall of the rich and powerful civilization of former days. There was a brief period, in the fifteenth century, at about the time of the English Wars of the Roses, when a Chinese army invaded and took the

[5] Lord Holden. *Ceylon.* George Allen and Unwin. 1938.

Sinhalese king prisoner to Pekin. By the end of 1500, however, the Chinese occupation had ended. Twenty-two years later an excited Sinhalese messenger presented himself before his king, and announced that:

> "there is in our harbour of Colombo a race of people fair of skin and comely withal! They don jackets of iron and hats of iron; they rest not a minute in one place . . . they eat hunks of white stone and drink blood, and they have guns with a noise louder than thunder, and the ball shot from one of them, after traversing a league, will break a castle of marble."

"They" were the crews of Portuguese ships driven by a strong current into Colombo harbour. Europe had arrived in Ceylon, more than two thousand years after the first kings began to build at Anuradhapura; twenty centuries during which a rich civilization had developed, flourished, and decayed. When the Portuguese, Dutch, and British began to explore the "Land without Sorrow" little remained of these former glories that was visible, though the natives said that in the jungles of the north there were ruins of mighty cities.

During the nineteenth century, after Ceylon had become a British possession, a number of travellers made adventurous journeys into the interior, and rediscovered these ancient cities. One such traveller, Major Forbes, published in 1840 a book called *Eleven Years in Ceylon,* in which he published a list of 165 Sinhalese kings. The first entry reads:

> 1. Wejaya . . . B.C. 543. Bud. I. Reigned 38 years.
> Founder of the Wejayan dynasty.

The last reads:

> 165. Sree Wickrema Raja-Singha (Kandy) A.D. 1798.
> Bud. 2341. Reigned 16 years. Son of the late King's wife's sister, deposed by the English, and died in captivity.

These records were, of course, compiled from the ancient Sinhalese chronicles. Shorn of their mythical elements, these records proved to be substantially true. Forbes and other explorers were bewildered and awe-struck by the evidence they found of cities which have no parallel among the ancient civilizations of Europe and Western Asia; cities, as Forbes wrote, "where now the growl of the elephant, the startling rush of wild hog and deer, the harsh screams of peacock and toucan, increase the solemn but cheerless feeling inspired by a gloomy forest waving over a buried city".[6]

> "All the ruins of Anuradhapura," he wrote, "even the lofty monuments which contain the relics of Buddha, are either entirely covered with jungle, or partly obscured by forests; these the imagination of the natives has peopled with unholy phantoms, spirits of the unrighteous, doomed to wander near their mouldering walls which were witnesses of their guilt, and are partakers of their desolation. . . . The only place clear of jungle was in front of the great temple, where a shady tree occupied the centre of a square, and a stone pillar, fourteen feet high, stood beside the figure of a bull cut in granite, and revolving on a pivot."

From this square a stair ascends to a large enclosure, in the centre of which stands the sacred bo-tree, almost certainly the same which was planted by Devanampiyatissa. "The tree," wrote Forbes, "is the principal object of veneration to the numerous pilgrims who annually visit Anuradhapura." It is still there, and is still revered by millions.

Forbes also described the "Brazen Palace", built by Dutthagamani, with its "sixteen hundred stone pillars placed in forty parallel lines, forty pillars in each, and occupying a square space, each side of which is two hundred and thirty-four feet in length." He mentions the dagobas of Anuradhapura, including the "Ruwanwelli-saye" built by Dutthagamani, standing "in the centre of an elevated square platform, which is paved with large stones of dressed granite, each side being about five hundred feet in length; and surrounded by a fosse seventy feet in breadth; the scarp, or sides of the platform, is sculptured to represent the

---

[6] Forbes, Major. *Eleven Years in Ceylon*. London, 1840.

foreparts and heads of elephants, projecting and appearing to support the massive superstructure."

Near the dagoba, the guides pointed out to Forbes, as they still do to-day, the granite slab to which the dying king was conveyed during his last illness, so that he could see his great works, the Ruwanwelli Dagoba and the "Brazen Palace" (the Lohapasada). Of this building, the columns of which still remain, the *Mahawamsa* says:

> "This palace is one hundred cubits square and of the same height. In it were nine stories, and in each of them one hundred apartments. All these apartments were highly furnished with silver; and the cornices thereof were embellished with gems. The flower ornaments were also set with gems, and the tinkling festoons were of gold. In this palace there were a thousand dormitories having windows with ornaments which were as bright as eyes."

Of the hall which was the central feature of the "Brazen Palace", the *Mahawamsa* says:

> "This hall was supported on golden pillars, representing lions and other animals as well as *devatas,* and was ornamented with festoons of pearls all around. Exactly in the middle of this hall, which was adorned with the seven treasures, there was a beautiful and enchanting ivory throne. On one side of this throne there was the emblem of the sun in gold; on the other the moon in silver; and on the third the stars in pearls. . . ."
>
> "The building was covered with brazen tiles; hence it acquired the name of 'Brazen Palace.' "

The buildings which Forbes and his contemporaries saw over a century ago have since been considerably cleared of jungle growth, repaired and partially restored. For many years British, and, later, Sinhalese archæologists have fought to save the lost cities from further damage and deterioration, to clear away trees and undergrowth from what were once the gracious parks and gardens of Anuradhapura, Polunnaruwa and other cities. To-day visitors can reach the sites via well-made roads, where once such pioneers as Cave and Forbes struggled along jungle tracks, and where, one hundred and fifty years earlier, the fugitive Robert Knox, escaping from his nineteen years' captivity, noticed "here and there, by the side of this river . . . a world of hewn stone pillars, and other heaps of hewn stones, which I suppose formerly were buildings. . . ."

They can admire the great Ruwanwelli, or "gold-dust" Dagoba, built by King Dutthangamani to enshrine the sacred Footprint of the Buddha, and a precious collection of relics. It is two hundred and seventy feet high and two hundred and ninety-four feet in diameter, built entirely of brick.

> "In the distance," writes Lord Holden, "it resembles a colossal red balloon crowned with a dazzling white and golden *tee,* and on nearer approach the intermittent scaffolding straggling across its bulbous face seems to increase its magnitude. . . ."

On the east side of the building are seven statues, probably the finest in Ceylon, one of which represents the king himself; the others are of the four Buddhas who have visited the earth.

> "A short distance from the temple stand two statues at the top of a short flight of steps. They represent King Dutthagamani and his mother. The outstanding feature of this beautiful representation of the king is the elegance of the folded hands, which incline imperceptibly towards the chest. The body of the mother is arrayed in bangles and necklaces and is crowned with a hat, apparently of Chinese origin. Her face is aloof and reposeful, and her profile is reminiscent of a primitive Italian Madonna. It would be impossible to exaggerate the beauty of these figures." [7]

Other examples of sculpture have survived here and there, at Anuradhapura, Polonnaruwa, and other places—a pitiful remnant of the many which once must have existed, but sufficient to hint at the beauty of ancient Sinhalese art. The sculptured figures

[7] Lord Holden. *Ceylon.*

are subtle and sensuous, representing a slightly-built race with well-formed bodies and delicate features. There is something fragile and flower-like about them, like the lotus-blooms they hold in their hands. A carved stela found at the Abhayagiriya Dagoba is described by Cave as follows:

> "The upper has a carved male figure . . . with a five-headed cobra as a sort of halo, holding flowers in his right hand and resting the left on his hip. In the lower panel is a female, with a single hood; the upper part of whose body is bare, with the exception of some jewellery, while below the waist the limbs are draped in a transparent robe; the ankles are encircled by bangles; and the palm of her right hand supports a vessel, containing a lotus-bud."

Strength and fragility; sensuality and asceticism; cruelty and gentleness; these opposed qualities in the art of ancient Ceylon may be the key to the character of its creators. Power and might are there, as in Nineveh, Babylon, and Hattusas. There is the Abhayagiriya Dagoba, a bell-like mound of brickwork which stood fifty feet higher than St. Paul's Cathedral; there is the broad granite stairway climbing the mountain of Mihintale to a height of a thousand feet; there is the galleried fortress of Sigri frowning from its crag; there is the Jetawanarama Dagoba, the materials of which, says one authority, would be sufficient to build eight thousand houses, each with a twenty foot frontage, or form a wall ten feet high and a foot wide, from London to Edinburgh.

But, combined with this monumental strength, there are other things; flower-garlanded streets along which the kings rode on elephants caparisoned in gold; the intricately jewelled shrines; the cross-legged Buddhas in serene contemplation; and the dancing girls, with faint smiles and swaying hips, moving with the same dreamy impassive grace which their descendants have inherited.

CHAPTER NINE

Death of a City

All of us who have had the good fortune to travel in ancient lands will have our favorite "lost cities". Mine is Palmyra, in the Syrian desert (described in *One Man's Journey*), but next to it comes the most obvious and frequently described of them all—Pompeii. If, therefore, this chapter is less objective than the rest, I must crave the reader's indulgence, because my memories of Pompeii are strongly personal, for reasons which will become apparent. They will also be shared, I believe, by many servicemen who fought in Italy during 1944.

I had not intended to visit the Campania in which Pompeii lies. In fact I was taken there in an ambulance. In the early summer of 1944 I had been accredited as a War Correspondent to the R.A.F., with the idea of producing radio documentary programmes about the R.A.F. Transport Command in North Africa, Italy and Burma. This was the first time I had ever been out of England, and the prospect was an exciting one. My chagrin, therefore, was considerable when, in Naples, I succumbed ingloriously to an obscure fever, which at first was regarded as a chill, but which turned out to be a virus type of pneumonia. I recollect an evening in the Officers' Mess of 214 Squadron, seen through a haze such as even the most generous hospitality could not have induced. It was followed by an ambulance journey along the coast-road of the Bay of Naples to a large pink-washed building set among gardens and olive-groves.

Early next morning I woke in a hospital ward, aware of a loud and disturbing rumble accompanied by tremors which I took to be an explosion in the near vicinity. When the Ward Sister came to take my temperature, I asked if we had been bombed in the night. Her reply was cool and casual:

"Oh, *that*. That was Vesuvius."

"Vesuvius?" I asked. "Are we near it?"

"Near it?" she replied. "We're on it," [1] and tripped off with the thermometer.

During convalescence, I used to sit on the balcony, looking at the cone of the volcano, from which wisps of smoke occasionally rose, and listening to the highly-coloured accounts of my companions who had seen the famous eruption which had taken place a few weeks before. I secretly and ashamedly hoped it would erupt again, but I am unlucky with volcanoes. The same thing happened nine years later in Mexico, when, after an arduous cross-country journey to see Paracutin—which had been erupting violently for several weeks, I arrived only to see a silent peaceful mountain of ash, which did not even deign to spit. . . .

I did once look down from a flying-boat at Stromboli in action, but am convinced that if we had descended, all activity would have ceased immediately.

This digression has been introduced only to demonstrate my unorthodox approach to the buried cities of Pompeii and Herculaneum, and subsequent visits to the sites in 1952 only proved the truth of the cliché about first impressions. In some ways 1944 was not the ideal time to visit Pompeii. The war had closed down excavations, and at night the gunflashes on the northern horizon made archæology seem a somewhat remote and esoteric pursuit. The ancient streets were thronged, not with earnest students of antiquity, but with troops on leave. One was not in the mood for serious study, and though I queued with the rest of the licentious soldiery to see the Roman Brothel (by far the greatest attraction), climbed the lower slopes of the mountain and clambered over the still-warm lava, my impressions seemed superficial.

Or so I thought at the time; but though, eight years later, I returned as a peace-time tourist and made a leisurely examination

---

[1] The hospital was at Torre del Greco, at the foot of the mountain.

of the ruins, my earlier memories remain the most vivid. Then the ash which powdered the streets, the occasional rumblings of the mountain, the stories one heard in the taverns of villages engulfed and people abandoning their homes, brought so much nearer the original tragedy which had destroyed Pompeii in A.D. 79.

Unlike the other cities described in this book, Pompeii did not decay and die gradually. It was killed by one terrible stroke. Moreover, through the words of Roman eyewitnesses, we can see that stroke fall. Pliny the Elder, for instance, who at that time commanded the fleet at Misenum, was killed in the disaster. In a letter to Tacitus, Pliny's nephew described the event in words so vivid that we can share the experience.

"On the 24th of August, about one in the afternoon, my mother desired him to observe a cloud of very unusual size and appearance. He had sunned himself, then taken a cold bath, and after a leisurely luncheon was engaged in study. He immediately called for his shoes and went up an eminence from which he might best view this very uncommon appearance. It was not at that distance discernible from what mountain the cloud issued, but it was found afterwards to be Vesuvius. I cannot give you a more exact description of its figure, than by resembling it to that of a pine-tree, which extended itself at the top into several branches; because, I imagine, a momentary gust of air blew it aloft, and then failing, forsook it; thus causing the cloud to expand literally as it dissolved, or possibly the downward pressure of its own weight produced this effect. It was at one moment white, at another dark and spotted, as if it had carried up earth or cinders.

"My uncle, true savant that he was, deemed the phenomenon worthy of a closer view. He ordered a light vessel to be got ready, and gave me the liberty, if I thought proper, to attend him."

The younger Pliny seems to have lacked his uncle's adventurous curiosity, for he replied that he would

"rather study; and as it happened, he had himself given me a theme for composition."

The older man's character comes out more clearly in what followed, for when Rectina, the wife of his friend Bassus, sent a note saying that her villa was threatened and she could only escape by sea,

"He changed his first design, and what he began with a philosophical, he pursued with an heroical turn of mind."

However even this, apparently, was not enough to drag the young man from his literary activities, so the Elder Pliny, having ordered large galleys to be launched, set off without his nephew:

". . . with the intention of assisting not only Rectina, but many others; for the villas stand extremely thick on that beautiful coast. Hastening to the place from whence others were flying, he steered his direct course to the point of danger, and with such freedom from fear, as to be able to make and dictate his observations upon the successive motions and figures of that terrific object.

"And now the cinders, which grew thicker and hotter the nearer he approached, fell into the ships, then pumice stones too, with stones blackened, scorched and cracked by fire, then the sea ebbed suddenly from under them, while the shore was blocked by landslips from the mountains. After considering for a moment whether he should retreat, he said to the captain who was urging that course, 'Fortune befriends the brave; carry me to Pomponianus'. Pomponianus was then at Stabiae, distant by half the width of the bay. . . . He had already embarked his baggage; for though at Stabiae the danger was not yet near, it was in full view, and certain to be extremely near, as soon as it spread; and he resolved to fly as soon as the contrary wind should cease. It was full favourable, however, for carrying my uncle to Pomponianus. He embraces, comforts, and encourages his alarmed friend, and desired to be conducted to a bathroom; and after having bathed, he sat down to supper with great cheerfulness, or at least (what is equally heroic) with all appearance of it.

"In the meanwhile Mount Vesuvius was blazing in several places with spreading and towering flames, whose refulgent brightness the darkness of the night set in high relief. But my uncle, in order to soothe apprehensions, kept saying that some fires had been left alight by the terrified country people, and what they saw were only deserted villages on fire. . . ."

Of his own experiences at this time the Younger Pliny wrote:

"There had been for several days before some shocks of earthquake, which the less alarmed us as they are frequent in Campania; but that night they became so violent that one might think that the world was not being merely shaken, but turned topsy-turvy. My mother flew to my chamber; I was just rising, meaning on my part to awaken her, if she was asleep. We sat down in the fore-court of the house, which separated it by a short space from the sea. I know not whether to call it courage or inexperience—I was not quite eighteen—but I called for a volume of Livy, and began to read, and even went on with the extracts I was making from it, as if nothing were the matter. . . ."

Meanwhile at Pompeii itself and the surrounding villas and villages, the terrified inhabitants thought they saw giants in the sky. As Dio Cassius wrote:

"Numbers of men quite surpassing any human stature—which creatures, in fact, as the giants are pictured to have been, appeared, now on the mountainside, now in the surrounding country, and again in the cities, wandering over the earth day and night, and also flitting in the air. . . . There were frequent rumblings, some of them subterranean, that resembled thunder, and some on the surface, that sounded like bellowings; the sea also joined in the roar and the sky re-echoed it. Then suddenly a portentous crash was heard, as if the mountains were tumbling in ruins; at first huge stones were hurled aloft, rising as high as the very summits, then came a great quantity of fire and endless smoke, so that the whole atmosphere was obscured and the sun entirely hidden. . . . Some thought that the giants were rising again in revolt (for at this time also many of their forms could be discerned in the smoke, and moreover, a sound as of trumpets was

heard) while others believed that the whole universe was
being resolved into chaos of fire."

The zestful Dio, writing one hundred and fifty years after
the eruption, was probably drawing on contemporary accounts now
lost, and on local traditions. But the young Pliny, reading Livy
while the villa shook and trembled, and his mother, thinking of
her brother out in the darkened bay, were eye-witnesses. Of the
following morning the young man wrote:

> "It was now six in the morning, and the light still
> ambiguous and faint. The buildings around us already
> tottered, and though we stood upon open ground, yet as
> the place was narrow and confined, there was certain and
> formidable danger from their collapsing."

They resolved to leave the town.

> "Being got outside the house, we halt in the middle
> of a most strange and dreadful scene. The coaches which
> we had ordered out, though upon the most level ground,
> were sliding to and fro, and could not be kept steady
> even when stones were put against the wheels. Then we
> beheld the sea sucked back, and as it were repulsed by
> the convulsive motion of the earth; it is certain at least the
> shore was considerable enlarged, and now held many sea-
> animals captive on dry land. On the other side (of the
> bay) a black and dreadful cloud bursting out in gusts of
> igneous serpentine vapour now and again yawned open to
> reveal long fantastic flames, resembling flashes of light-
> ning but much larger. . . ."

At Stabiae, where he had spent the night with his friend
Pomponianus, the Elder Pliny was dying. Later his nephew was
told that the old man had slept for a while until "the court which
led to his apartment now lay so deep under a mixture of pumice
stones and ashes, that, if he had continued longer in his bedroom,
he would have been unable to get out. On being roused, he came
out, and returned to Pomponianus and the others, who had sat up
all night. They consulted together as to whether they should hold
out in the house, or wander about in the open."

Eventually it was decided that it was better to stay in the open, and risk being felled by stones or choked by ash and fumes, than be crushed by falling buildings, and there is a tragically ludicrous description of these high Roman officials and their followers, who "tied pillows upon their heads with napkins; this was their whole defence against the showers which fell round them."

Finally they wandered to the shore, but it was impossible to put to sea as the waves and wind were still contrary.

> "There my uncle, having thrown himself down upon a disused sail, repeatedly called for, and drank, a draught of cold water; soon after, flames, and a strong smell of sulphur, which was the forerunner of them, dispersed the rest of the company in flight; him they only roused. He raised himself up with the assistance of two of his slaves, but instantly fell; some unusually gross vapour, as I conjecture, having obstructed his breathing and blocked his windpipe, which was not only naturally weak and constricted, but chronically inflamed. When day dawned again (the third from that he last beheld) his body was found entire and uninjured, and still fully clothed as in life; its posture was that of a sleeping, rather than a dead man."

Across the bay, in the country outside the shattered port of Misenum, from which the Elder Pliny had set out, his sister struggled to persuade her son to escape as best he could.

> "a young man could do it; she, burdened with age and corpulency, would die easy if only she had not caused my death. I replied, I would not be saved without her, and taking her by the hand I hurried her on. . . . Ashes now fall upon us, though as yet in no great quantity. I looked behind me; gross darkness pressed upon our rear, and came rolling over the land after us like a torrent. . . . We had scarce sat down to rest when darkness overspread us, not like that of a moonless or cloudy night, but of a room when it is shut up and the lamp put out. You could hear the shrieks of the women, the crying of children, and the shouts of men; some seeking children, others their parents, others their wives or husbands, and

only distinguishing them by their voices; one lamenting
his own fate, another that of his family; some praying to
die, from the very fear of dying; many lifting their hands
to the gods; but the greater part imagining that there were
no gods left anywhere, and that the last and eternal night
had come upon the world."

Pliny and his mother survived, but of the thousands who died,
choked by fumes, smothered by ashes, or crushed beneath fallen
buildings, many must indeed have believed, as the young Roman
says, "that the last and eternal night had come". On the wall of a
Pompeian villa unearthed by archæologists eighteen centuries later
someone had written:

SODOMA GOMORA

In the above chapter the translation of Pliny the Younger ("Letters"
Book VI) is by William Melmoth, Loeb Edition, William Heinemann, 1927;
of Dio Cassius (Book LXVI) by E. Cary, Loeb Edition, William Heinemann,
1925.

CHAPTER TEN

The Resurrection of Pompeii

"Such, Marcellus, is the story I am singing on the Chal-
cidic strand, where Vesuvius hurls forth broken rage,
outpouring fire that would rival Trinacrian flames. Marvellous, but true! Will future ages believe, when once
more crops are growing, and these wastes are green again,
that cities and people lie beneath, and that their ancestral
lands have suffered a like fate?"

So wrote Publius Papinius Statius, the Roman epic poet, who
was a contemporary of Pliny the Younger. To-day his rhetorical
question is answered. During the past two hundred years excavators have removed much, though not all of the volcanic ash
which smothered Pompeii, and have revealed the streets, shops,
taverns, workrooms, public buildings and villas from which their
inhabitants fled, or tried to fly, more than eighteen hundred years
ago. They have also partially uncovered the neighbouring port of
Herculaneum—a much stiffer task, since this town was buried
under showers of volcanic mud to a depth of 50 or 60 feet. In
time this solidified into *tufa* as hard as rock.

The first excavators were the Pompeians themselves, who,
returning to their city when the eruption had ceased, dug down
through the roofs of their buried homes and salvaged what they
could find of their furniture and belongings. The tunnels they
drove through the solidified ash can still be seen in places. But a
time came when Pompeii and Herculaneum were forgotten.
Throughout the Middle Ages they lay undisturbed, and it was not
until 1709 that an Austrian prince sank a shaft at Herculaneum,
and then, by means of underground tunnels, robbed the buried

theatre of marbles and statues. Twenty years later systematic excavation began on the same site, but Charles III of Naples, under
whose orders the work was carried out, merely used the site as a
mine from which to obtain archæological specimens for his collection. A few years after, an accidental find at Pompeii led to excavations there; at first by tunnelling, but afterwards by the actual uncovering of the city.

From the latter part of the eighteenth century to the present
day, digging has gone on practically continuously, though slowly,
and often with slender resources. Perhaps this slowness has not
been entirely a disadvantage, since it has resulted in large, un-
touched sections of both cities being left preserved for modern,
scientific excavation. Archæological techniques have advanced so
far in the past fifty years that a site can be made to reveal far more
archæological information than was possible under the older, cruder
methods of digging.

To-day four-fifths of Pompeii and a substantial, though much
smaller, section of Herculaneum have been cleared. They are the
best-known archæological sites in Europe, and for the layman by
far the most wonderful. For here, and nowhere else on earth, are
ancient cities in which life did not die out but was suddenly ar-
rested. "Behind those walls," as one writer has said, "lies an ancient
Italian town, stilled in a moment of time. To enter the gates of
this city is to walk two thousand years into the past." [1]

In the preceding chapters I have tried to describe the methods by which archæologists gradually pieced together a picture of
ancient Assyrian, Sumerian, Hittite and Indian cities from fragmentary remains and by deciphering inscriptions in forgotten
tongues. In Pompeii and Herculaneum this was not so. The streets,
houses, shops, inns, business premises were there, waiting to be
found; the dining-room with the furniture still in it; the bedroom
with bed and bedside table, the kitchen-stove with a cooking-pot
still on it; the bakery with its corn-mills and ovens, the inn with the
bibulous scrawls of its patrons still on the walls, the brothel with

[1] R. C. Carrington, in B.B.C. television broadcast on Pompeii.

its neat little cubicles for the girls, and the cash-desk at which their guests paid their money. As for inscriptions—1,500 of which were found on the walls of the city—election messages, lover's scrawls, children's exercises, announcements of gladiatorial games —there was no difficulty over decipherment, as all were in Latin. To complete the picture, on the walls of the richer houses were painted frescoes, some of which depicted in fascinating detail the everyday life of the citizens of Pompeii eighteen centuries ago.

Before we look at the cities, let us take a quick backward glance at their history, because it is important to realize that both Pompeii and Herculaneum existed six centuries before the Romans occupied them, and many of their buildings are pre-Roman. In the seventh century before Christ, when the Greek colonists were establishing themselves along the coast, the country was occupied by a tribe called the Oscans. Later the Etruscans, from Northern Italy (Tuscany takes its name from them) possessed the land, until, in 420 B.C., another Italic tribe, the Samnites, took over, and under the Samnite influence both cities prospered. Both the Samnites and the Etruscans were in many ways a more civilized people than the Romans, who at this time were merely a small tribe living beside the Tiber, constantly at war with their neighbours. But throughout the pre-Roman period the cultural influence was Greek. The very name Torre del Greco (where the R.A.F. had their hospital in 1944) means "the town of the Greeks"—a reference to the nearby city of Herculaneum, named after the Greek hero Hercules. Greek art, Greek religion, Greek literature, permeated the peoples of Campania.

When, in 80 B.C., the Roman general Sulla captured Pompeii and settled his veterans there, the Romans became possessors of attractive and flourishing little provincial towns with a history going back more than six hundred years. The new-comers, by comparison with the Hellenized Samnites, were at a lower cultural level, though, when they conquered the Greek world and absorbed its much richer civilization, they too became Hellenized. As time went on the wealthier Romans, attracted by the beauty of the Bay

of Naples, and by its climate, built villas near such towns as
Pompeii, Herculaneum, Baiae, and Misenum, either as holiday
residences or as permanent homes. Such were the villas occupied
by Pliny and his nephew, by their friends Bassus and Rectina, and
by Pomponianus.

Of the two towns we are considering, Pompeii was by far the
larger, supporting a population which has been variously estimated at between 15,000 and 25,000 inhabitants. The fluctuation
in population was probably due to the fact that when the wealthy
Roman "vacationists" arrived at their villas with an army of
slaves and attendants, they also attracted tradesmen and artisans to
the town. The great amphitheatre at Pompeii, where the gladiatorial
sports and animal shows were held, could accommodate 20,000
people, which looks as if the games attracted many spectators from
other towns in the neighbourhood; this would account for the
large number of hotels and inns which have been unearthed in
Pompeii.

Pompeii was built on an isolated ridge formed by volcanic
activity in very ancient times; it is about five miles south-east of
Vesuvius. Herculaneum, less than five miles from the mountain,
lay on the shore. "While Herculaneum," writes Corti, "was at first
merely a transit point, pleasantly enough situated, it was soon evident that Pompeii, built somewhat further off on the lava hill, ad-
jacent to the mouth of the navigable Sarno, with its possibilities
as a harbour, and at the crossing of important roads, was emi-
nently suited to be an important commercial town. So the Greeks
turned their attention to this place." [2] And Herculaneum remained
a small town.

This, obviously, is not the place in which to give detailed descriptions of either town, to which many books have been devoted. As one who has read or at least "dipped into" most of those
written in English, may I recommend, as by far the best written,
most readable (as well as accurate) account, *The Destruction and*

[2] Corti, Egon Cæsar Conte. *The Destruction and Resurrection of Pompeii and Herculaneum.* Routledge and Kegan Paul. 1951.

Resurrection of Pompeii and Herculaneum, by Egon Cæsar Conte
Corti, first published in Germany in 1940, and in England in 1951.
"Dog does not eat dog", and I am reluctant to criticize the writings
of fellow-craftsmen working in the same field—especially as most
are by archæologists whose learning far exceeds mine. But too many
of such works are marred, in my view, by what appears to be a
wilful blindness to an aspect of Pompeii which immediately strikes
any visitor who sees it with unprejudiced eyes; its lusty eroticism,
its sheer vulgar vitality. Of all "dead cities" Pompeii is by far the
most alive; yet, some writers on the subject have smothered the
unfortunate city under an accumulation of dusty facts about bakeries and laundries as heavy as the lava-dust which first buried it.

When, very occasionally, they do approach the more earthy
manifestations of Pompeian life—which stare at them from practically every painted fresco, or carved phallus embedded in a wall
—they do so either with embarrassing coyness or a primness which
would be maddening if it were not so laughable. Thus one writer,
wagging a deprecating forefinger, says:

> "There were dark alleys, too, where depravity
> lurked, and at the end of this sinister street stood a two-
> storied building . . . noteworthy to the Pompeians for
> ladies of easy virtue." [3]

And rapidly averting his and our eyes he hurries on to the
baths.

> "Less reprehensible was the Roman indulgence in
> bathing . . ." etc., etc.

Writing of the amusing *graffiti* (wall-scribblings) which the
common people of Pompeii were fond of scratching or chalking on
any convenient space, Professor Mau writes:

> "The cultivated men and women of the ancient city
> were not accustomed to scratch their names upon the
> stucco or to confide their reflections and experiences on
> the surface of the wall; we may assume that the writers

[3] B.B.C. television broadcast, September 18, 1956.

were . . . not representative of the best elements of society."

We may indeed, but the "cultivated men and women" wrote memoirs, letters and chronicles which have survived. Our only written records of the common people are such inscriptions as those found at Pompeii; "expressions of infantilism" as another scholar describes them, but at least no more tedious than many a pompous Roman bore whose dull observations are now chastely bound between the covers of a Loeb edition.

I also strongly suspect that one of the reasons for this academic aloofness is that some of the Pompeian *graffiti* refer to human activities of which some (though not all) scholars may disapprove. This one, for instance, chalked by the revellers on the walls of a Pompeian inn, some eighteen hundred years ago:

> *"Greetings! We are most valiant drinking men!*
> *When you came, we paid the bill!"*

This occurs three times, and always signed by the same man, Eupor, who was clearly the life and soul of the party.

Another inscription, on a painted fresco, depicting an inn-scene, reads:

> *"Curse you, Landlord. You sell water for wine and*
> *drink unmixed wine yourself!"*

One of the most interesting monographs on these *graffiti* is *The Common People of Pompeii,* by the American scholar, Helen H. Tanzer,[4] and others are listed in the Bibliography; all these contain valuable information, especially Carrington's *Pompeii,* but Corti's book alone, in my opinion, combines authority, scholarship, and a fluent, almost dashing descriptive style. It is also mercifully free from the priggishness of the sheltered mind.

Entering Pompeii through the Porta Marina on the south, you climb a steep, stone-surfaced road, worn by chariot and wagon-wheels, to the great Forum, or public square, at one end of which

---

[4] Published by the Johns Hopkins Press, Baltimore. 1939.

stand substantial remains of the great temple of Saturn. Nearby, also fronting the Forum, are the remains of the Basilica, an imposing, pillared building which in Roman times served both as a Court of Justice and a Town Hall. Here the public business of the town was done, and one imagines the Pompeians lounging under the shady colonnades, or perhaps buying sweetmeats from the food-pedlars who thronged the public places. A painting on the walls of one of the larger houses shows such a scene; an old man has fallen asleep beside his tray of dainties. A young boy, accompanied by a man, presumably his father, stands holding out a plate. Another young man, probably the pedlar's son, touches the old man's shoulder to awaken him.

From this elevated spot the eye takes in the vine-covered slopes of Vesuvius on the north, and the smiling Campania on either side, following the sweetly curving line of the Bay. The sun is hot on your shoulder, the sea is blue as the sky, the spaces between the white, sunlit columns etched in deep shade. All that we feel when we hear the word "Mediterranean" is contained within the walls of this once-bustling little city; its white-toga'd citizens, babbling in Latin, laughing, arguing, bargaining, gossiping, seem much nearer in that friendly sunshine than do, say, the long-dead inhabitants of Babylon and Hattusas.

From the Forum you continue on your way until you reach a cross-roads. Here one of the most important streets, the Strada di Nola, crosses Pompeii from north-east to south-west. Another street, the "Street of Abundance", ran parallel with it to the southeast, and a third, the Strada Stabiana, crossed them both, running in a north-west to south-east direction. Between these thoroughfares minor streets were laid out in a grid, some lined with shops, inns, and business premises, others with villas of varying sizes. From the outside these private dwellings look rather forbidding; high walls pierced by an entrance guarded by a porter's lodge, and few windows in the exterior. But once through the gates the visitor sees, usually, a suite of rooms set around an open space, above which a square opening gives light, and allows rainwater to fall into an open basin in the centre—the *impluvium*. Beyond that he passes through a second gateway to a courtyard, the peristyle, which is sometimes planted with flowers and shrubs, and surrounded by a shady arcade, beyond which more rooms open off. Further still, if the villa is a large one, he comes to the garden, in which among the flower-beds are figures of nymphs and satyrs, and sometimes fountains.

Around the city was a girdle-wall, but after the Romans were established at Pompeii in 80 B.C., defence was unnecessary, and villas were built outside the wall, particularly on the southern side of the slopes overlooking the sea. Nine of the gates survive, the Sea Gate through which we entered, the Stabian Gate at the south-eastern end of the Stabian Way, the Vesuvian Gate at the opposite end of the same street, the Porta di Nola at the northern end of the Strada di Nola, and so on. There was a large amphitheatre at the north-eastern corner, within the walls, and this area seems to have been occupied mainly by those concerned with the games; gladiators, organized in schools with their instructors, animals and their keepers, etc.

Apart from being a residence for the wealthier Romans (and enriched business men of the locality) Pompeii was essentially a commercial and trading centre. The famous Falernian wine was made from vines grown on the slopes of Vesuvius, and there were other, cheaper, local wines, some of which were exported. Then, as now, there were extensive olive-groves, and olive oil was one of the staple products. Volcanic ash produces a fertile soil, and the Campanian countryside grew corn, fruit and vegetables (Pompeii had a separate vegetable market). Cattle were raised and poultry kept, providing rich dishes for the Pompeian gourmets. The main impression one receives of Pompeii is of a rich, leisured, sybaritic life lived in the sunshine, with an abundance of food, good wine, and the other sensual pleasures unashamedly enjoyed.

Another impression is one of vulgarity. The painted frescoes, the statuary, the decoration of Pompeian houses vary in quality, but even the best are poor and derivative compared with Greek art, and one suspects that Greek Pompeii was probably æsthetically superior to its Roman successor, even if the sanitation was not. There is something coarse and *nouveau riche* about much Pompeian art, but it provides the most vivid illustration we have of Roman provincial life in the first century A.D.

Re-peopling ancient Babylon or Nineveh requires a considerable effort of imagination, particularly if one is not an archæologist. Pompeii and Herculaneum present no such difficulties, even for the layman, because in many of the streets the walls still stood to a considerable height, and in some cases, where the upper storeys collapsed during the eruption, the Italian archæologists have rebuilt them exactly as they were. One walks along the same pavements the Pompeians used, crosses the same raised "stepping-stones" designed to enable pedestrians to avoid the ruts, and in bad weather, the mud. The shops where the Pompeians bought their food and clothing, the "quick-lunch bars" where they took snacks before going to the theatre, the restaurants and wine-shops, all are still to be seen. The public baths with their hot and cold chambers, their changing rooms with cupboards for the bathers' clothes, their plunge baths and their exercise grounds are very much as the Roman inhabitants knew them. In the gardens of the villas grow the same types of flowers which their Pompeian owners planted. This has been made possible by the fact that the roots of the original plants left an impression in the compressed volcanic ash, enabling botanists to identify them. Specimens of the same flowers were then replanted.

One's first visit to Pompeii is a unique, uncanny, almost alarming experience. Nowhere else in the world, save at Herculaneum, does one get such a sense of immediate contact with the remote past. In a narrow street one turns into a doorway and there is a bakery. You see the grinding mill—two heavy stones, the lower one conical, the upper shaped like an hour-glass and fitting over the lower. Grain was poured in through the top, and the upper millstone was turned by donkeys walking round a circular platform. Nearby is the stable for the animals, the kneading room, the ovens, and a store-room for loaves. There were twenty such bakeries in Pompeii, and carbonized specimens of loaves have been found. They are usually circular, and scored across the top like a large "hot-cross-bun". You walk on a little farther and enter a fulling establishment, where the Pompeians' togas were washed (this was compulsory) and raw cloth from the looms was first cleaned by treading in troughs, then treated with fuller's earth, washed, shrunk and bleached with sulphur, before being delivered to the cloth-merchants. The vats used in the various processes are still in position, and can be compared with those found in a Roman villa at Chedworth, Gloucestershire, in England.

In many ways life in first-century Pompeii was not unlike that of an Italian provincial town to-day. One notices, for example, the number of cafés, eating places, and bars. I prefer the word "bar" to the guide-book "wine-shop". A bar is a place where drink is served "for consumption on the premises" as well as "to take away"; such was the Pompeian *taberna,* except that it also had adjoining rooms in which meals could be served if required. There was the usual bar-counter, and the frescoes show customers being served at such establishments. One of them records the disgusted comment of an unsatisfied client—quoted earlier—and another shows the figure of a soldier carrying a spear, over which stands the legend "ADDE CALICEM SETINIUM"—"Give me a cup of Satian". Satian wine was imported, so evidently the warrior did not want the *vin ordinaire.*

In another picture a serving-girl is handing wine to her customers with the words "You can drink here for one *as"* (a small coin), "if you pay double you can have better wine, but if you pay four you can have Falernian". Yet another picture depicts a landlord pushing two drunks out of his inn, with the words ITAS FORSA RIXATIS—which can be translated:

"Scram! You can do your quarrelling outside."

On archæological sites in Egypt are similar pictures depicting scenes from everyday life, but in Pompeii one may stand in the actual buildings in which tradesmen, soldiers, gladiators, dancing girls, and animal trainers caroused after the day's sport, took wagers on their favourites, insulted the landlord, pinched the serving-girl's bottom, and got steadily drunk. Later, as the moon rose over Vesuvius, no doubt, they roared out songs which would have confirmed Professor Mau's belief that they were "not representative of the best elements in society".

Perhaps it was after a night spent at one such *taberna* that an unknown Pompeian wrote on a nearby wall:

"Romula stayed here with Staphyclus."

As in our own day, Pompeian lovers wrote their names on walls, sometimes accompanying them with scraps of very bad verse, which, in translation, recall a modern popular song "lyric" of the "June-moon-tune" variety; indeed they may have been snatches from the "hit-tunes" of the period. Here is one:

"Anyone could as well stop the winds blowing
And the waters from flowing
As stop lovers from loving. . . ."

Not all the verse scribbled on the Pompeian walls is as banal as this. There are scraps of Ovid, Lucretius, Propertius and Virgil, often misquoted, as the writers were obviously relying on memory. Names of gods and goddesses, echoes of Greek myths, stand side by side with sententious observations such as:

"A little evil grows great if disregarded."

Schoolchildren provided their quota on the lower parts of the walls. One child had laboriously written the alphabet in an infantile scrawl, while another had set down the days of the week . . . Solis, Lunae, Mardis, Jovis, etc.

These chalkings and scratchings, puerile though most of them are, at least indicate that even the meanest citizen was literate. As Helen Tanzer observes:

"Everybody could read and almost everybody could and apparently did write."

Or as one brilliant Pompeian wit inscribed on the side of a house—

"Everyone writes on the walls—except me."

The walls were also used for election notices. Pompeii was governed by a City Council. The elected officials, called *Quinquennales,* were voted into office every five years. Evidently an election had taken place, or was in progress when disaster overtook the city, for chalked on the walls are fervent recommendations of the contesting candidates, with the names and trades of their supporters. These inscriptions are valuable, because they indicate some of the many trades and occupations; among those mentioned are farmers, muledrivers, innkeepers, fishermen, bakers, shoemakers, dyers and cleaners, porters, soldiers, gladiators, etc.

Foodshops, called *alimenta,* were numerous, and in one a shopper had written down his or her provision list, which included oil, wine, cheese, vegetables and bread. There were also dealers in specialized produce, such as *aliarii* (dealers in garlic) and *galinarii* (poultry dealers). Apparently boiled eggs for breakfast were used in Pompeii as to-day, and in one of the richer houses archæologists came upon a breakfast set in silver, complete with silver tray and two egg-cups.

Wine-merchants not only supplied wine to the *tabernas* and private homes, but exported it, especially the *Vinum Vesuvinum,* which was grown on the slopes of Vesuvius. However, Pliny thought that Pompeian wines caused headaches. Other wines were imported from Taormina and Sorrento.

I have mentioned the *tabernas*—equivalent to the modern cafés; but there were many other places in which the Pompeian could obtain food, hospitality and entertainment. These can be seen in many places in the resurrected city; for instance the *hospitiæ* or hotels, which included bedrooms and dining-rooms; the *themopalia,* or hot-drink shops (like American "quick-lunch stands"), in which the bar-counters have deep recesses for vessels containing hot soups or stews. One could stop at one of these places on the way to the theatre, when there was insufficient time for a full meal in a restaurant. They are usually found on busy thoroughfares near the theatres. The lowest eating houses were the *papinæ*—which supplied meals from meat left over from the sacrifices. But, as Helen Tanzer observes, "no gentleman would be seen in one."

If I appear to have overstressed the gastronomic element in Pompeian life, I can only reply that all the available archæological evidence—wall-paintings, character of the buildings and the objects found in them—points to an unashamedly hedonistic existence. Judged by this evidence the first-century citizens of Pompeii appear to have had two main pursuits, (*a*) profits, and (*b*) pleasure. As an example of the first, an inscription in the villa of one wealthy Pompeian businessman reads:

WELCOME PROFITS!

In another the visitors were greeted with the words:

PROFITS MEAN JOY!

As an example of the second pursuit, there exists, in the beautiful house of Caius Incundus, who lived on the Stabian Way, a quotation from Ovid which reads:

"Long live the lover! Perish the one who does not know how to love! And accursed be he who will forbid us to love!"

Caius Iucundus was a freedman who had made a large fortune as a banker, but, as Corti observes, "with all this keen sense of business, he was also an artist in living."

Again judging solely from the archæological evidence, the main sources of pleasure appear to have been good food, fine wine, pleasant houses, luxurious houses, and of course sex. This applied to all social classes. At the lowest level, if you were a Staphyclus without a Romula, or too poor to afford a mistress, there was a convenient establishment near the street of Mercury which still exists. It is a two-storied building with an attractive balcony. Entering, you paid your money at a stone cash-desk and took your choice of the available attractions. You can still see, to-day, the little cubicles for the girls, whose names are written above each recess.

On the walls behind the alcoves are paintings, concerning which most books on Pompeii are deliberately evasive, if they do not ignore them altogether. Surely this attitude puts us on the same moral level as the leering guides who, after showing the building to the gentlemen, accept a few extra lire to allow the lady visitors inside. The paintings, of which there is one in each couched alcove, portray the various positions in which sexual intercourse may be enjoyed. They have been described as "pornographic" or "obscene". In my view they are nothing of the kind. If they had been painted on the wall of a public square, or in a drawing-room, they might be so described, but in a brothel they are perfectly suitable as a form of functional decoration. Æsthetically they are execrable, but morally neither more or less offensive than the "Doll Tearsheet" scenes in Shakespeare's *Henry IV*. I suggest it is high time we ceased to be hypocritical about them.

If, on the other hand, you were wealthy and did not need to patronize the public stews, you would include in your villa a small apartment set apart for such pursuits (usually described by the local *ciceroni* as "little rooms for fornication"). After a party, at which dancing-girls formed part of the entertainment, such chambers were available for the private gratification of the host and his guests. Such a chamber can be seen in one of the most luxurious of the Pompeian villas, "The House of the Vettii". The Vettii were two wealthy brothers, new-rich freedmen who had bought a noble patrician house which they remodelled and refurnished. "The two freedmen who dwelt there," writes Corti, "were unashamed hedonists. One little room proved beyond any doubt, being obviously dedicated to the joys of Venus, for its walls were covered with pictures which were capable of exciting lovers to the utmost."

Sex in a more sophisticated form is represented in the wall-paintings in the "House of Mysteries", a large and wealthy villa built outside the city walls, overlooking the sea. The owner's mistress was, or had been, a priestess of Dionysus, and the walls of the principal room were adorned with paintings portraying, in sequence, the various stages in the initiation of a girl novice.

> "Perhaps," writes Corti, "they represent the conse-
> cration of the former mistress of this wonderful house, so
> that the novice who plays the chief part may be the mis-
> tress herself."

In the first scene, a naked boy, probably a hermaphrodite, reads from a scroll the regulations for the initiation into the mysteries. Next, a priestess is shown carrying a dish with offerings towards a group of three women who are about to perform some symbolic rite. Next, a priestess, with her back to the spectator, pours purifying water over the consecrated object, which is hidden, while near her a naked Silenus plays on a lyre, and a shepherd boy plays the Syrinx. In the following scene the young girl novice, seized with terror, turns away from the group and tries to wrap herself in her veil. Further on the same girl, now unclothed, leans her head on the knees of a priestess while at her back another figure stands with a raised whip. While the flagellation is proceeding, a nude Bacchante, already initiated, dances before the novice, as if to show the pleasures which await her when the ordeal is over. The climax is reached in the following tableau, in which the sacred phallus, the symbol of male generative power, is unveiled.

The main public entertainment was provided in the huge amphitheatre, built at the expense of a wealthy Pompeian citizen, which could seat 20,000 people. Here were given public shows in which gladiators fought to the death, and animals were either goaded into fighting each other, or else pitted against human opponents.

There were, however, two other places of public entertainment, and these were *theatres,* not sports-arenas. The larger had a capacity of about 5,000, the smaller of 1,500. There are several wall-paintings representing scenes from the comedies played in the larger theatre, but neither the plays nor the situations can be identified. In one, which may be a scene from *Miles Gloriosus* (The Braggart Soldier) of Plautus, there is a masked actor holding a spear, while another masked figure approaches him. On each side of the scene is a bored-looking seated figure, each with a stick. These, says Miss Tanzer, "were not a part of the caste, but represent members of the police, who sat in niches in the proscenium facing the audience". Another painting shows a dance scene from a comedy, in which four actors are performing, one playing the tambourine, another the clappers, and others the double and single flute.

The names of some of the Pompeian actors appear on inscriptions. The favourite was Paris; and another was Actius. There is a farewell notice about him which reads:

"Actius, beloved of the people, come back soon;
fare thee well!"

But the gladiators seem to have been even more popular. One is described as *Dominus puparum*—"squire of dames", and another as *suspirium puellarum*—"answer to a maiden's prayer." Notices announcing forthcoming shows in the big amphitheatre have survived, one of which informs the population that:

"The troupe of gladiators owned by Suettius Centus
will give a performance at Pompeii on May 31st.
"There will be an animal show.
"The awnings will be used."

The function of the little theatre, seating only 1,500, is not known, but it may well have been patronized by the more intellectual section of the population. Perhaps we have, in these three buildings, amphitheatre, middle-sized theatre, and small theatre, the Pompeian equivalent of the Light, Home and Third Programmes!

Herculaneum was only one-sixth the size of Pompeii, and, due to the fact that it was buried under a sixty foot layer of hard *tufa*, has been much more difficult to excavate. Its sole industry was fishing; hooks, nets, lines and floats have been found in abundance, but the town had little economic importance. Probably, also, its political life was less vigorous, for as Carrington observes, not a single election notice has been discovered there. The streets were narrower, and showed no car-ruts; it was evidently a very quiet little town.

It had a theatre, which was first discovered in 1750, but it can still only be approached by underground tunnels, and is now lit by electricity. In one of the villas, also found in the eighteenth century, some fine Hellenistic and Greek bronzes were found, and are now in the Naples Museum. In the same building excavators came upon a rare find; nearly two thousand papyrus fragments, a rich man's library. From the fragments which have been unrolled and deciphered, the bulk contain writings on Epicurean philosophy, mostly in Greek.

> "The preponderance in the collection of works by Philodemus has led some authorities to believe that it formed the library of that philosopher, and perhaps that the villa belonged to his patron, L. Calpurnius Piso Cæsoninus, father-in-law of Julius Cæsar." [5]

From 1927 onwards new excavations have been carried out at Herculaneum, which have revealed streets, more villas, and a set of public baths. Perhaps the most interesting find was a tenement building about twenty feet in height. It is a timber-framed building built around a small courtyard. In front there is a portico supporting a balcony, beneath which are three entrances. One leads to a narrow staircase ascending to upper rooms; a second admits to the ground floor apartments, while a third opens on to a shop which also communicates with the ground floor rooms. It is a simple apartment house, not a luxurious villa.

In one of the upper rooms the discoverers found the original furniture; a wooden bed, a table and a cupboard. This modest apartment may have been a bed-sitting room. A larger room at the front of the house, opening on to the balcony, may have been occupied by the landlord. One wonders what happened to him, and to his tenants, on the day they had to vacate these "attractive furnished premises", leaving their chattels behind them.

Most of the inhabitants of Herculaneum did get away, but this was not so at Pompeii, where 2,000 perished. Even so, most of those whose skeletons have been found had had time to take cover. They were discovered in cellars, under colonnades, in the doorways of private houses, and in public shelters.

The city was not destroyed by lava streams, which would have completely demolished the houses, though such lava may have been ejected at the time, since Pliny mentions fires on the slopes of the mountain. Evidently, however, it did not reach the

[5] Carrington, R. C. *Pompeii*. Clarendon Press. 1936.

towns. In 1944 I climbed the lower slopes of Vesuvius and clambered over the cooled lava, which was like a mound of furnace-slag.

In Mexico, in 1952, I saw a lava stream, fifty feet high, which had driven straight through the side of a large church, leaving only the towers at one end and the High Altar at the other. The jagged lumps, weighing tons, were like iron; they had a metallic ring when struck. Such a mass would have pushed down the Houses of Parliament, let alone the comparatively fragile buildings of Pompeii.

The substance which buried the city was *lapilli,* lava in a fragmentary condition pounded by friction inside the volcano and then shot with explosive force into the air. The fragments vary in size from lumps the size of a walnut to fine ash. They did not burn the city but smothered it.

Pliny's description is terrifying enough, but he was not at Pompeii, but some distance away, at Misenum. What the Pompeians themselves experienced can only be imagined from the grim evidence unearthed by the excavators when they dug down into the buried streets. I cannot do better than quote from Mr. Corti's brilliant chapter reconstructing the disaster from a close study of the site, and from contemporary accounts:

"Suddenly, in the forenoon of 24th August, there followed a fearful clap of thunder. The ear-splitting detonation came from the direction of Vesuvius, to which all eyes turned, terror-filled. And lo, the mountain-top had split open, and amid the crash of thunder fire seemed to be breaking from its heart. But no, the glow disappeared, and an immense black smoke-cloud rose to heaven, deafening crashes followed one another in quick succession, dark pillars of stone disintegrated high in the air and sank down in heaps. And suddenly, no one knew how and from where, there was tearing rain everywhere, and with it showers of stones, fragments of earth, tiny pieces of light pumice stone, interspersed with great lumps like bombs, and all so thick and continuous that the sun was darkened. All at once it was night in the midst of day, while intermittent lightning-flashes lit up the dreadful scene. Killed or stunned, the birds fell from the air, and dead fish were cast on the shores by the raging sea."

Herculaneum was the first to be engulfed by "a rolling wall of mud reaching at places a height of thirty to forty feet, flooding over everything, burying houses and temple and filling the cellars. There was only one thing to do, to flee as quickly as possible. . . . Those who had horses and wagons swung themselves up, whipped the horses, tried to hold up burning torches, and took flight. Away, away towards the sea or towards Naples."

Then came Pompeii's turn, but here, as the catastrophe was not immediate, precious time was lost; many people, watching with horror the convulsions of the mountain, hoped and prayed that the ash-cloud, rising like a giant pine tree a thousand feet into the sky, might be deflected by the wind away from them. Those of us who have experienced aerial bombardment in the Second World War well know the instinct to cling to one's home and possessions as long as possible.

But the north-west wind drove the deadly cloud towards the town, and the inhabitants began to seek safety in flight.

> "The *lapilli* were piling up in great heaps, the small light pebbles forcing their way in everywhere, while now and then the wind deflected boulders weighing as much as 14 lbs. over the town. In no time everything was en-gulfed, and many roofs collapsed under the weight. . . . While the fugitives struggled through the nine or ten foot high heaps of *lapilli*, the white ash mingled with the rain fell remorselessly, hindering the general flight; and count-less Pompeians were suffocated even in the open street by the terrible sulphurous fumes. The damp ash clung to their hands and feet, and those who had not taken to flight immediately after the eruption suffered a terrible death."

In that sudden, terror-stricken flight everything was left just as it was. In one house a sucking-pig was left roasting in its pot, in another bread was in the oven. In one fine house, owned by a wealthy banker called Cæcilius Iucundus, his two sons, Quintus and Sextus, decided to abandon their home and seek refuge in the house of a friend, Vesonius. But he had already gone, with his family, forgetting, in their haste, to release their watch-dog which was chained near the entrance to the *atrium*.

"The stones rained through the opening of the *atrium*, and the poor beast jumped as high as the chain attached by a bronze ring attached to his collar would let him, straining to get free. In the end he was miserably throttled, and lay with his four legs stretched out in the agony of death."

Now the streets were packed with a struggling crowd of fugitives, most of whom were making for the Gate of Herculaneum, in the west. Those who lived at this end of the town, for example Caius Sallustius, who owned a beautiful villa on the corner of Mercury Street, managed to get away.

"Only the mistress of the house seems to have lost too much time in the gathering of her valuables; she collapsed in the damp and sticky ash of the street, not far from her home; strewn around her were her jewellery, her money and her silver mirror, and near her were her three serving-women."

But the ash and stones rained down out of the darkness, and sulphur-fumes stung the eyes and rasped the throat, and the struggling mass of men and women were jammed near the gate, where the bodies of the suffocated were found piled in confusion.

"One after another sank down in the ocean of stone and ash; many went to eternity with a sack of gold and silver coins on their back."

Perhaps the grimmest scene of all was disclosed in a house in the Street of Tombs. Here, evidently, a party had gathered at a funeral feast for a recently deceased relative. Death had struck the mourners so quickly—probably through poisonous fumes—that they had not even risen from the couches on which they reclined at their funeral feast. There, in their painted dining-room, the excavators found them "celebrating not only their kinsman's burial but their own as well".

We will leave Pompeii with one last picture. The scene is the beautiful "Villa of the Mysteries" already described; the opulent house of a rich Roman whose mistress had been a priestess of Dionysus. It stood outside the gate, near the sea, and one would have thought that its inhabitants would have had a better chance of escaping than those inside the town. When the excavators unearthed it they found, beautifully preserved, the series of painted frescoes depicting the initiation of the novitiate. But they also found the bodies of three women who had been trapped in an upper room:

> "They could not flee," writes Corti, "since the floors as well as the roof had collapsed, and they fell through to the ground floor. There they lay with their lovely jewellery, their rings and chains of gold adorning their broken limbs, and were poisoned by the sulphurous fumes. One of them, a young girl, still clutched, convulsively, a little bronze mirror. . . . One girl had reached the entrance of the villa, then her strength left her. A man, perhaps the porter, first wandered through the many rooms of the great house, then took refuge in his little watchroom, there to perish in its darkest corner. Still in death he gazed, as though enchanted, on the little finger of his left hand, on which he wore an iron ring with a stone chalcedony, with a tiny female figure engraved on it." [6]

[6] Corti, E. C. C. *The Destruction and Resurrection of Pompeii and Herculaneum.* Routledge and Kegan Paul. 1951.

CHAPTER ELEVEN

The Sacred Well of Chichen-Itza

When we cross the Atlantic to look at the Lost Cities of Central and South America we return again to the mood of the early nineteenth-century explorers, whose adventures were described in the early chapters of this book. For though the cities of the Aztecs, the Mayas and the Incas are of a much later date than Nineveh and Babylon, the attitude of the men who first found and explored them was far more like that of Claudius Rich and Henry Layard than, say, Sir Leonard Woolley or Sir Flinders Petrie.

Reading some of their books, one re-enters a world of adventure, hardship and danger, and wide-eyed wonder. This is not to suggest that they were necessarily unscientific or inaccurate in their observations, but there is an atmosphere of almost schoolboy excitement about them which is at the same time naïve and refreshing. For a taste, here is Mr. T. A. Willard describing the first sight of Chichen-Itza, the great city of the Mayas in the jungles of Yucatan, as told to him by his old friend Edward Thompson, who spent a large part of his life excavating it.

> "For days I had been travelling, first by train, then by *volan,*—that satanic contrivance which leaves one bruised from head to foot,—and finally in the saddle, dozing over the head of a somnolent horse.
> "Even the witchery of the moonlight could not long hold alert my fatigued body and mind. On and on we plodded, hour after hour. Midnight passed and how many hours I do not know, when I heard an exclamation in the vernacular, from my guide. Startled out of my half-conscious dream I came erect in the saddle.

"My Indian was earnestly pointing up ahead. I raised
my eyes and became electrically, tinglingly awake. There,
high up, wraith-like in the waning moonlight, loomed
what seemed to be a Grecian temple of colossal propor-
tions, atop a steep hill. So massive did it seem in the half-
light of the approaching morning that I could think of it
only as an impregnable fortress high above the sea, on
some rock, wave-dashed promontory. As this mass took
clearer shape before me and with each succeeding hoof-
beat of my weary steed, it grew more and more huge.
I felt an actual physical pain, as if my heart had slipped
a few beats and then raced to make up the loss."

This sort of thing is acceptable in small doses, but after a
few pages the sophisticated reader may feel an impulse to take a
machete and lop down some of the more luxuriant growths of Mr.
Willard's highly vegetative style. His knees "shook a little" . . .
as he "glanced apprehensively" over his shoulder "awaiting the terrible, majestic wrath of the gods whose temple was profaned". He
sees in imagination a beautiful Maya maiden flung into the Sacred
Well of Chichen-Itza, as a sacrifice to the Rain-God.

"And what is this embroidered bower borne so rever-
ently by sturdy, sun-browned lesser priests? Is it a bier, a
stately catafalque? Is the pitiful victim already dead?
Ah, no! she moves, beautiful, flawless—the most lovely
maiden to be found in the land . . . there is terror in
those lovely eyes, a benumbing, cold fear of the Unknown. . . . Her gauzy garments reveal the tender flesh
and adolescent contours of a girl in her early teens. . . .
A last forward swing and the bride of Yum Chac hurtles
far out over the well. Turning slowly in the air, the lithe-
some body falls faster and faster till it strikes the dark
water seventy feet below. . . . An echoing splash and
all is still. Only the widening ripples are left. The child
bride has found favour in the eyes of her Lord, the great
god Noh-och Yum Chac."

But however one may smile at his literary exuberance, Willard
was painting a true picture. Without any doubt the scene which
Thompson saw in his imagination and which Willard described,

did in fact take place at this spot; not once but many times. The proof was provided by Thompson himself years later, when, at the risk of his life, he explored the seventy-foot deep well of Chichen-Itza in a diving-suit. To explain why and how this happened it is necessary first to say something of what is known of Maya history and legend.

The Mayas, the aboriginal inhabitants of the province of Yucatan, in Mexico, were the most advanced of all the Indian peoples of Central America. They had a hieroglyphic system of writing, and have left records both on paper and in stone-carvings. In religion they had a great deal in common with their northern neighbours, the Aztecs, worshipping the sun and other elemental gods, building great temples and pyramids not unlike those of the Aztecs, and, like them, practising human sacrifice. Their general level of culture was roughly parallel with that of the other great Indian tribes, to whose languages the Mayan tongue was related. Weapons and tools, mainly of stone and wood, were also similar. The Mayas were primarily an agricultural people, whereas the Aztecs were more warlike.

It is far more difficult to trace the history of these American Indian peoples than those of Egypt and Western Asia. Until the arrival of Columbus no one in Europe had heard of them. When, a century later, the Spanish conquistadores arrived, they were more intent on plunder than on preserving records of the ancient cultures they had discovered and were rapidly destroying. Much as one may admire the courage of Cortez and his adventurers, their story is as vile a record of greed and cruelty as any in the blood-stained history of the human race.

It might be said in partial defence of the Spaniards that the Mayas too were cruel; that, for instance, they practised human sacrifice. Shocked by these pagan customs, the Spanish priests who accompanied the conquerors converted the Mayas to the merciful religion of Christ, sometimes, perhaps, by methods indicated in the following extract from an old Maya chronicle:

"It was then that the teaching of Christianity began, that shall be universal over our land. . . . Then began the execution by hanging, and the fire at the end of our hands. Then also came ropes and cords into the world. Then the children of the younger brothers passed under the hardship of legal summons and tribute. . . . Then the seven sacraments of the Word of God were established. Let us receive our guests heartily; our elder brothers come!" [1]

On the other hand, some of the Spanish clergy undoubtedly did their best to mitigate the worst excesses of the soldiers, and protected the Indians from them. But unfortunately, in their bigoted enthusiasm they also destroyed most of the ancient Indian writings which, had they been preserved and translated, might have told us almost as much concerning the aboriginal Americans as we know of Egypt and Babylon. Some records were kept. An exiled Inca wrote, in his old age, a history of his people in Spanish, and a number of Spanish writers described the manners and customs of the peoples they conquered.

These Spanish records, therefore, remain our main written source of information concerning the original inhabitants of Central and South America, and these have been supplemented by the work of archæologists, from pioneers like Edward Thompson, Teobert Maler, Désiré Charnay, to workers trained in a more recent scientific school of research, such as Vaillant, Swanton, Spinden and others.

This is not the place to discuss the complex problems of dating the early American culture—Aztec, Toltec, Mayan, etc., which is still controversial. However, according to the late Dr. George Vaillant, the first men to enter the American Continent came from Asia via the Bering Straits. The date of their arrival is unknown, but as recently as 1947 Dr. Helmuth de Terra found, near Tepexpan, in Mexico, the remains of a prehistoric hunter,

[1] Thompson, Edward Herbert. *People of the Serpent.* G. P. Putnam's Sons. London, 1933.

"well-preserved in unmistakable association with the extinct Archi-diskodon elephant. This man, who lived by hunting elephants in Mexico 15,000 years ago, was very like the more 'primitive'-looking Indians of the Mexican plateau to-day. Yet he was contemporary with the late Palæolithic (Old Stone Age) cave-painters of Europe." [2]

In America, as in Egypt, Mesopotamia and the Indus Valley, the first civilization arose in places where men were able to domesticate plants, grow food-crops and settle in one place. In the New World there were two such centres, Middle America and the Andean region of South America. In these areas the Indians reached the highest peaks of their social and material culture.

In both places men learned to domesticate plants. Dr. Vaillant says:

> "The highlands of Peru yielded the white potato, but at the time of the conquest the great basic American foods, corn and beans, were diffused over most of agricultural America. Whether they were first domesticated in Peru or Middle America is a point still arguable. However, the great principle to bear in mind is that *no plant cultivated by the American Indians is known to Asia, Europe or Africa prior to the white settlement of America. The introduction of these plants more than doubled the available food supply of the older countries.*" [3] (Our italics.)

Another point to bear in mind, particularly when we come to consider the monumental architectural achievements of the American Indians, is that, except for the Peruvians, they had no animals for haulage and transport; no horses, mules, or oxen. The Andean peoples raised llamas both for transport and wool. The only animal which was universally domesticated was the dog, which in the north was used as a beast of burden and in Mexico for food. The cow and sheep were unknown.

[2] Vaillant, G. C. *The Aztecs of Mexico*. Penguin Books. 1951.
[3] Ibid.

This lack of animals for transport may have been one of the reasons why there was no extensive migration, and the population pressures which often caused wars in the Old World hardly existed in America, before the arrival of the white man. It would also help to explain why a number of separate cultures and separate languages developed independently. The Mayas, the Olmecs, the Zapotecs, the Toltecs, the Aztecs, the Incas, all had a common origin in the first Asiatic invaders of the American continent; their language was related, their social customs and religious beliefs, their art, dress, tools and weapons were often similar; yet they tended to keep to themselves, and, though they did make war upon each other, "war techniques . . . were little developed in the Indian cultures, and the killing and rapine which took place during the white colonization did not have their origin in the usual Indian political attitude".

Accurate dating is impossible because, although the Mayans had an elaborate and accurate calendric system, it has not yet been found possible to co-relate it accurately with Christian dates. However, the consensus of archæological opinion now gives about A.D. 400 as the approximate date of the beginning of full independent civilization in America, and many of the surviving monuments are very much later, between about A.D. 800 and 1400.[4] The earliest of these independent civilizations, therefore, began roughly towards the end of the Roman Empire; the latest were contemporary with the later Middle Ages in Europe. For example the most magnificent buildings of Chichen-Itza, the Mayan capital, were probably erected at the same time as Salisbury Cathedral was being built in England.

The Maya cities of Yucatan were primarily religious centres, as were the cities of ancient Ceylon. Extensive remains exist at several places, Holmul, Uaxactun, Palenque, San José; but the most impressive are those of Chichen-Itza the capital. Here, rising out

---

[4] This does not mean, of course, that there were no civilized communities in America before A.D. 400. The so-called "Middle Cultures" can be traced back to the beginning of the Christian era.

of the jungle, are enormous structures, built of huge blocks of finely-masoned stone. Edward Thompson first saw them some sixty years ago.

> "Chichen-Itza is really two cities. The more ancient is overgrown by a thick forest, and its location is indicated only by an occasional grassy, thicket-covered mound, out of which grow great trees and whose sides are covered with scattered carved stones. The newer city is clearly defined by the buildings which are still standing. The whole, including the older and newer city, covers an area of about twelve square miles. . . . In the area which I designate as new Chichen-Itza are twelve buildings in an almost perfect state of preservation, as though built not more than twenty or thirty years ago. Ten of them are still covered with their original ponderous stone roofs and are entirely habitable. . . . The only evident plan is that the present buildings, which are temples and perhaps palaces for the kings and those of high religious or noble rank, are centrally located. Beyond these for miles about are the remains of small rectangular foundations, evidently the sites of what were once the dwelling-places of the large population of the city."

Thompson first came to Yucatan as the American Consul. He became so fascinated by the country, its people, and especially their ancient cities, that he bought the *hacienda* or estate on which Chichen-Itza stands, and spent thirty years of his life there, studying and excavating the remains. His pioneer work has since been superseded by that of the Carnegie Foundation, but his book, *People of the Serpent,* and that of his friend Willard, *City of the Sacred Well,* are entertaining popular accounts of the early discoveries, written with burning enthusiasm and love of the subject. Like Schliemann, discoverer of Troy and Mycenæ, and like Layard of Nineveh, Thompson was an amateur of archæology in the literal meaning of the word—a lover.

His chronology is now out of date (his dates are far too early), and some of his conclusions have since been proved wrong. But his passionate absorption, not only in the ancient monuments, but

in the legends and traditions of the Maya people among whom he
lived, and whom he loved, more than counterbalance these defects. The record of his thirty years' devoted work, undertaken
largely at his own expense, breathes a humanity and a sense of
dedicated purpose which is sometimes lacking in the writings of
later archæologists.

Among the ancient Maya stories which most fascinated him
were those concerned with the Sacred Well of Chichen-Itza. One
of the high clergy who came to Mexico with the conquistadores was
Bishop Diego de Landa, who wrote a book called *Relacion de las
Cosas de Yucatan.*

In it he stated that:

> "From the court in front of these theatres (at
> Chichen-Itza) runs a wide and handsome roadway as far
> as the Well, which is about two stone's throws off.
> "Into this Well they have had and still have the cus-
> tom of throwing men alive as a sacrifice to their gods in
> time of drought, and they believed that they would not
> die, though they never saw them again. They also threw
> in many other things like precious stones and things they
> prized, and so if this country had possessed gold it would
> have been this Well that would have the greater part of
> it, so great is the devotion that the Indians show for it."

There were other legends which told how, on certain occasions, the most beautiful virgin in the land was thrown into the
well as an offering to Yum Chac, the Rain God, whose palace was
said to be at the bottom of the pit. Sometimes women were flung
into the water unbound, and then, some hours later, those which
survived were hauled out by ropes and questioned. Don Diego Sar-
miento de Figueroa, writing in 1579, gave this account in a report
to his sovereign, Charles V of Spain:

> "The Lords and principal personages of the land had
> the custom, after sixty days of abstinence and fasting, of
> arriving at daybreak at the month of the *Cenote* and
> throwing into it Indian women belonging to each of these
> lords and personages, at the same time telling these

women to ask for their masters a year favourable to his particular needs and desires.

"The women, being thrown in unbound, fell into the water with great force and noise. At high noon those that could cried out loudly and ropes were let down to them. After the women came up, half dead, fires were built around them and copal incense was burned before them. When they recovered their senses, they said that below there were many people of their nation, men and women, and that they received them. When their heads were inclined downwards beneath the water they seemed to see many deeps and hollows, and they, the people, responded to their queries concerning the good or the bad year that was in store for their masters."

There are three large natural wells (*canotes*) at Chichen-Itza and several minor ones. In the Mayan language *"Chi"* means "mouth" and *"Chen"* means "well", and the site must have been chosen because of its abundant water-supply. The Sacred Well is an enormous natural cavity in the rock, about one hundred and sixty feet across its widest point—a small lake, in fact. From the brink of this great pit is a sheer drop of seventy feet to the surface of the water, the depth of which is about sixty feet. The colour is jade-green, usually with a film of fine limestone dust on the surface of the water.

When Thompson first came to Chichen-Itza, the Sacred Way, the stone causeway leading to the great well, was in bad repair, its outline broken by the roots of trees. But it could be traced to the brink of the well, near which, on the side nearest one of the huge pyramidal structures of the Mayas, were the remains of a small, ruined building in which apparently the last rites were performed before the victims were thrown into the pit.

Thompson decided to explore the well in order to find out if the Maya traditions were true. The task was a formidable one. From the beginning he seems to have planned diving operations as the ultimate method of securing the small objects which might lie at the well-bottom, but first it was necessary to clear the centuries-old accumulation of mud at the base of the pit, and for this dredging machinery would be necessary. While this was being ordered he went to Boston and took lessons in deep-sea diving from Captain Ephraim Nickerson of Long Wharf.

"Under this expert and patient teaching," writes Thompson, "I became in time a fairly good diver, but by no means a perfect one, as I was to learn some time later. My next move was to adapt to my purpose an 'orange-peel bucket' dredge with the winch, tackles, and ropes of a stiff-legged derrick and a thirty-foot swinging boom."

When at last this equipment had been shipped to the nearest port and transported with great difficulty over jungle tracks to Chichen-Itza, Thompson had it erected at the brink of the well. But first he had to decide at which point he was to sink the dredging bucket, since, as the well was one hundred and sixty feet wide and about eight feet broad, obviously it would not be practicable to dredge the whole area. In order to establish the spot at which he would be most likely to find remains he made a somewhat macabre experiment. In his own words:

"I . . . established what I called the 'fertile zone' by throwing in wooden logs shaped like human beings and having the weight of the average native. By measuring the rope after these manikins were hauled ashore, I learned the extreme distance to which sacrificial victims could have been thrown. In this way I fixed the spot where the human remains would probably be found." [5]

The first part of the operation was disappointing. For day after day the dredge disappeared below the surface of the water, and, after its steel teeth had clawed at the bottom, was hauled up again, only to discharge an evil-smelling mass of muck and slime, decayed vegetation, and tree-stumps. Each disgusting load had to be carefully examined and sifted to discover if it contained any object of antiquity. But, apart from a few scraps of ancient potsherds,

[5] Thompson, Edward. *People of the Serpent*. G. P. Putnam's Sons. London, 1933.

which could well have been thrown in by small boys of any period, there was nothing. Thompson's Indian workmen naturally thought their master was mad, but, as they were being paid for the job, did not complain, but continued to work the dredge throughout the long, hot days, while the brightly beady eyes of frogs and lizards watched them from the crevices in the limestone walls of the pit.

> "several times we brought up the skeletons of deer or of wild dogs and once the tangled skeletons of a jaguar and a cow, mute evidence of a long-past forest tragedy. . . . Then, for a long while, finds even as interesting as these ceased. Absolutely nothing was brought up but mud and leaves, with an occasional stone. My high hopes dwindled and became less than nothing. The work was interminable, nauseating. . . ." [6]

Until one dank, rainy day, when things seemed darkest, the dredge brought up "what at first appeared to be two ostrich-eggs, cream coloured and oval against the black in which they rested". Thompson examined them, and found they were of aromatic resin (copal). He scraped off a piece, dried and lit it. It burned with a pleasant smell. And he remembered that Don Diego had written, in his report to the King of Spain:

> "After the women came up . . . fires were built around them and *copal incense* was burned before them."

From that time on more and more of these balls of copal incense came up in the dredge, some of them bearing the impress of the baskets in which they had been enclosed. There were also tripod vessels filled with copal and rubber incense, wooden fragments of unknown use, and then, one day, Thompson came upon a well-preserved wooden object in the form of a bill-hook or pruning-knife.

"No sword of damask steel," writes Willard with his customary enthusiasm, "could compare in historical value with these simple wooden implements." They were the first examples found of the

* Willard, T. A. *The City of the Sacred Well*. Heinemann. London.

hul-che or throwing-stick of the ancient Mayas, often seen depicted in their carvings, but never previously found intact. The water had preserved them for many centuries. These weapons were used by the Mayas and some other Indian tribes for hurling darts.

Soon after being exposed to the air the throwing-sticks began to decompose, but Thompson had preservatives ready, and these valuable specimens were saved. Next, with more balls of copal, came great quantities of rubber incense and rubber objects. Torquemada had said of the Mayas, "they light fires in their vessels containing copal in their sacrificial ceremonies with rubber". Many of the masses of copal Thompson found had nodules of rubber embedded in their surfaces, and in some cases slivers of wood projecting from rubber insets. These, he believed, were intended as lighters for the copal.

It was shortly after these discoveries that a black object turned up in the dredge which caused considerable alarm among the Indian workers.

> "One of my natives had, as usual, pushed his arms, clear to the elbows, into the oozy mass, when he leaped back with a cry of terror. . . . He pointed to the head of a small dark-coloured serpent, with a white-ringed neck, which stood up menacingly among the muck. It was precisely the shape, size and appearance of a small and extremely poisonous viper which is native to Yucatan."

But there was no need for alarm. The snake was made of rubber.

Confirmation of the grim truth of the old traditions came when "the dredge brought up a perfect skull, bleached and polished to whiteness. Later came other skulls and human bones, scores of them. Most of the skeletons were of youthful maids, but every now and then one was raised which had the breadth of shoulders, and the thick skull, and the heavy frame of a powerful man—no doubt some mighty warrior, sacrificed in the flower of his vigour, sent to grace the court of the Rain God." [7]

[7] Willard, T. A. *The City of the Sacred Well.* Heinemann. London.

Comparing these skulls with those found in the cemeteries of modern Mayas, Thompson found no difference between them. The female skulls found in the well belonged to girls aged between fourteen and twenty.

For months the steel grab continued to bring up human remains and archæological treasures. The balls of copal used as incense by the ancient Mayas were so numerous as to become monotonous, though they testified to the number of sacrifices and offerings which had been made throughout the centuries. One of Thompson's Maya friends, a *H'Men,* or Wise Man, told him that "In ancient times our fathers burned the sacred resin—*pom*—and by the fragrant smoke their prayers were wafted to their God whose home was in the Sun". But other archæological treasures also appeared in the dredge; temple vases and incense burners, lanceheads, arrow-heads, axes and hammer-stones of flint and calcite, copper chisels, and discs of beaten copper, some of them embossed with figures of the ancient gods of the Mayas. There were also golden objects, especially a large quantity of small golden bells, which had been deliberately flattened with a heavy maul before being thrown into the water. Lovely jade ornaments were also found, but these too appear to have been deliberately broken; not pulverized, but snapped apart by a skilled hand, so that it was not difficult to put them together again.

Thompson suggested that these objects had been ritually "killed", just as the human victims had been slain so that their spirits could go to the Rain God, Yum Chac. He cited as a modern parallel a Maya funeral he had seen in which the gown and slippers of the dead woman had been deliberately slit before she was buried. Although Thompson does not mention the fact—indeed he may not have been aware of it—the Ancient Egyptians of the early Dynasties observed a similar custom. I myself have seen vases buried under the pyramid of King Djoser (2800 B.C.) at Sakkara in Egypt, which had also been deliberately smashed before being placed in the store-chambers under the king's pyramid.

At last, after months of labour, the steel jaws of the grab

began to bring up splinters of rock, indicating that it had dug down through the thick layers of mud and reached bedrock. Now came the next and most fantastic part of the operation. Thompson guessed that the floor of the well would be uneven, and that possibly within its hollows would be other objects which the grab could not reach. The only way in which they could be found was by descending the well in a diving suit and groping for them by hand. This he proceeded to do, accompanied by a Greek professional diver, one of two whom he hired for the operation.

A pontoon was launched on the surface of the water, and in this Thompson rigged the air-pump, the Greeks having trained Indian workmen to operate it.

> "When they considered that the men were letter perfect," writes Thompson, "we were ready to dive. . . . We rode down to the pontoon in the basin of the dredge, and while the assistant took his place by the men at the pump to direct them, we put on our suits, outfits of waterproof canvas with big copper helmets weighing more than thirty pounds and equipped with plate-glass goggle eyes and air-valves near the ears."

Thus began what must surely be the most extraordinary feat of underwater archæology before Cousteau. Thompson's dredge had scooped out a huge hole in the layer of mud on the well's bottom, until it reached the rocky floor. Into that hole Thompson and his Greek assistant now descended.

> "During the first ten feet of descent, the light rays changed from yellow to green and then to a purplish black. After that I was in utter darkness. When I gulped and opened the air-valves in my helmet a sound like 'pht-pht' came from each ear and then the pain ceased. Several times this process had to be repeated before I stood on the bottom. . . . I felt . . . a strange thrill when I realized that I was the only living being who had ever reached this place alive and expected to leave it again still living. Then the Greek diver came down beside me and we shook hands. . . ."

At this depth the electric torches which the divers had brought with them were useless, but, feeling around him, Thompson realized that he was surrounded by precipitous walls of compressed mud. The dredge had bitten out a large cavity in the mud, some thirty feet deep, the lower part of which was so highly compressed that it held large rocks, fallen columns and tree roots. These, he tells us, were embedded in the walls of the dredged-out pit "as raisins are embedded in plum puddings", and every now and then one of the rocks would work loose and plunge down on Thompson and his assistant as they groped in the darkness.

> "As the rock masses fell," he writes, "the push of the water before and around them reached us before the rock did and struck us like a huge soft cushion and sent us canonning, often head down and feet upward, balancing and tremulous like the white of an egg in a glassful of water, until the commotion had died down and we could get on our feet again."

On the floor of the well the archæologist came upon large, smooth-faced stones, some of which were carved, as he was able to detect by touch. These were attached to chains and hauled to the surface. One had carved on it a seated figure of a god or priest. Once these heavy objects were cleared Thompson was able to explore the crevices and hollows in the bottom. As his fingers probed they touched small objects of stone and metal, which he stuffed into a pouch at his side. On the surface he emptied out the pouch and saw the gleam of gold and the glistening green of jade. There were jade beads, beautiful embossed rings, and scores of small bells, also of gold. In one day two hundred of these specimens of Maya workmanship were brought to the surface. There were two golden tiaras representing feathered serpents, emblematic figures, and what appear to have been golden tops of official wands. There were also many articles of copper, or copper and gold alloy; copper circlets and copper chisels.

Reading Thompson's account, I was reminded of the discovery

by D. G. Hogarth of the cave-sanctuary of Zeus in Crete.[8] There the explorers found hundreds of tiny votive offerings stuck in the cracks of the stalactites by worshippers of the god between two and three thousand years ago. There is, of course, no possible connection between the two finds except man's age-old habit of making offerings to his gods.

With regard to the intrinsic value of the objects found in the Sacred Well, there is a curious discrepancy between the account given by Willard and that of the discoverer himself in his own book *People of the Serpent*. Willard mentions, for example, "one golden bowl . . . nine inches in diameter" and "several smaller ones about three inches in diameter . . . many golden figures of animals and insects . . . twelve plain discs of gold which I imagine are blanks, originally intended by the goldsmith for some craftsman to ornament with designs", flint knives with handles of gold, and scores of tiny bells of which "the clappers were, like the bells themselves, made of pure gold."

He also illustrates a number of these lovely objects, some of which are described as "massive gold bowls and cups" and "gold embossed disks in many designs". And he represents Thompson as having said:

> "The golden objects brought up, if simply thrown into the goldsmith's melting pot, would net several hundreds of thousands of dollars in bullion—dividend enough, if one were sufficiently sordid in mind, to justify all my investment of time, effort, and money in the undertaking." [9]

However, in his own book, *People of the Serpent,* Thompson writes:

> "Objects of nearly pure gold were encountered, both cast, beaten and engraved in repoussé, but they were few in number and relatively unimportant. Most of the so-

[8] *See* the present author's *The Bull of Minos.*
[9] Willard, T. A. *The City of the Sacred Well,* p. 131.

called gold objects were of low-grade alloy, with more copper than gold in them. That which gave them their chief value were the symbolical and other figures cast or carved upon them. . . . The value in money of the objects recovered from the Sacred Well with so much labour and at such expense, is, to be sure, insignificant. . . ." [10]

If I have dwelt at some length on the Sacred Well, rather than the great buildings which surround it, this is not only because Thompson's operation is unique in archæology, but because the Well, and the gruesome ceremonies performed at its brink, emphasize the essentially religious and ritualistic character of those buildings. Like other ancient peoples, e.g., the Sumerians and Egyptians, the Mayans were an agricultural people whose existence depended on their crops. They knew that the fertility of their soil lay at the mercy of elemental forces outside their understanding or control; a prolonged drought, a series of bad harvests, could cause famine which might, and sometimes did, necessitate wholesale migration. Mayan traditions, preserved by the Spaniards, state that Chichen-Itza was deserted and then reoccupied more than once, and the truth of these traditions is confirmed by archæology. Sometimes the people were stricken down by diseases which slew thousands, apparently without cause. Who could be responsible but a god, who must be propitiated by gifts? There was a war-god to help them overcome their enemies. There were gods of rain and wind, gods of fire, creative deities and gods of death.

Like the related Indian races, such as the Aztecs and the Nahuatls, the Mayas seem to have honoured above all a Chief God, who was a deity of civilization, learning and priesthood, and was called by the Aztecs Quetzacoatl, and by the Mayas Kukulcan. He is usually represented as a feathered serpent, and at Chichen-Itza each corner of the great terraced pyramid, the "Castillo", has a stone serpent undulating from the base of the building to the platform on which stands the temple. On each side of this pyramid, which is built in nine terraces, is a broad stairway, 111 feet long,

[10] Thompson, Edward. *People of the Serpent,* p. 288.

28·7 feet wide, and rising in 104 steps to the platform. At Te-
nochtitlan, the Aztec capital, we know from the writings of Cortez
and others that captured prisoners were dragged up these stairways and sacrificed in a particularly barbarous manner; the living
heart of the victim was torn out of his body. These ceremonies are
vividly depicted in Aztec art, and probably took place also at
Chichen-Itza.

Architecturally this pyramid is splendid, a majestic blending
of Maya and Mexican elements. The huge stones are accurately
hewn and laid with fine precision. Like those of the Egyptian
pyramids, they were hauled into place by manpower alone. The
Mayas had no animals for haulage, not even the ass. The building
stands on an artificial platform ten feet high, with a level top of
crushed stone, extending northwards for three hundred yards to
the Sacred Well. West of the Castillo is a huge ceremonial court
between two parallel moles of masonry each 270 feet long, 34 feet
wide and 25 feet high. Within this space ritual games took place,
in which the object seems to have been to project a rubber ball
through stone rings set in the masonry. These rings still survive at
Chichen-Itza, and on other Mayan and Aztec sites. Similar games
are still played in Latin America to-day. When I was in northern
Mexico a few years ago I noticed that every village, however small,
had its ball-court with an iron ring on a post. Ironically, the innocent game of "net-ball", which in Britain is played almost ex-
clusively by schoolgirls, originated in the rituals performed in
honour of the fierce gods of the American Indian.

Some of the buildings of Chichen-Itza are richly carved, and
some bear the remains of wall paintings. There is the so-called
"Tiger Temple" with its frieze of jaguars alternating with shields
and ornaments. Inside this temple is a painted battle scene showing
Mayan warriors, armed with spears and throwing sticks, attacking
a city. Swords were of wood inset with flint, and the spears were
flint-tipped. Metal was not used for weapons, which is one of the
reasons why the Spanish warriors, who had crossbows, steel swords
and firearms, were able to conquer Mexico with such small forces.

Other reasons were (1) that they possessed horses, which the Indians had never seen before, and (2) the disunity of the Indian tribes, some of whom allied themselves with the Spaniards, hoping that the Europeans' superior arms would help them to defeat their fellow-Indians. Thus, by playing off one tribe against another the invaders were able eventually to control their whole country.

A strange structure, forty feet high, with a winding stairway and annular chambers, is believed by some archæologists to have been an astronomical observatory. The Mayas possessed a calendar system of such accuracy that the astronomer, Humboldt, could not at first believe that it was of native origin. Another huge monument which at a distance looks like a fortress, is the only storeyed building which has survived in Chichen-Itza. The local Indian name for it is *La Casa del Monjas* or the "Nunnery". Nearly three hundred feet wide, it rises at the centre to a height of ninety feet, in three tiers, each smaller than the one below it. It bears the marks of several reconstructions. The second storey, the floor of which is more than thirty feet from the ground, is approached by a massive stone stairway, more than twenty feet wide, and above this was a third storey served by a second stairway.

The main part of the structure has five doorways but, like the rest of the buildings of Chichen-Itza, no windows. Inside are many narrow chambers, with connecting doorways. There are also a large number of shallow recesses which may possibly have been used to store the sacred writings—perhaps the same which the fanatic Bishop de Landa burned in the public square in the Pueblo de Mani, when, as one Spanish chronicler naïvely records, the people "made a great cry of woe". As Thompson comments: "Is it to be wondered at? They saw not only the sacred things calcining in the fervent heat, but also the written lore, the accumulated knowledge of their race, going up in smoke and cinders."

The real purpose of this strange building remains a mystery, though its local name may preserve a true tradition. It is known that, among some Indian peoples, the Aztecs, for example, communities of women and girls were segregated and took part in religious rites. The highly ritualistic nature of the Mayan religion, with its elaborate ceremonies, would call for a high degree of training. Possibly this building was occupied by priestesses.

One of the most dramatic discoveries made by Thompson at Chichen-Itza was a series of tombs, one below the other, in the heart of a small pyramid west of the "Nunnery". When he first investigated the site it was a mere shapeless mound covered with scrub and trees, with the ruins of a miniature temple on the top. There was the usual stairway on each of the four sides, badly broken, flanked by balustrades formed by the bodies of stone serpents. He sounded the stone floor of the temple with a steel rod and found that one part rang hollow. Prising up the stones, he found underneath a large, square shaft choked by a tangle of rootlets which had first to be hacked away, dislodging the vermin which they harboured. At the foot of the shaft lay portions of a human skeleton much gnawed by rats, and some earthen vessels. Having cleared these he sounded the floor, and again heard the hollow ring which indicated a second chamber below the first. Part of the floor was lifted and, sure enough, there was yet a third shaft, also containing skeletal remains in a better state of preservation, together with offering-jars and small ornaments.

At this point he was still high up inside the pyramid. Suspecting that there were still further tombs beneath the two he had found he continued down, and each time he lifted the floor-tiles yet another chamber was discovered, each containing a human skeleton. There were, in all, five graves superimposed one upon the other, and in some Thompson found copper bells, polished rock-crystal beads and other objects. The floor of the last grave he found was level with the base of the pyramid, and he naturally assumed there would be no more graves. But no, the sounding-rod again gave out the familiar hollow ring; up came the floor, and this time, instead of a shaft, the excavators found a series of steps hewn out of the living rock. Both the stairway and the chamber beneath were choked with wood ashes which had to be laboriously removed. "The only way I could enter the chamber," writes Thompson, "was by lying flat on my back and pushing my feet ahead of me through the ashes and into the chamber, which I did."

When at last this chamber was cleared he found polished jade beads, some of which had been half-fused by great heat, and a number of potsherds. Thompson suggested that it had been a repository for objects taken from previous burials. In shape the chamber was like a funnel, fairly wide at the entrance, but narrowing towards the other end, where it ended in a wall of rock. And now the archæologist was quite sure that he had reached the end.

> "The week was drawing to a close and with it, so appeared, our task. The work within that deep-down, badly ventilated shaft was not too pleasant. The air was close; the place was frightfully hot, and the big wax candles, dim and smoky, did not tend to make the place more comfortable.
>
> "We three—Manuel, Pedro and I—were stripped to the waist and looked more like chimney sweeps than delvers after scientific lore. The work seemed nearly at an end so that we kept doggedly on, the boys digging and sifting while I stopped frequently to make notes. Late in the day, all seemed finished except for a few isolated ash-heaps and a big flat stone that leaned against the very end of the wall."

Before leaving, Thompson decided to move the stone and sweep the ashes behind it in case there were still a few beads and small objects to be found.

> "I grasped the stone slab with both hands and pulled it towards me. It yielded so suddenly that I fell back with it. My companions also fell back, for, instead of uncovering a pile of ashes, it disclosed a big, circular, pitch-black hole, and from that unsuspected hole came a long soughing rush of cold, damp wind. Our candles went out at once, leaving us in inky blackness. . . . The two natives were simply glued to their places in sheer terror.
>
> "Finally Pedro spoke. 'It is the mouth of Hell,' he said, and I heard his teeth chatter as he said it. . . . For the ancient Mayas hell, called by them Metnal, was not a

burning pit of fire and brimstone but a dank, cold place where lost souls, benumbed with chill, struggled forever in thick, dark mud."

By letting down a tape with a lantern attached to it, Thompson found that the pit was fifty feet deep. He does not mention whether it was hewn out of the rock, or was a natural cave. I suspect the latter. I also suspect that, since the cave apparently had no other outlet, the "soughing rush of wind" was a pardonable exaggeration. Next day the excavator was lowered into the hole, armed, he tells us, with a "sharp hunting-knife between my teeth, thus leaving my hands free for action if needed", and found, among other things, a beautiful alabaster vase containing jade beads and a pendant. Beside the vase, which was broken, lay many other objects, terra-cotta votive urns three feet high, incense burners, a large plaque carved with conventionalized human figures, a polished jade globe, carved ear-ornaments, and mother-of-pearl objects set in polished shell "apparently intended to be the eyes of some figure". There were also oval pearls, evidently part of a necklace, but these were badly decayed by contact with the earth or calcined by burnt copal incense. Thompson did not have to use his knife, though he mentions that the crevices of the cave swarmed with "Tzeentum spiders, which can give an ugly sting producing a fever hard to subdue". These big, flat, crab-like spiders move quickly and are hard to catch and kill.

Thompson suggested that this tomb might have been that of a High Priest, and that the upper graves may have been "the acolytes or servants of the High Priest, whose bodies were so placed as to guard in death, as they served in life, this high and sacred personage". However, neither he nor Willard state that human bones were found in the pit beneath the pyramid, though each of the chambers above it had its skeleton. The question has not been conclusively answered.

Thompson's latter years at Chichen-Itza were clouded with tragedy and disappointment. At one period local revolutionaries burned down his house, destroying valuable documents and antiquities. Later, after he had rebuilt his home, he ran into trouble with the Mexican Government.

> "Extravagant reports had been circulated as to the value of the objects taken by me from the Sacred Well at Chichen-Itza. Some enthusiastic friends had estimated the value of the golden finds to be five hundred thousand dollars, and these statements, reaching the ears of the Government officials, caused them to sit up and take notice."

The plantation was "attached by the Mexican Government for the sum of 1,300,000 pesos", and became the subject of a lawsuit, the result of which I have not been able to trace.

But the tough old New Englander's work had its reward, if only by attracting American archæologists to study more closely the ancient civilizations of their own continent. His work was supported partly by the Peabody Museum of Harvard, and the Field Columbian Museum of Chicago. Later, the work was continued by the Carnegie Foundation, using Thompson's hacienda as their headquarters. Archæologists have continued to clear and excavate this magnificent site, using methods and resources more scientific than Thompson could command. To-day Chichen-Itza has become a "tourist attraction". The modern visitor, driving to the site along well-surfaced roads, can see the great grey temples and pyramids cleared of vegetation; restored and repaired, they rise resplendent above the miles of jungle through which the early explorers had to stumble along rough tracks.

Nevertheless, despite the increase in knowledge, we still know less about the civilizations of the American Indians than we know of the more ancient cultures of Egypt and Mesopotamia. More knowledge is continually being added, thanks largely to American archæologists, but the destruction of most of the old written records by the Spanish invaders was an irretrievable loss. Though separated from us in time by a few centuries only, the Mayas, Incas, Aztecs, and the rest are more remote than the people of Babylon, Hattusas and Ur of the Chaldees. However, they have their memorials. Every time we eat potatoes, Indian corn, tomatoes, bounce a rubber ball, take quinine or smoke tobacco, we are linked, however tenuously, with people who sacrificed to the gods of rain and wind and fire, and who built such cities as Chichen-Itza.

CHAPTER TWELVE

The Tragedy of the Incas

Stories of lost cities hidden in remote inaccessible valleys, or buried by impenetrable jungle, are a favourite theme of romantic fiction. The city "never seen by a white man" appeals to that starved sense of wonder which dies as more and more of the earth's surface is opened by exploration. It was different for the great navigators of the sixteenth and seventeenth centuries, to whom the "New World" really was new. But, during the past century, the steady improvement in communications, culminating in air-travel, has meant that, save for the Arctic and Antarctic regions and a few areas in Asia and South America, most of our planet is known and mapped.

But sometimes the map-makers have made mistakes. It was due to one such mistake, plus the mountainous, inaccessible nature of the country, that one Lost City did remain unknown to white men until the year 1911. The date is significant; just before the beginning of air travel. The Inca city, now called Macchu Picchu (though that was not its original name), stands on a high crag of the Andes, in Peru. The man who discovered it was Hiram Bingham, sometime Director of the Peruvian Expedition of Yale University and the National Geographic Society, Member of the American Alpine Club, Professor of Latin-American History in Yale University. These titles are significant, for Professor Bingham combines the learning of the historian with the adventurous spirit of the explorer and courage of the mountaineer. Although he pays generous tribute to the fellow members of his expeditions, and to others who assisted him—topographers, naturalists, archæologists, doctors—the honour of this extraordinary achievement belongs principally to him, and there can be no adequate substitute for his personal account of it given in *The Lost City of the Incas*. In a fairly wide acquaintance with the literature of travel and exploration, plus a not inconsiderable amount of world travel, I have yet to find a more gripping and romantic story of discovery *which is also true*. I have therefore drawn liberally on Professor Bingham's books, especially the above mentioned one,[1] to the author and publishers of which I offer my grateful acknowledgements. This chapter must necessarily be only a bare summary of the story, leaving out much fascinating detail which should be read in the discoverer's own account.

First it is necessary to know a little about the ancient chronicles which provided the slender clues to Bingham's discovery. When the *conquistador* Francisco Pizarro entered Peru in 1531, the country was ruled by an ancient race of kings called the Incas. Although in time this word came to be applied to the people as a whole, its original meaning was "King" or "Ruler". Thus the ancient Peruvians spoke of "the Inca Tupac Amaru" as we speak of "King Charles II". The first Inca was Manco Capac, who lived in about A.D. 1000. The last, Tupac Amaru, and his family were put to death by the Spaniards in 1572. Our knowledge of Inca history, and especially that of the last four Incas, depends largely on Spanish writers of the sixteenth and early seventeenth centuries, who entered Peru at, or shortly after the period of the conquest. The Incas themselves had no system of writing, but one of them, Titu Cusi, dictated to a *Mestizo* [2] secretary the story of his father Manco's life and death. This man wrote down his account in crude Spanish, which was later revised by an Augustinian friar, Marcos Garcia. There was also Garcilasso Inca de la Vega, of Spanish-Inca parentage, who left Peru when he was twenty, lived in Spain for the rest of his life, and in his later years wrote a book called *Royal Commentaries,* setting down what he knew of the history

---

[1] Bingham, Hiram. *The Lost City of the Incas.* Phœnix House. London, 1951.

[2] *Mestizo:* person of mixed Spanish and Indian blood.

of his race. Prescott's classic book on the conquest of Peru is based partly on this. Other writers were Pedro Sancho, one of Pizarro's secretaries, Fernando Montesinos, who went to Peru in 1629 as adviser to the Viceroy, and wrote several works, including a history of the Incas; and a rather tedious priest named Father de Lancha, who produced a long *Moralizing Chronicle of the Activities of the Augustinian Order in Peru.* Nine-tenths of it is almost unreadable, but the remainder is valuable historically, because it describes in detail the adventures and misfortunes of two missionary priests, Friar Diego and Friar Marcos, who visited the Inca Titu Cusi in the mountain retreat to which he had fled from the Spaniards.

We also possess an account by Don Diego Rodriguez de Figueroa, who, in 1565, attempted to convert the Inca Titu Cusi to Christianity; a description by Captain Balthasar de Ocampo of Titu Cusi's funeral; and the courageous Captain Garcia has left a vivid record of his pursuit and capture of the last Inca, Tupac Amaru. From these and other documents it is possible to reconstruct in broad outline the history of the last four Incas, and their desperate and pathetic attempt to retain what was left of their shrunken dominions before the invaders took everything.

The country now called Peru lies on the western seaboard of South America, fronting the Pacific, with Ecuador and Colombia in the north, Brazil to the east, and Bolivia to the south-east and Chile to the south. From the coast the land rises first to high plateaux of from 6,000 to 12,000 feet, and then to the triple chain of the Andes, 250 miles wide, and rising in places to peaks of more than 20,000 feet. Some of the passes through the Andes are higher than the highest mountain in Europe.

It is a country of fantastic contrasts, from hot, fœtid jungles to an Alpine landscape of glaciers and snow-capped mountains. Before the coming of the Incas the land seems to have been occupied by highly civilized peoples, the Aymaras and the Chimus. We know little about them, but when the Spaniards arrived in 1531 they found the Incas ruling a people among whom the arts and sciences were highly advanced, and these imply a long period of growth, certainly a longer period than the five hundred years separating the Incas of Pizarro's time from the first Inca, Manco (*circa* A.D. 1000).

These early peoples had developed, over perhaps two thousand years, a system of agriculture in advance of any in use on the American continent. Undeterred by the mountainous country, which has few plains, they made tiers of terraces along the steep slopes to hold back the soil, which they kept productive by fertilization. In this soil they grew corn, several species of tomatoes, beans, cassava, sweet and white potatoes and other crops, all of which they bred from wild plants. The wild ancestor of the potato, for instance, still grows in the Andes. Its tubers are about the size of a pea, yet from this the Indians of South America developed twelve varieties of the potato we know to-day. Before the Spanish conquest, none of these food plants were known outside the American continent.

Most of the agricultural soil in the Peruvian Andes was placed there by the Incas and their predecessors; it is still in use, but nowadays wheat and barley are usually grown where the Incas raised potatoes and maize. The Incas also used *guano* fertilizer from the bird-islands off the coast, and placed such a high value on it that it was an offence to kill one of these birds. In the bottoms of the valleys which cross the desert between Ecuador and Chile, these skilful farmers deflected rivers and constructed irrigation ditches, fed by the melting snows of the Andes.

They also discovered the medicinal value of quinine (obtained from the bark of the cinchona tree, which gives the drug its name) and of cocaine, which they extracted from the coca-plant.

In the domestication of animals they were far more successful than the Indians of Central and North America. They bred the guinea-pig for food, and from the native American camel, the *guanaco,* they bred the llama and the alpaca, which were used for transport. When we order an alpaca coat we are using an Inca word. At one time such garments were made from the fine, soft hair of the alpaca, but nowadays the word is not used to describe the real article, since, as Bingham says, "shrewd cloth merchants, many years ago, adopted the name for a rather coarse material made from sheep's wool."

Thousands of miles of well-made roads linked the cities of the Inca Empire, which once included not only Peru, but extended over Bolivia and Ecuador; its influence was felt even as far as the forests of the Gran Chaco in Brazil. As the Incas did not use wheeled vehicles these roads did not need an even surface, and the gradients are often steep. Tunnels and bridges were wide enough to take a man or a llama, no more. The bridges, slung across swift rivers and deep canyons, were perilous structures suspended from ropes of twisted lianas—the rope-like vines which grow in the Peruvian jungles. Some of these bridges were three hundred feet long, sagging in the middle and swaying in the wind, so that non-Indian travellers often crawl across them on their hands and knees. They terrified the Spaniards, one is happy to note. If only the Incas had been as expert at military strategy as they were at agriculture they would have cut the bridges and hindered, if not prevented, the final conquest of their country.

Along this network of roads moved the slow caravans of llamas, and swift runners carrying messages from city to city. They were not written messages; the Incas had no writing system, but they used knotted cords called *quipus;* the arrangement of knots gave the information required. Sometimes the couriers carried delicacies for the royal table. An old chronicle states that fish caught in the Pacific Ocean could be carried over the mountains by these couriers and delivered in an edible condition at the Inca capital of Cuzco.

Like all highly civilized peoples, e.g. the Ancient Egyptians and the Sumerians, the Incas used mind-transforming drugs to mitigate the stresses and strains of life. Of these alcohol was chief. They brewed a very potent drink called *chicha,* on which they sometimes got drunk for days on end. Rodriguez wrote an amusingly shocked commentary on this after he had visited Titu Cusi at his headquarters and tried to convert him to Christianity. The Inca partiality for liquor is indicated by the numerous expressions in their language describing the various stages of intoxication.

The Inca governmental system was a benevolent despotism. No one went hungry. No one was without a home. The land was held communally, and each inhabitant had an allotment to farm. When he married and had children, the allotment was increased proportionally, and there was an equitable distribution of food. But this involved a high degree of regimentation. There were regulations governing every aspect of life and interfering with the subjects at every point. Idleness was punished. Yet, on the whole, the common people seem to have been fairly and justly treated, and, unlike the Indians of Central America, when the Incas conquered another people they did not treat them as slaves, but encouraged them to become part of their own system. In this they were not unlike the Romans.

Their religion was based principally on the worship of the sun. At Cuzco, the capital, and at other places, one can still see Sun-temples, but at the time of the Spanish conquest the Incas had ceased the practice of human sacrifice, although it seems to have been continued among the coastal tribes over whom they ruled.

Besides the sun and moon, they worshipped an "Unknown God" an all-pervading spirit who was represented, at Cuzco, as a large flat plate of fine gold. But sun-worship seems to have been predominant. Like the Mayas, the Incas had "convents" or "boarding-schools" for some of their high-born women and girls, who were called "Virgins of the Sun". The Inca priests had a charming custom of "tethering the sun" at the time of the winter solstice. In several Inca temples, e.g. at Macchu Picchu, there are stone posts for this purpose. During the autumn and winter, the Incas saw the sun—on which they depended—moving farther and farther north. If he was allowed to continue on his northward path there was danger that he would never return, and then their crops would fail. The priests, skilful astronomers, knew the date of the winter solstice, and at that time they performed ceremonies at which the sun was ritually "tethered" to a post, as an animal is tied. When the great disc appeared to halt and retrace its path the people would be delighted and the priests' power and prestige confirmed. Presumably a similar ritual took place at the time of the summer solstice.

Such was the civilization which existed in Peru when the first Spanish ships arrived off the coast with their steel-clad soldiers, their horses, their officials and their priests—eager to convert the heathen to a religion which had originated in western Asia, half the world away. The tragic story, which should be read in full in the pages of Prescott and the Spanish chroniclers, can only be summarized here. When, in 1533, Pizarro took the Inca capital of Cuzco, he selected from among the Incas a young nobleman named Manco and made him king. At first Manco was pleased, but when he discovered that he was expected to be a mere puppet of his masters he led a revolt, hoping that by superior numbers the Indians could drive the invaders from their country. But spears, clubs, bows and slings were no match for Spanish firearms, particularly when the invader was backed by disaffected Indians who refused allegiance to the Inca.

Manco's forces were defeated, and with his wife, family, and followers he fled from the great city of his ancestors with its fortress, palace, and temples, and marched into the Valley of the Urubamba. With him went his three sons, one of whom was Titu Cusi, then six years old. Later, when he became king, Titu Cusi dictated the story of his father's life.

The temperate valley of the great river Urubamba was Manco's first line of retreat, but soon the Spaniards followed him there. After several fierce battles he retreated to Ollantaytambo, the last important Inca town in the valley before the high mountains began. Here, unfortunately, some of Manco's soldiers got drunk at a party he had given for the Indians of the district, and were surprised and routed by a small Spanish force. The invaders captured, among other things, the mummies of the Incas' ancestors which he had taken from Cuzco, and many jewels and precious things. Manco's wife was taken prisoner, together with the boy Titu Cusi and other members of the royal family. But Manco himself managed to escape and retreated into the high mountains where his position was impregnable.

> "Everyone is familiar," writes Bingham, "with the story of how hazardous it was for Hannibal and Napoleon, in different epochs, to bring their armies into Italy over the comparatively low passes of the Alps. It is not surprising that Pizarro found it impossible to follow the Inca Manco over passes which were higher than the very summit of Mount Blanc. In no parts of the Peruvian Andes are there so many beautiful snow peaks. Veronica (19,342 feet), Salcantay (20,565 feet), Soray (19,437 feet) and Soiroccocha (18,197 feet) are outstanding features of the landscape. Some of them are visible for a hundred miles. None of them have been climbed so far as it is known." [3]

The old chronicles state that Manco established himself at a fortress on a hill-top; this fortress is variously described as "Vitcos", "Uiticos", and "Pitcos". There are also references in contemporary writings to a second Inca stronghold called "Vilcabamba". These places were in a dry, well-watered region in the mountains; corn and potatoes were grown, and the Inca and his followers lived well. Titu Cusi, successor to Manco, says that his father used to lead raiding parties to ambush and plunder the Spanish merchants on the road between Cuzco and Lima. To do this he would cross the great Apurimac river (Apurimac means "Great Speaker") on rafts and then lie in wait near the highroad. These attacks were successful, in spite of Spanish superiority in arms. The Inca's troops used spears, clubs, and powerful slings which could kill a horse or break a steel sword at fifty paces. They were also skilful with the bolas,[4] a weapon consisting of three stones tied to a cord which when flung could wrap itself

[3] Bingham, Hiram. *Lost City of the Incas.* Phœnix House. London, 1951.
[4] Similar weapons have been dug up on prehistoric sites in Europe and Asia.

round the legs of a horse, or pinion a man's arms to his sides. After each raid Manco and his followers returned to their hill-top fortress of Vitcos.

Infuriated by these raids, Pizarro sent a force to capture Manco. Exhausted by the long climb over the mountains, and overcome by "mountain sickness" caused by the high altitude (over 15,000 feet), they were ambushed and cut to pieces. Only a handful escaped. After this disaster the Spaniards left Manco alone for a time. Then, in 1542, Pizarro was assassinated by the followers of his partner Almagro. In the civil war which followed, the "Almagrites" were defeated and some of the refugees fled to Vitcos and joined Manco, who received them kindly. The leaders of these Spanish rebels were Gomez Perez and Diego Mendez, of whom Father Calancha wrote, "they were rascals, worthy of Manco's favour". They were certainly rascals, but whether worthy of the Inca's favour may be judged by the horrible incident which occurred later. At first all went well. The refugees taught Manco the use of firearms and horsemanship, and when, in 1544, King Charles V of Spain sent out a new Viceroy with strict orders that the Indians should have better treatment, Gomez and Mendez persuaded Manco to write a letter to the new Viceroy asking if he might appear before him; he also asked for the pardon of the Spanish rebels who had taken refuge with him. Gomez went to Cuzco with Manco's note, was pardoned, and returned to Vitcos with the good news. Manco then prepared to return with his followers to Cuzco, and would have done so but for an incident which illustrates how one act of human folly can alter the course of history.

We have several versions of the story; the two most convincing are those of Garcilasso Inca de la Vega (though he wrote his account fifty years after it happened) and Titu Cusi, second son of Manco, who was living at Vitcos at the time, having escaped from the Spaniards and rejoined his father. Garcilasso says that the refugees had taught the Inca a number of games, such as bowls, quoits and chess. They took these games very seriously and quarrels sometimes occurred (probably inflamed by *chicha*). One day, after Gomez's return from Cuzco, he was playing bowls with Manco, and a dispute arose over the measure of a certain cast. "This," writes Garcilasso, "often happened between them; for this Perez, being a person of hot and fiery brain, without judgement or understanding, would take the least occasion in the world to contend with and provoke the Inca."

> "Being no longer able to endure his rudeness, the Inca pushed him on the breast, and bid him to consider to whom he talked. Perez, not considering in his heat and passion either his own safety or that of his companions, lifted up his hand, and with the bowl struck the Inca so violently on the head that he knocked him down." [5]

This is Garcilasso's version. Titu Cusi, who was fifteen at the time, tells a different story.

He says that, during a game of quoits, while Manco had a quoit raised in his hand, several Spaniards rushed upon him with drawn swords and killed him, and that, when Titu Cusi rushed to defend his father "they hurled a lance which only just failed to kill me. I was terrified and fled among the bushes. They looked for me but could not find me."

A third version says that the quarrel took place over a game of chess between the Inca and Diego Mendez, in which the Spaniard lost his temper and called Manco a dog. Angered by the insult, the Inca struck Diego Mendez with his fist, whereupon Mendez stabbed him.

The Spaniards tried to escape, but, it is good to know, were overtaken, pulled off their horses and put to very unpleasant deaths. Manco died three days later, leaving three sons, Sayri Tupac, Titu Cusi, and Tupac Amaru. They were the last three Incas, and their history throws an interesting light on their char-

[5] Translation by Sir Clements Markham.

acters. Of the three, Titu Cusi was by far the strongest and most formidable. An eye-witness of his father's death, he harboured a justifiable bitterness against the Spaniards. His two brothers trusted them and were destroyed.

After a time Sayri Tupac, apparently a gentle creature, was persuaded to return to Cuzco, where he became a Christian and married an Inca princess. He died two years later; according to the Spaniards of disease, though the Incas said he was poisoned. Titu Cusi, who was thirty years old when he heard of his brother's death, fled to the inaccessible valley of the Cordillera Vilcabamba, and assumed the throne. The old chronicles tell us that he put his younger brother, Tupac Amaru, into "The House of the Sun with the Chosen Virgins and their Matrons". This sanctuary was not at Vitcos, but at a place called Vilcabamba which, as Professor Bingham remarks, "since its whereabouts were unknown to the Spaniards would also be a favourite residence of Titu Cusi himself".

A few Spanish emissaries reached Vitcos and were received with natural suspicion, but there is no record of them having seen Vilcabamba, though two friars were once permitted to go very near it. One of the most interesting accounts by a Spaniard is that written by Don Diego Rodriguez de Figueroa, who made an unsuccessful attempt to convert Titu Cusi to Christianity. It contains a fascinating description of the Inca, the last but one of his line, in his full panoply of state, surrounded by his court and his warriors.

> "The three hundred Indians with their lances, and others from the surrounding country, had made a great theatre for the Inca, of red clay. They were waiting his arrival, and wished me to go out to meet him. . . . Many lances were drawn up on a hill, and messengers arrived to say that the Inca was coming. The Inca came in front of all, with a head-dress of plumes of many colours, a silver plate on his breast, a golden shield in one hand, and a lance all of gold. He wore garters of feathers and fastened to them were small wooden bells. On his

head was a diadem and another round his neck. In one hand he had a gilded dagger, and he came in a mask of several colours." [6]

Thus Rodriguez described the formal dress of the Emperors of Peru as it had been worn in the days of Inca power and majesty, when they had ruled an Empire which had extended from the forests of the Amazon to the Pacific coast; now that Empire had shrunk to a small mountainous region of the Andes. But Titu Cusi was still the Inca, in all the pride of his ancestors.

I have said that the character of the three Incas comes out very clearly in their history. Titu Cusi, the strongest personality, must have been an embittered and revengeful man, and a highly intelligent one. His behaviour towards Rodriguez and the unfortunate clerics who followed him later can easily be explained by this assumption. Probably he knew he could never hope to defeat the Spaniards, but in the meantime he determined to torment and ridicule them.

In this he certainly succeeded, and one reads with pleasure the bewildered accounts of the humourless Spaniards, who seem to have been unaware of the tricks which were being played on them by the subtle king.

First the Inca invited the dignified Rodriguez to his quarters.

"His mien," writes Rodriguez, "was rather severe and manly. He wore a shirt of blue damask, and a mantle of very fine cloth. He is served on silver, and there are also twenty or thirty good-looking women, waiting behind him. He sent for me to eat where he was with his women and his governor."

After asking the Spanish emissary whether he had "made the acquaintance of his captains", the Inca departed, "exactly in the same order as when he had arrived, with music of silver flutes and trumpets. That night there was a guard of a hundred Indians who were divided into watches, and flutes and drums were played to call each watch."

[6] Translated by Sir Clements Markham.

Next morning the king recalled Rodriguez to watch his troops, who apparently had drunk freely, no doubt with the Inca's encouragement. From a rising ground the Spaniard watched "the festivities made by the Inca, and heard the songs. The dances were war dances with spears in their hands, throwing them from one to the other. I believe that they did these things by reason of the quantity of *chicha* that they had drunk."

He was right. Part of the entertainment which Titu Cusi had devised for his guest was a display by 600 Anti Indians, wild warriors from the Amazon jungle, well fortified with *chicha*.

> "They advanced in good order, making reverence to the sun and the Inca and took their positions. Then the Inca again began to brandish his lance, and said that he could raise all the Indians in Peru, he had only to give the order. . . . Then all those Antis made an offer to the Inca that, if he wished it, they would eat me raw. They said to him 'What are you doing with this little bearded one here, who is trying to deceive you? It is better we should eat him at once.'
>
> "Then two renegade *orejones* came straight at me with spears in their hands, flourishing their weapons and saying 'The bearded ones! Our enemies.' [7] I laughed at this, but at the same time commending myself to God. I asked the Inca to have mercy and protect me, and so he delivered me from them, and hid me until morning."

Apparently the Inca was sufficiently impressed by his guest's courage and tact to permit a few crosses to be set up, though against the wishes of his Indian followers. He appears to have considered leaving Vitcos and returning to Yucay in the lower valley, where Sayri Tupac had lived. But, when, encouraged by the apparent success of their ambassador, the Spaniards sent another emissary, with thirty troops, along the road to the Inca stronghold, Titu Cusi wisely destroyed the bridge and they had to return. Rodriguez was sent back to Cuzco, though the Inca

[7] The Incas were clean-shaven.

retained in his service a Spanish-speaking secretary, Martin Pando, who later took down Titu Cusi's life-story.

Later came the two unfortunate Augustinian friars, Friar Diego and Friar Marcos, whose story is tragic-comic. This was in 1565, when the bigoted King Philip II had determined to enforce Christianity throughout his Empire. At first Titu Cusi appeared to adopt the faith, and allowed one of the friars to erect a church at a place called Puquira, "where the Inca King held his court and his armies". Puquira was near Vitcos, and the name is important because it provided one of the clues which led Professor Bingham to the discovery of the lost Inca cities. For the story of the two Augustinians we have to rely on the moralizing Father Calancha, who is naturally biased. From this account, however, that while Father Diego was a gentle, kindly soul who won the love of the Indians by healing the sick, Friar Marcos was an intolerant bigot who railed against the Indian fondness for *chicha*, "leading," says Calancha, "to incest, sodomy and homicide". His culminating act of folly (though it must have required courage) was to desecrate the Temple of the Sun near Vitcos, described in Calancha's book as "in a village called Chuquipalpa," and containing *"a white rock over a spring of water"*. (Our italics.)

This brief description provided Professor Bingham with another clue.

It speaks much for the toleration of the Inca that he did not immediately order the execution of the two friars; perhaps Father Diego's popularity among the poor caused him to stay his hand.

But he put the two holy men to a very severe test. From a careful study of Calancha's account, I suspect that Titu Cusi, having, no doubt, been told that two of the principal Christian virtues were fortitude and chastity, decided to make a practical experiment, Calancha does not say this, of course, but the Inca was an intelligent man, and the ludicrous situations in which he involved the two friars look to me like the whims of a cynical philosopher with a taste for practical joking.

The two Augustinians had repeatedly asked to be taken to
Titu Cusi's "principal seat", Vilcabamba, which no Spaniard had
seen, and where, according to Calancha, there was a "University
of Idolatry" in which lived the Chosen Women of the Sun. At last
Titu Cusi agreed that they should see Vilcabamba. "Come with
me," he said, "I desire to entertain you". It was, the missionaries
reported, a long and tiresome journey of three days' duration between Puquira, the Inca's Army Headquarters, and the great sanctuary in the mountains. It was during the rainy season, and the
friars had a cold, miserable journey. When they reached "a place
called Ungacacha" they found the road flooded.

> "Shortly after daylight," Calancha says, "on de-
> scending to a plain, the monks thought that they had
> come to a lake. The Inca said to them, 'all of us must
> pass through the water.' O cruel apostate! [8] He travelled
> in a litter and the two priests on foot without shoes!
> The two ministers went into the water and proceeded
> joyfully, for they knew they were receiving these insults
> and torments because of the Inca's hatred of their
> preaching. . . . Cold and covered with mud, they came
> out on dry land, and there the Inca told them that he had
> come by that difficult route because he had thought it
> would so disgust them with the attempt that they would
> go from thence to Cuzco."

Father Calancha says that "they" (the Indians) "covered
the roads with water, the country being inundated by turning the
river from its course, because the fathers desired and often attempted to go to Vilcabamba to preach, because it was the chief
town, and the one in which was the University of Idolatry and
the professors of witchcraft, teachers of the abominations."

Neither of the priests ever saw the great city. "The Inca,"
writes Calancha, "did not wish the fathers to live in the town and
ordered that they be given lodgings outside so that they might
not see the worship, ceremonies and rites in which the Inca and
his captains participated daily with their sorcerers." There they

[8] Evidently Titu Cusi's "conversion" to Christianity had not been serious.

had to remain, preaching against idolatry, and there Titu Cusi put them to a second trial, this time of their chastity. Calancha's account of this is one of the choicest examples of unconscious humour I have ever encountered, all the funnier because of the solemnity with which it is written.

Apparently the Inca carefully selected some of the most beautiful of the Chosen Women of the Sun, particularly those from the warm, humid valleys near the coast, where "modesty and chastity were unknown." They were the most beautiful and pleasing of those regions, the most elegantly adorned and doubtless the most seductive. "The women made use of all that the devil knows how to teach them, practising all the arts of sensuality and the most dangerous gifts of seduction. But these apostolic men defended themselves so valiantly that the women returned, defeated and abashed. . . ."

But the Inca was not defeated yet, and brought up reserves. Throughout the night beautiful women, disguised in friars' habits, were sent to the friars' quarters, and "since the Indians' rooms nor their taverns had any keys or doors, the women were able to reach the friars' beds. . . . This battery of women continued by day and night, the habits being changed and different Indians always being sent. If the monks left their houses and went into the country, they sought them out. The attackers did not cease to contrive new wiles and to present terrible temptations."

After this trial, from which the friars apparently emerged victorious, Titu Cusi seems to have become more tolerant of them, and allowed them to return to Puquira to continue their ministry. It was during this period, however, that they attempted to desecrate the Sun Temple, "a white rock over a spring of water". Friar Marcos was stoned out of the province, but Friar Diego was permitted to remain. His end was a tragic one. After what Professor Bingham describes as "a wet party", Titu Cusi contracted double pneumonia. Friar Diego attempted to cure him with his simple medicines, or at least to secure his confession and absolution. But Titu Cusi died, and one of his wives accused the priest of causing the Inca's death. Father Diego was put to death "with great cruelty", and Father Calancha devotes many pages to the details.

The end of the last Inca, Tupac Amaru, followed soon. The young man was brought from the House of the Chosen Women, where Titu Cusi placed him, and made king. But he lacked either his father's courage or his brother's cunning. Untrained in statesmanship or war he was no match for the Spaniards. His downfall was hastened by an unfortunate combination of circumstances. At first the Viceroy asked Tupac Amaru to return to Cuzco, but the Ambassador bearing the invitation was murdered on the road to the Inca stronghold. Enraged, the Viceroy sent a punitive expedition under a Captain Garcia, with orders to capture the Inca. Whereas Manco or Titu Cusi would have destroyed the bridges and garrisoned the defensive forts guarding the approaches to the Inca kingdom, Tupac Amaru left the bridges open and the forts unmanned. Garcia, after first storming and capturing "the young fortress" (apparently Vitcos), pursued the Inca and his few remaining followers down the valley of the Pampaconas, deep into the Amazon jungles. It was a stern chase in which the Spanish soldiers showed great courage. Garcia and his men, half-starved and barefoot, forded rapids, constructed rafts, hacked their way along jungle trails, until at last, Garcia says in his own account, the Inca preferred to trust himself to the Spaniards "rather than perish of famine".

The end was inevitable. The last Inca was carried in triumph to Cuzco, where, after a mock trial, he, his wife, and his followers were put to death "with fiendish cruelty". If Titu Cusi the "idolator" had been alive, he could have told his brother what mercy he could expect from the Spaniards.

CHAPTER THIRTEEN

The Discovery of Vilcabamba

The principal clues which led Bingham to discover the lost cities of the Incas are contained in the foregoing account. These, and local traditions, were all with which he had to work when, in 1911, he led an expedition into Peru. A keen mountaineer, he had climbed his first mountain, with his father, when four years old. As a young man, he tells us, "in a desire to qualify myself to teach South American history, and to write about the great General Simon Bolivar, I followed his route across the Andes from Venezuela to Colombia." Later, as a delegate to the First Pan American Scientific Congress in 1908, he made a journey into the Andes, following the old Spanish trade route from Buenos Aires to Lima. From Cuzco he penetrated the Andes on mule-back, and came for the first time in contact with the land of the Incas. He became so fascinated by the story, and by the magnificent, unexplored mountain country, that he determined to return with an expedition organized, he says, "in the hope that we might check the highest mountain in America (Mt. Coropuna, over 23,000 feet), collect a lot of geological and biological data, and above all try to find the last capital of the Incas". He was not at this time an archæologist.

He was accompanied by Professor Isaiah Bowman, the geologist-geographer of the expedition; Professor Harry W. Foote, a naturalist; Dr. William G. Erving, surgeon; Kai Hendrikson, topographer; H. L. Tucker, engineer; and Paul B. Lanius, assistant.

He was not of course the first explorer to visit the area; Castelnau, Marcou, Wiener, Squier and others had travelled in it. In 1834 the Count de Sartiges had made a long adventurous journey into the Andes, and so had Raimondi in 1865. Both had left descriptive accounts, and Raimondi a map, which Bingham carried on his travels, together with more recent maps. Leaving Cuzco, with its splendid Inca temples and palaces, the expedition moved along the Urubamba Valley, past Ollantaytambo, until it reached Torontoy, the end of the cultivated temperate valley, and the beginning of the Grand Canyon of the Urubamba.

In the late 'nineties, some twelve or fifteen years before Bingham's expedition, a road had been blasted out along the edge of the canyon, following the river. Before that time it had been impossible to travel along the foot of the canyon.

> "The Urubamba river, in cutting its way through the granite ranges, forms rapids too dangerous to be passable and precipices which can be scaled only with great effort and considerable peril, if at all. At one time a footpath probably ran near the river, where the Indians, by crawling along the face of the cliffs and sometimes swinging from one ledge to another on hanging vines, were able to make their way to the alluvial terraces down the valley." [1]

Before the river road was made there were only two passable approaches from Cuzco to the lower valley of the Urubamba. One was via the pass of Panticalla, to the north. The other was over a pass between Mount Salcantay (20,565 feet) and Mount Soray (19,437 feet). In each case the passes ascended to more than 12,000 feet, and were frequently impassable, especially in winter. Before the making of the river-road the mountainous mass between these two divergent routes was practically unknown. It had not been accessible for nearly four hundred years.

There are many Inca sites in Peru, some in remote places, and several had been put forward as possibly the sites of the lost cities of Vitcos and Vilcabamba. Bingham had examined several of these, including Choqquequirau, a mountain fortress controlling

---

[1] Bingham, Hiram. *Lost City of the Incas*. Phœnix House. 1951.

the upper valley of the Apurimac—the "Great Speaker". To reach Choqquequirau Bingham had to cross a 270 foot suspension bridge, three feet wide and highly unstable, across rapids of such terrifying power and sound as to drown all speech. "No one bothers to learn to swim in the Andes," he comments.

But the explorer was not satisfied that Choqquequirau was one of the Inca cities described in the sixteenth-century chronicles, and a Peruvian scholar, Don Carlos Romero, agreed with him, saying that "the chronicles contained enough evidence to show that the last Inca capital was not at Choqquequirau but probably over the ranges in the region where I had seen snow-capped peaks".

Thanks to the new road Bingham and his companions were able to travel along the Urubamba river, looking for "a great white rock over a spring of water".

> "The road runs through a land of matchless charm. It has the majestic grandeur of the Canadian Rockies, as well as the startling beauty of Nuuanu Pali near Honolulu, and the enchanting vistas of the Koolau Ditch Trail on Maui, in my native land. In the variety of its charms and the power of its spell, I know no place in the world which can compare with it. Not only has it great snow peaks looming above the clouds more than two miles overhead, and gigantic precipices of many-coloured granite rising sheer for thousands of feet above the foaming, glistening, roaring rapids, it has also, in striking contrast, orchids and tree ferns, the delectable beauty of luxurious vegetation, and the mysterious witchery of the jungle. One is drawn irresistibly onward by ever-recurring surprises through a deep winding gorge, turning and twisting past overhanging cliffs of incredible height." [2]

Here and there they came upon ancient tracks, and later, when they passed the lower mouth of the gorge, wonderful examples of Inca terracing rose up the valley sides. There were also a number of Inca towns and forts, but none which fitted the description of Vitcos. However, Bingham did find one mountain

[2] *Lost City of the Incas.*

stronghold of a size and splendour which made him wonder, but, as he did not immediately realize its significance, I shall follow his example and leave its description to the end of this chapter.

Bingham and his colleagues travelled on down the Urubamba, halting at villages and isolated farms to question the inhabitants about Inca remains. Bingham had taken with him extracts from the old chronicles, which he showed or read out to his Indian hosts. Usually he drew a blank; there were Inca ruins here, or there, or over the mountain, but when examined they did not tally with any of the descriptions. At one place a *mestizo*, hearing the words "Yurak Rumi" (white stone), raised the expedition's hopes by saying there was a place of that name some distance away. It was necessary to cut a trail through the jungle to reach it, but when at last they arrived at the spot the weary travellers found only a simple primitive Inca house of no importance.

At the town of Santa Ana, at the head of the canoe naviga- tion of the Urubamba, they met Don Pedro Duque, a Colombian who had lived for many years in Peru. He was keenly interested in the quest, but did not know of any place within the area with a name remotely resembling Vitcos. Don Pedro invited to his plantation house all his friends and neighbours and put the question to them. Again—no success. It was all very discouraging. Bingham now decided to search the valley of the Vilcabamba, as- sisted by the map drawn by the distinguished cartographer Rai- mondi, who had surveyed the area more than seventy years earlier. Bingham felt that, from the contemporary accounts of Balthasar de Ocampo and Captain Garcia, the Vilcabamba valley was probably the "valley of Vitcos" along which the last Inca, Tupac Amaru, had attempted to escape. But Raimondi made no mention of any Inca ruins in this area, so "it was with feelings of considerable uncertainty that we proceeded on our quest". Eventually they reached the valley, which is flanked by high, jungle-covered moun- tains and very steep. At the village of Lucma they met *Gobernador* Mogrovejo, a local official who knew the district well, and to whom Bingham offered a Peruvian silver dollar for every ruin to which he could take them. The old man agreed, somewhat dourly, to help, although he had never heard of any place called Vitcos, nor could he recognize any of the other localities mentioned in Father Calancha's four-hundred-year-old chronicle. In fact the *Gobernador* did not disguise his contempt for the whole enterprise.

Next day they left Lucma, forded the river, and saw ahead of them "a truncated hill a thousand feet high, its top partly covered with a scrubby growth of trees and bushes, its sides steep and rocky". Mogrovejo said there were ruins on the top, and that the hill was called *Rosapata,* a hybrid word compounded of *pata,* which is a Quichua (Indian) word for "hill", and *rosas,* the Spanish word for roses. This at first only interested Bingham moderately, until someone mentioned casually that the village at the foot of the hill was called *Puquiura.*

Puquiura . . . that was the name of the place at which Titu Cusi had received Rodriguez in state, the place at which the two friars had built a church. Could this be the same Puquiura? If so, then Vitcos could not be far away, for had not Friar Marcos and Friar Diego walked in procession from Puquiura to the "House of the Sun" which, says Calancha, was "close to Vitcos"? But when the explorers reached the village they found no clues. None of the buildings was of any great age.

Crossing the Vilcabamba and its tributary, the Tincochaca, Bingham and his companions followed Mogrovejo up the slopes of the hill called Rosapata. They came first to "an old and very dilapidated structure in the saddle of the hill on the south side of Rosapata. It was evidently an Inca structure, probably a small fort, but not Vitcos. As they continued to climb the hill Bingham remembered the description of Vitcos given by Captain Garcia, "on a very high eminence surrounded with rugged crags and jungles, very dangerous to ascend and almost impregnable".

When he reached the top he found that it was indeed "a very high eminence surrounded by rugged crags". On the most approachable side a long wall had been built, so carefully that a besieger could not even have obtained a toehold. And on the very summit of the hill were the ruins of buildings surrounding a compound measuring 160 feet by 145 feet. Around this were thirteen or fourteen buildings set out in a rough square, with one large and several smaller courtyards. They were obviously of Inca construction, but so badly damaged by treasure-seekers that Bingham could not establish their exact dimensions. But what struck him most forcibly were the remains of a huge structure, 245 feet long and 43 feet wide, with thirty doorways, fifteen on each side, but without windows. Running from front to back were three passages, and in between were ten large chambers. The entrances to the corridors or hallways were well-made of fine granite, and the lintels also were of blocks of white granite, eight feet long. "This indeed was," writes the explorer, "a residence fit for a royal Inca, an exile from Cuzco." And he recalled the Spanish chronicler Ocampo's description of Vitcos:

> "There is an extensive level space with a very sumptuous and majestic building erected with great skill and art, all the lintels of the doors, the principal as well as the ordinary ones, being elaborately carved."

By "carved" Ocampo may not have meant "adorned with carvings", but "well cut". The buildings on the top of the hill of Rosapata seemed to meet most of the requirements of Ocampo's "fortress of Pitcos". But still Bingham could not be quite sure. Where was the *Yurak Rumi,* "great white rock over a spring of water" which should be nearby? That night, at Tincochaca, an Indian friend of Mogrovejo said, quite casually, in reply to the oft-repeated question, "Oh, yes, there is a great white rock over a spring. It's in a valley not far from here. I'll show you to-morrow."

But again the explorers were disappointed. Their guide led them to a large white boulder, with a carved seat on one side. Nearby was a cave, which may have contained Inca mummies. But there was no spring answering to Calancha's description, nor could this, though it was certainly an Inca monument, possibly be described as a "Temple of the Sun". By this time Bingham and his colleagues must have begun to share the disgruntled pessimism

of their guide, whose only interest in the Inca ruins was in earning
a silver dollar for every example he found, and who thought the
whole quest futile and pointless. After all, he had lived most of his
life in the district, and, if he knew of no such place, why should
a group of Americans expect to find it?

Perhaps Bingham himself had begun to lose faith, although
he does not say so. But, on the same afternoon, after following
a trickling stream through the thick woods he came into an open
space, and there, shining in the evening sun, was a great white rock,
and beneath the trees, the remains of an Inca temple, "flanking and
partly enclosing a gigantic granite boulder, one end of which overhung a small pool of running water". It was late on the afternoon
of August 9th, 1911.

> "There was not a hut to be seen, scarcely a sound
> to be heard, an ideal place for practising the mystic cere-
> monies of the ancient cult. The remarkable aspect of this
> great boulder and the dark pool beneath its shadow had
> caused this to become a place of worship. Here, with-
> out doubt, was 'the principal *mochadero* of those
> forested mountains'. It is still venerated by the Indians
> of the vicinity. At last we had found the place where,
> in the days of Titu Cusi, the Inca priests faced the east,
> and greeted the rising sun, 'extended their hands towards
> it', and 'threw kisses towards it'. . . . We may imagine
> the sun priests, clad in their resplendent robes of office,
> standing on the top of the rock at the edge of the steepest
> side, their faces lit by the rosy light of the early morning,
> awaiting the moment when the great divinity should ap-
> pear above the eastern hills and receive their adoration.
> As it rose we may imagine them saluting it and crying:
> 'O sun! Thou who art in peace and safety, shine upon us,
> keep us from sickness, and keep us in health and safety.
> O Sun! Thou who has said let there be Cuzco and
> Tampu, grant that these thy children the Incas may con-
> quer all other peoples. We beseech thee that thy children
> the Incas may be always conquerors since it is for this
> end that thou has created them." [3]

[3] Bingham, Hiram. *Lost City of the Incas*. Phœnix House. 1951.

So Rosapata *was* Vitcos. Puquiura was *the* Puquiura. And this was the Temple of the Sun which the friars had desecrated. But there remained Titu Cusi's principal seat, Vilcabamba, with its House of the Chosen Women and other monuments of idolatry which the two brave priests had failed to enter, and which, as far as is known, no Spaniard ever saw. Where was Vilcabamba? Calancha had said that it was three days' journey from Vitcos. But in which direction?

Before continuing his journey, Bingham made a careful survey of Vitcos. On the side of the compound opposite the Inca's palace he found a number of buildings, roughly constructed, which he thought might have been built to accommodate the Spanish refugees whom Manco had sheltered, and who eventually betrayed him. In these buildings were found "articles of European origin, heavily rusted horseshoe nails, a buckle, bridle and saddle ornaments, and three 'Jews' ' harps". At first Bingham thought that these might have been left by modern Indians who had occupied the hill-top, though, as he points out, the necessity of carrying water supplies up the steep hill would seem to make this unlikely. Could they, perhaps, be the remains of some of the articles which Manco had taken from the Spanish merchants whom he plundered on the Cuzco-Lima road? Or could they have belonged to the Spanish refugees, Gomez, Mendez and the rest? Rodriguez de Figueroa mentions two pairs of scissors which he gave as a present to Titu Cusi. In the ruins of Vitcos Bingham picked up a rusty pair of scissors.

This is not, perhaps, scientific archæology; it leaves room for the sceptic to doubt. Yet one envies the experience of Hiram Bingham and his companions, standing in the broad compound facing the ruined palace of the Inca Manco, reflecting that here, almost certainly, occurred the tragic quarrel when the drunken Gomez struck down his royal host.

*   *   *

In their search for Vilcabamba the explorers moved down the humid valley of the Pampaconas, penetrating into the jungles

where lived wild, naked Indians—descendants of the flesh-eating
Antis who had threatened to eat Rodriguez de Figueroa, the "little
bearded one". Here in the forest of the Upper Amazon, far from
his mountain home, the unhappy Tupac Amaru, last of the Incas,
surrendered at last to the ruthless Captain Garcia, who brought
him back to Cuzco and to his death. Garcia says that the Inca
preferred to trust himself to the Spaniards rather than die of
famine. This may have been because the Antis lived on the flesh
of monkeys, which are plentiful in the area. Probably Tupac
Amaru, delicately nurtured in the "House of the Chosen Women",
could not accustom himself to the diet of savages; or perhaps he
feared the Antis themselves. But, as Bingham says, "it is doubtful
whether his Indian allies would ever have permitted Captain
Garcia to capture the Inca had they been able to furnish Tupac
with such food as he was accustomed to."

Bingham had been led to explore the valley of the Pampaconas by reports of an Inca city called *Espiritu Pampa*—"the
Pampa of Ghosts". Helped by a friendly planter, Saavedra, the
expedition eventually located Inca buildings in the jungle on the
banks of a tributary of the Pampaconas. But, says the explorer,
"it did not seem to me reasonable to suppose that the priest and
Virgins of the Sun who fled from cold Cuzco with Manco and were
established by him somewhere in the fastnesses of Vilcabamba would
have cared to live in this hot valley. The difference in climate is as
great as that between Scotland and Egypt. They would have found
in Espiritu Pampa no food which they liked. Furthermore, they
could have found the seclusion and safety which they craved just as
well in several other parts of the province, together with a cool,
bracing climate and foodstuffs more nearly resembling those to
which they had been accustomed."

The fact was that Bingham, although at the time he had not
realized it, had already found Vilcabamba. He found it in July,
1911, when, as described earlier in this chapter, he had travelled
through the great canyon of the Urubamba below the Inca fortress
of Salapunco, near Torontoy. After passing a place called Maquina

the expedition came upon "a little open plain called Mandor Pampa. Except where the rapids roared past it, gigantic precipices hemmed it in on all sides."

Here Bingham met and talked to a man called Melchor Arteaga, who told him that there were some very good ruins in the vicinity—in fact they were on the top of the mountain opposite. This, as I have explained, was in an area which had only been opened to explorers since the cutting of the river-road through the canyon; earlier explorers, including the Spaniards, could only have approached it over the high mountain passes. It had therefore remained unknown, except to the Indians. On the morning of July 24th Bingham set out, accompanied only by Arteaga and a Peruvian soldier, Sergeant Carrasco. The other members of the expedition were disinclined to make the steep climb. The naturalist said there were "more butterflies near the river" and the surgeon had clothes to wash. So Bingham had the honour of being almost certainly the first white man to see this mountain stronghold of the Incas.

First Arteaga led him across a primitive "bridge" consisting of half a dozen slender logs, spliced together with vines. Then began the climb.

> "A good part of the distance we went on all fours, sometimes holding on by our fingernails. Here and there, a primitive ladder made from the roughly notched trunk of a small tree was placed in such a way as to help one over what might otherwise have proved to be an impassable cliff. In another place the slope was covered with slippery grass where it was hard to find handholds or footholds. Arteaga groaned and said there were lots of snakes there. Sergeant Carrasco said nothing but was glad he had good military shoes. The humidity was great. We were in the belt of maximum precipitation in eastern Peru. The heat was excessive and I was not in training."

At noon, utterly exhausted, Bingham came to a small hut about 2,000 feet above the river. Here Arteaga introduced him to two Indians, Alvarez and Richarte, who, for some yet unexplained reason, had chosen to make their home in this remote spot. The reason became apparent when, higher up the mountainside, the Indians led the travellers to a series of fine, broad terraces filled with fertile soil. They were Inca terraces. When Richarte and Alvarez had first found them they were thickly overgrown with trees, but many of these had now been cut down, and the two farmers had begun to grow crops of maize, sweet and white potatoes, sugar cane, beans, tomatoes and gooseberries.

> "They said there were two paths to the outside world. Of one we had already had a taste; the other was 'even more difficult', a perilous path down the face of a rocky precipice on the other side of the ridge. It was their only means of egress in the wet season when the primitive bridge over which we had come could not be maintained. I was not surprised to learn that they went away from home only about once a month."

Still, there was nothing very extraordinary about Inca terraces, though the view was almost worth the climb.

> "Tremendous green precipices fell away to the white rapids of the Urubamba below. Immediately in front, on the north side of the valley, was a great granite cliff rising 2,000 feet sheer. . . . Beyond, cloud-capped, snow-covered mountains rose thousands of feet above us."

Reluctant to move, fatigued by the long climb, Bingham lay for a long time in admiration. At last he stumbled to his feet again and followed the Indians up the slope, climbing over fallen trees and scrambling through bamboo thickets. Then, quite suddenly, he found himself among buildings of finely masoned stone. First came "a semi-circular building whose outer wall, gently sloping and slightly curved, bore a striking resemblance to the famous Temple of the Sun in Cuzco. . . . It followed the natural curvature of the rock and was keyed to it by one of the finest examples of masonry I have ever seen. . . . Furthermore it was tied into another beautiful wall, made of very carefully matched ashlars of pure white granite, especially selected for its fine grain. . . . The flowing lines, the symmetrical arrangement of the ashlars, combined to produce a wonderful effect . . . this structure surpassed in attractiveness the best walls in Cuzco, which had caused visitors to marvel for centuries. . . . It fairly took my breath away. What could this place be? Why had no one given us any idea of it?"

This was only the first of many wonders. As the Indians urged Bingham to climb higher, he came upon a great granite stairway leading to two great buildings of white stone, of which the walls were composed of Cyclopean blocks, higher than a man. They were temples, each with only three walls, the fourth side being open. The larger temple had walls twelve feet in height, lined with niches, probably for the mummies of the dead Incas. There was no evidence either building had ever been roofed. "The top course of beautifully smooth ashlars was left uncovered so that the sun could be welcomed. . . . I examined the larger blocks in the lower course and estimated that they must weigh from ten to fifteen tons each."

South of the main temple was an open courtyard, flanked on its east side by an even more amazing structure. This again appeared to be a temple, "containing three great windows looking out over the canyon to the rising sun. Nothing like them in design and execution has ever been found. . . . This was clearly a ceremonial edifice of peculiar significance."

Then Bingham remembered that Salcamayhua, a Peruvian chronicler who had described the antiquities of his country in 1620, had said that Manco I, the first Inca, had ordered "works to be executed at the place of his birth, consisting of a masonry wall with three windows". Manco I had lived round about A.D. 1000, five centuries before Manco II, who had resisted the Spaniards. Bingham says that at first he suspected that he had found the city of the first Inca. It was not until later that he realized it could also have been the home of the last.

In the following year, 1912, Bingham returned at the head

of an expedition formed to survey and excavate these ruins on the heights above the canyon of the Urubamba; the heights called Macchu Picchu. That is the name now given to the city, but there seems little doubt that it is Vilcabamba, the principal seat of the last Inca kings, their ultimate refuge which even the conquistadors never discovered. The excavators worked hard, cutting down the entire hardwood forest which smothered the city. The splendour of the buildings, the Olympian magnificence of the site, and its romantic associations, aroused in the discoverers a sense of dedicated purpose. They had found one of the wonders of the world, the more amazing in that it had kept its secret down to the first decade of the twentieth century.

The ruins straddle a narrow ridge or "saddle" below the peak of Macchu Picchu. On three sides the city is protected by the rapids of the Urubamba, roaring through the canyon two thousand feet below. On the fourth side the massif is approachable only along another razor-like spur of mountain. The eastern side of the ridge is impassable, and on the western side there is a footpath which runs along a narrow horizontal cleft in the side of the precipice. A handful of men could defend it against an army. On the eastern and western side of the ridge are 1,500 foot precipices, down which rocks could be rolled on to intruders.

Where breaks occurred in the face of the cliffs, these were walled up to deny any foothold to attackers. The ridge is guarded by a small but powerful fort, as Bingham says, "a veritable Thermopylæ. No one could reach the sacred precincts unless the Inca decreed, as Friar Marcos and Friar Diego found to their cost."

On Macchu Picchu itself and on neighbouring peaks the explorers found remains of Inca signal stations, by which messages could be sent and received across the mountains.

As will be seen from the photograph in center insert, Vilcabamba was built on steeply terraced slopes; there are over one hundred stairways within the city, connecting these terraces in which the inhabitants grew their crops. Water was supplied from springs which rise within a mile of the town, and led by stone conduits under the city wall and thence to a series of stone tanks. From the last basin the aqueduct runs into the moat. Bingham does not mention springs within the city itself, and he suggests that one of the reasons why Vilcabamba was eventually abandoned may have been the shortage of water.

There are many garden plots, sometimes in association with small houses. Other houses were arranged in groups, and in some the excavators found stone mortars for grinding.

The finest buildings are on the west side of the city. After ascending a series of steep terraces one comes to the top of a hill where stands a small temple and a fine *intihuatana* or "place where the sun is tied". . . . Nearby are "the ruins of two attractive houses, built, like the rest, of white granite blocks squared as nicely as could be done without instruments of precision unknown to the builders, and fitted together without clay". South of this hill-top, at a lower level, is an open space which Bingham named the "sacred plaza", flanked on two sides by the largest temples. The granite blocks of which they are built are of enormous size, some weighing fifteen tons and more. They are exquisitely cut, and fitted together with extreme precision without mortar. The walls slope inwards, as in some Egyptian buildings, to give stability to the structure, and the doorways are usually narrower at the top than at the bottom.

Since the Incas did not possess any lifting tackle, or tools of iron or steel, these granite monoliths must have been manœuvred into place by little bronze crow-bars (of which examples have been found). The construction, as Bingham remarks, must have taken generations, perhaps centuries of effort.

A number of cemeteries were found and excavated. These were usually in caves on the steep rocky slopes, covered in dense jungle. Finding them was difficult and sometimes dangerous, as poisonous snakes live in the undergrowth, and several of Bingham's Indian workers were bitten. Within the caves the skeletons lay on the floor where they had fallen when the mummy wrappings had decayed. Originally the bodies had been buried in a sitting position, the knees drawn up under the chin. Usually they were accompanied by pottery and simple implements of bone or occasionally bronze. Sometimes the graves had been disturbed by wild beasts, bears or jaguars.

The most interesting cemetery was a group of caves half-way down the mountain-side to the north-east of the city. Here lay the bodies of fifty Incas, of which only four were male. "This was a very exciting discovery," writes Bingham. "Apparently the last residents of Macchu Picchu were Chosen Women, the 'Virgins of the Sun' associated with the sanctuaries where the sun was worshipped. Some distance to the south of this group are more caves in which some fifty more skeletons were found; all except five or six were female."

Later a most interesting single interment was found, also a woman, but evidently of higher rank than the rest. The grave was overhung by an immense boulder some fifty feet high. Beside the skeleton there were the remains of a dog, two large shawl-pins of bronze, sewing needles, tweezers, fragments of fabric and a concave bronze mirror. Bingham suggests that this grave may have been that of the High Priestess or *Mama-Cuna,* the "Mother Superior" of the convent. "We know," he says, "that on certain ceremonial occasions the *Mama-Cuna . . .* is reported to have ignited a tuft of wool by concentrating the sun's rays with a concave bronze mirror," though he adds, "whether this can actually be done I do not know."

It seems almost incredible that a city of such size and magnificence could have remained hidden for nearly four centuries after the first Europeans arrived in Peru; but it is true. The reason, as the discoverer explains, is:

"because this ridge is in the most inaccessible corner of the most inaccessible part of the Andes. No part of the highlands of Peru is better defended by natural bulwarks —a stupendous canyon whose rock is granite, and whose precipices are frequently a thousand feet sheer, presenting difficulties which daunt the most ambitious modern mountain climbers. Yet here, in a remote part of the canyon, on the narrow ridge flanked by tremendous precipices, a highly civilized people, artistic, inventive, well-organized, at some time in the distant past built themselves a sanctuary for the worship of the sun."

Not only were the sites of Vitcos and "Old Vilcabamba" [4] unidentified until Bingham discovered them, but they were in a region which was not even mapped. When, in the search for Vitcos, Bingham and his colleagues climbed out of the pass westward of the Vilcabamba river, they saw, to the west, a great chain of snow-capped peaks which were not marked on any map. According to Raimondi's chart there was no room for such a range between the rivers Apurimac and Urubamba. And yet, instead of finding themselves at the junction of the Apurimac and the Pampaconas the explorers stood on a lofty mountain pass surrounded by high peaks and glaciers.

Next year the chief topographer of the expedition, Alfred H. Bumstead, solved the mystery. "He determined the Apurimac and the Urubamba to be thirty miles farther apart at this point than anyone had supposed. Our surveys opened an unexplored region, *1,500 square miles in extent,* whose very existence had not been guessed before 1911. It proved to be one of the largest undescribed glaciated regions in South America. Yet it is less than a hundred miles from Cuzco, the chief city of the Peruvian Andes. That this region could have so long defied investigation and exploration shows better than anything how wisely Manco had selected his refuge."

[4] There is a comparatively modern town of the same name near the source of the Vilcabamba river.

Postscript

In the introduction to this book I stated that its main function was to entertain, and that the Lost Cities I had chosen to illustrate my theme were selected by one criterion, their capacity to excite wonder. Whether or not I have succeeded the reader must judge, but before I write the last full stop I am tempted to make a few purely personal observations based on conclusions I have reached during the writing of this book. I put these forward tentatively, not as facts, but as opinions with which the reader may or may not agree. Nor do I claim that they are in any way original.

The first is that, by comparing the growth, development and decline of such varied cultures as those of Sumeria, Assyria, the Hittite Empire, the Indus Valley, Ceylon and America, one can detect a fairly uniform pattern. In each case the beginning was agriculture, whether based on the irrigation of river valleys, as in Mesopotamia and the Indus Valley, or the Inca terraces of Peru, or the great hydraulic engineering works of the ancient Sinhalese. In each case such development could only take place under a strong centralized power which, by organization and discipline, could create large, integrated societies. And in each case such power was focused in a priesthood consisting of the educated and intelligent, who provided the nucleus of technicians, engineers, scientists, who preserved and transmitted a body of knowledge, whether in written or oral form. Sometimes the chief priests were also kings. Sometimes the kings were drawn from a military class who gained power, in the first place, by their courage and skill in battle, and their ability to protect the state against its enemies. But even when kings ruled, they were usually closely allied with the priesthood, though occasionally kings and priests were rivals for power.

The second observation, arising from the first, is that the central core of all these ancient civilizations was religion; the cities themselves reveal this clearly, since in every case the wealth of the community—in labour, land, materials, technical and artistic skill—was concentrated on the building of religious edifices. Compare the sun-temples of the Mayas and the Incas with those of the Sumerians, or the *dagobas* of Anuradhapura with the pyramids and temples of Egypt. The only other great buildings were the palaces of the kings, but these were also closely connected with the worship of the gods. The palaces of Sennacherib and Ashur-ban-pal in Assyria were adorned with sculptured reliefs of Assyrian deities; the palaces of the Sinhalese kings were in close association with their temples; the palaces of the Maya and Inca rulers were also linked with religious worship, and the kings themselves took a prominent part in religious rites.

Nearly all these early religions were based on the propitiation of what we call "natural forces", but which to the ancient peoples were deities; sun, rain, wind, gods of vegetation and fertility, etc. Compare Yum Chac, the Maya god of rain, with the Sumerian Enki, god of the waters; or the Egyptian sun-god, Re, with the Maya and Inca solar deities. In most cases the propitiation of such deities involved sacrifice, often human sacrifice. The Buddhist religion of Ceylon seems at first to provide an exception, but though, among the intellectual *élite,* Buddha was a spiritual leader and not a god, he was and still is worshipped as such by the masses; offerings were and are made at his shrines just as they were to the gods of Mesopotamia, Mexico and Peru.

In the case of Roman Pompeii, where a sophisticated society was becoming decadent, the gods were probably taken less seriously, but the primitive gods and goddesses of the Greeks, whom the Romans adopted after their conquest of Greece, were also mainly nature-deities to whom human sacrifice was sometimes offered by the primitive ancestors of the classical Greeks, e.g.

Agamemnon's sacrifice of his daughter Iphigenia. In fact it would appear that all or nearly all human societies pass through this phase. The "royal tombs" at Ur of the Chaldees show that the Sumerians practised human sacrifice in 2500 B.C. The Aztecs and Mayas, whose civilization developed much later, were still offering human victims to their gods in A.D. 1500.

There are other interesting parallels between these widely separated cultures, e.g. the evidence of a complex bureaucratic system of control in Sumeria, possibly at Mohenjo-daro and Harappa, and certainly in Peru; systems which, while providing for the material welfare of the people, left them very little liberty of action. In fact the Inca system bore some resemblance to the modern Communist state, with its emphasis on communal ownership, and the same applied to some of the Indian civilizations of central America.

The parallels and resemblances do not necessarily indicate any close physical connection between the various civilizations which produced the cities described in this book. Contact, even between Egypt and Sumeria, and between Sumeria and the Indus Valley, was relatively slight, and, unless one is prepared to accept the highly controversial theory of a "lost Atlantic continent", there can have been no possibility of contact between the early civilizations of the Old World and the New. Surely the most likely explanation is that, given conditions which enable man to settle permanently in one place, he tends to develop on broadly similar lines, though subject to differences due to race, climate and geography.

My third conclusion is one with which some readers may disagree; it is that even the highest religions have not made men more tolerant, merciful or humane. The Assyrians, a pagan people denounced by the Hebrew prophets, behaved with the most abominable cruelty. But their worst barbarities were no fouler than those perpetrated against the American Indians by some European Christians three thousand years later. Conversely, some ancient people, also pagan "idolators", were comparatively humane. There is little deliberate cruelty in the Hittite records. The Incas gave up human sacrifice, and from their behaviour towards their conquerors they seem to have been more just and tolerant than the Spaniards. Nor, among the Europeans, were cruelty and inhumanity confined to Catholic Spain. Protestant England conducted a profitable and barbarous slave-trade between West Africa and her American colonies.

Even in ancient Ceylon, where the lofty religion of Buddhism forbade the taking of life, human or animal, the Sinhalese rulers ordered execution by impalement, mutilation, being crushed beneath the feet of elephants. And, as we know, all these barbarities have been exceeded in the twentieth century both in Christian Europe and atheist Russia.

Yet, in its 3,000 years of existence, the civilization of Ancient Egypt, which ended more than twenty centuries ago, contains fewer records of cruelty and intolerance than any other, despite the fact that the Egyptian religion was animistic, and contained little if any ethical teaching. There seems to be no necessary connection between morality and religion.

The Lost Cities of the world, dried skeletons from which life had departed, stand as mute witnesses of Man's varied attempts to find security and fulfilment in an organized society. Some were successful for a time. All, in the end, failed, leaving one with a sense of doubt and omen. As Mr. Giorgio de Chirico has written, in the passage which introduces Dr. George Vaillant's *Aztecs of Mexico:*

> *One of the strangest feelings left to us by prehistory is the sensation of omen. It will always exist. It is like an eternal proof of the* non sequitur *of the universe. The first man must have seen omens everywhere, he must have shuddered at each step.*

Bibliography

MESOPOTAMIA

Budge, E. A. W., *The Rise and Progress of Assyriology.* London, 1925.

Cottrell, Leonard, *The Anvil of Civilization.* Mentor Books Ltd., New York, 1957.

de Burgh, W. G., *The Legacy of the Ancient World.* Penguin Books, London, 1953.

Gadd, C. J., *Stones of Assyria.* London, 1936.

Hilprecht, H. V., *Excavations in Assyria and Babylonia.* Philadelphia, 1904.

Hilprecht, H. V., *Explorations in Bible Lands.* Edinburgh, 1903.

Koldewey, R., *The Excavations at Babylon.* London, 1914.

Layard, A. H., *Autobiography and Letters.* London, 1903.

Layard, A. H., *Early Adventures in Persia, Susiana and Babylonia.* London, 1887.

Layard, A. H., *Nineveh and Babylon.* London, 1853.

Lloyd, Seton, *Excavations on Sumerian Sites.* London, 1936.

Lloyd, Seton, *Foundations in the Dust.* Penguin Books, London, 1955.

Pritchard, J. B., *Ancient Near Eastern Texts.* Princeton University, 1950.

Rawlinson, G., *A Memoir of Major-General Sir Henry Creswick Rawlinson.* London, 1898.

Rich, Claudius, *A Narrative of a Journey to the Site of Babylon,* 2 vols. London, 1839.

Rich, Claudius, *Narrative of a Residence in Koordistan by the late Claudius James Rich, Esq.* London, 1836.

Woolley, Sir Leonard, *Ur of the Chaldees*. Penguin Books, London, 1954.

ASIA MINOR

Barnett, R. D., "Karatepe. The Key to the Hittite Hieroglyphs," *Journal of Anatolian Studies,* III (1953), p. 53.

Bossert, H. Th., "Found at last—a bilingual key to the previously undecipherable Hittite Hieroglyphic inscriptions." *Illustrated London News,* 14 May, 1949.

Bossert, H. Th., and U. B. Alkim, *Karatepe* (First Report, 1946, and Second Report, 1947). Istanbul.

Bittel, K., and H. Cambel, *Boghazkoy* (Guide in English). Istanbul, 1951.

Burckhardt, J. L., *Travels in Syria and the Holy Land.* London, 1821.

Cottrell, L., *The Anvil of Civilization.* Mentor Books, New York, 1957.

Garstang, J., *The Hittite Empire.* London, 1929.

Garstang, J., *The Land of the Hittites.* London, 1910.

Gurney, C. R., *The Hittites.* Penguin Books, London, 1954.

Hogarth, D. G., "The Hittites of Asia Minor," *Cambridge Ancient History,* II, xl. Cambridge, 1931.

Hrozny, B., "Hittites", Article in *Encyclopædia Britannica,* 14th edition, 1929.

Lloyd, Seton, *Early Anatolia.* Penguin Books, London, 1956.

Mercer, S. A. B., *The Tell el-Amarna Tablets.* Toronto, 1939.

Messershmidt, L., *The Hittites.* London, 1903.

Ozguc, T., "Where the Assyrians built a commercial empire in second-millennium Anatolia". *Illustrated London News.* 14 January, 1950.

Pritchard, J. B. *Ancient Near Eastern Texts.* Princeton University, 1950.

Sayce, A. H., *The Lost Empire of the Hittites.* London, 1910.

Sayce, A. H., "What happened after the death of Tutankhamun?" *Journal of Egyptian Archæology,* XII, 168–70, 315.

Wright, W., *The Empire of the Hittites.* London, 1884.

INDUS VALLEY

Wheeler, Sir Mortimer, *The Indus Age*. Cambridge University Press, 1953.

Mackay, Ernest, *The Indus Civilization*. Lovat, Dickson & Thompson Ltd., 1953.

(And specialized works listed in Sir Mortimer Wheeler's book.)

CEYLON

Cave, H. W., *The Ruined Cities of Ceylon*. Sampson Low, Marston & Co. Ltd., London, 1900.

Forbes, Major, *Eleven Years in Ceylon*. London, 1840.

Holden, Lord, *Ceylon*. George Allen & Unwin Ltd., London, 1937.

Knox, R., *Historical Relation of Ceylon*. London, 1696.

Paranavitana, Dr. S., *Archæological Survey of Ceylon*. Annual reports for 1947, 1948, 1949, 1950, 1951, 1952, 1953, 1954.

Skinner, T., *Fifty Years in Ceylon*. W. H. Allen, London, 1891.

POMPEII AND HERCULANEUM

Barker, E. R., *Buried Herculaneum*. Adam & Charles Black, London, 1914.

Corti, E. C. C., *Destruction and Resurrection of Pompeii and Herculaneum*. Routledge & Kegan Paul, London, 1951.

Carrington, R. C., *Pompeii*. Clarendon Press, Oxford, 1936.

Dio Cassius (Book LXVI), translated by E. Cary. Loeb Edition. Heinemann, London, 1925.

Engelmann, W., *Guide to Pompeii*. Leipzig, 1925.

Horne, J. F., *The Mirage of Two Buried Cities*. Hazell Watson & Viney, London, 1900.

Pliny the Younger, *Letters,* Vol. I and II, translated by William Melmouth. Heinemann, London (Loeb Edition).

Tanzer, Helen, *The Common People of Pompeii*. Johns Hopkins Press, Baltimore, 1937.

MEXICO

Charnay, Désiré, and Viollet-le-Duc, E. E., *The Ancient Cities of the New World*. New York, 1887.

Gallop, R., "Ancient Monuments of Mexico", *The Geographical Magazine,* Vol. 7. London, 1938.

Gann, T., and Thompson, J. E., *The History of the Maya*. New York, 1931.

Joyce, T. A., *Maya and Mexican Art*. London, 1927.

Prescott, W. H. P., *The Conquest of Mexico*. London, 1843.

Spence, Lewis, *The Gods of Mexico*. London, 1923.

Spinden, H. J., *Ancient Civilizations of Mexico and Middle America,* American Museum of Natural History Handbook Series, No. 3. New York, 1928.

Thompson, Edward, *People of the Serpent*. G. P. Putnams, London, 1933.

Thompson, J. E., *Civilization of the Mayas,* Leaflet 25, 2nd edition. Field Museum of Natural History, Chicago, 1932.

Thompson, J. Eric, *Mexico before Cortes*. New York, 1933.

Totten, G. E., *Maya Architecture*. Washington, 1926.

Vaillant, G. C., *The Aztecs of Mexico*. Penguin Books, London, 1951.

Willard, T., *City of the Sacred Well*. William Heinemann Ltd., London.

Wissler, C., *The American Indian*. New York, 1938.

PERU

Bingham, Hiram, *Inca Land*. Constable & Co. Ltd., London, 1922.

Bingham, Hiram, *Lost City of the Incas*. Phœnix House, London, 1951.

Bowman, I., *The Canon of the Urubamba*. Bulletin of the American Geographical Society, December 1912.

Charnay, Désiré, and Viollet-le-Duc, E. E., *The Ancient Cities of the New World*. New York, 1887.

Markham, Sir Clements, Translations of the Spanish chronicles published in numerous volumes by the Hakluyt Society.

Means, P. A., *Ancient Civilizations of the Andes*. New York and London, 1931.

Prescott, W. H. P., *The Conquest of Peru*. London.

Pizarro, Pedro (translated and edited by P. A. Means), *Relation of the Discovery and Conquest of the Kingdom of Peru*. New York, 1921.

Rowe, J. H., *Inca Culture at the Time of the Spanish Conquest*.

ABOUT THE AUTHOR

LEONARD COTTRELL, a world-renowned archaeologist and senior writer-producer for the British Broadcasting Corporation, was born in Wolverhampton, England in 1914. He has worked in advertising and served as a war correspondent with the R.A.F. in the Mediterranean area.

Mr. Cottrell has traveled nearly half a million miles gathering authoritative material for his many books, making them "come alive" with on-the-spot reporting even though the civilization about which he writes may have long since vanished.

Mr. Cottrell's devotion to the study of archaeology, and especially of Egyptology, culminated in his highly praised B.B.C. series on Ancient Egypt. His many books on the ancient world have been widely acclaimed in this country and abroad. These include: *Lost Cities, Wonders of the World, The Lost Pharaohs, The Mountains of Pharaoh, Hannibal: Enemy of Rome,* and *The Bull of Minos.*

A SELECTED LIST OF *Universal Library* TITLES

HISTORY AND POLITICAL SCIENCE

LITERARY CRITICISM, DRAMA, AND POETRY

TITLES OF GENERAL INTEREST